# Enterprise Java Developer's Guide

## S. Narayanan
## Junhe Liu

**McGraw-Hill**

New York   San Francisco   Washington, D.C.   Auckland   Bogotá
Caracas   Lisbon   London   Madrid   Mexico City   Milan   Montreal
New Delhi   San Juan   Singapore   Sydney   Tokyo   Toronto

# McGraw-Hill

*A Division of The McGraw-Hill Companies*

1 2 3 4 5 6 7 8 9 0  AGM/AGM  9 0 4 3 2 1 0 9

P/N 0-07-134674-0
Part of ISBN 0-07-134673-2

The sponsoring editor for this book was Simon Yates, and the production supervisor was Clare Stanley. It was set in Vendome by **TIPS** Technical Publishing.

Printed and bound by Quebecor/Martinsburg.

McGraw-Hill books are available at special quantity discounts to use as premiums and sales promotions, or for use in corporate training programs. For more information, please write to the Director of Special Sales, McGraw-Hill, 11 West 19th Street, New York, NY 10011. Or contact your local bookstore.

Throughout this book, trademarked names are used. Rather than put a trademark symbol after every occurrence of a trademarked name, we use names in an editorial fashion only, and to the benefit of the trademark owner, with no intention of infringement of the trademark. Where such designations appear in this book, they have been printed with initial caps.

 This book is printed on recycled, acid-free paper containing a minimum of 50% recycled, de-inked fiber.

# Contents

# Contents

Contents

Contents

Contents

# Table of Listings

# Dedication

## S Narayanan

To my parents, who want to see their son always soaring high.

## Junhe Liu

For my family, and especially my wife Jiong, whose encouragement makes this book possible.

# Acknowledgments

We would like to take this opportunity to thank the whole team—their hard work and dedication were crucial to the production of this book.

Many thanks to our agent and project manager, Robert Kern, for giving us the opportunity to put our expertise and knowledge into book form, and for his continuous help and encouragement from beginning to end. We would also like to thank development editor Vicki Hertz and copy editor Rachel Pearce Anderson, who scrutinized all of the text and made numerous suggestions that improved the readability of this book. Our thanks also go to proofreader Paulette Miley, indexer Tim Griffin, and compositors Sarah O'Keefe and Sheila Loring of Scriptorium Publishing Services, Inc., and Caroline McKenzie, for their help pulling everything together. Under a very tight schedule, these professionals worked on all aspects of the book and made a lot of suggestions that improved its quality.

We sincerely appreciate the efforts of our technical reviewer, Derek Hamner, for his helpful tips and suggestions for improving the code and its presentation.

We would also like to thank all of our friends who helped us, directly or indirectly, to write this book. These friends include Camile Olcese, of North Park University; David Brownell, of JavaSoft; Fred Delse, of Hewlett Packard; Hitesh Bosamiya, of Wipro Infotech; Kirk Chen, of JavaSoft; Jay Song, of Ford Motors; Nick Daily, of Netscape Communications; Paul Dreyfus of Netscape Communications; Robert Weltman, of Netscape Communications; Rupesh Chhatrapati, of Netscape Communications and Vinay Badami, of Netscape Communications.

Lastly, we'd like to thank Simon Yates, of McGraw-Hill, for making this book a reality.

# Introduction

Welcome to *Enterprise Java™ Developer's Guide*. We are writing this book to fill a huge gap in the Internet/intranet application development arena using JavaBeans™. Few books discuss (much less demonstrate) developing bean-based client/server applications, and not a single book available at the time of this book's writing discusses Internet/intranet-based applications using JavaBeans, especially Beans on the server side.

The preponderance of existing books approach JavaBeans from the beginner's perspective, ignoring the fact that most of us working with beans are either seasoned developers or experienced programmers. Because of this beginner's orientation, these books can only cover so much ground, and they tend to gloss (if cover at all) the topics and type of coverage needed to build bean applications for the enterprise and Internet/intranet.

Once a JavaBeans programmer learns about Java component technology, he or she wants to know how to build reusable components for faster/better application development. To achieve this, we need to begin first with the requisite discussion of how component technology fits into the enterprise arena. In the second section, we build a few well-chosen fundamental beans needed for enterprise development. This gives the reader a contextually-based, clear picture of building such things as enterprise JavaBeans. In the last section of the book, we extend from the practical knowledge gained in the second section to constructing full-blown enterprise Internet/intranet applications.

## Who Should Use This Book?

*Enterprise Java Developer's Guide* should be read by anyone seeking to learn how to develop real-life Internet/intranet applications using the various available Java technologies. We wrote this book primarily for people who already have Java and have at least a beginner's level of JavaBeans programming knowledge. Additionally, two other sets of people who will benefit from reading this book are (1) those who want to leverage off of the programming contained in existing beans to develop applications by using high-level tools to hook beans together, and (2) corporate managers who need to understand the increasingly important role of Java technology in the enterprise environment.

# What Do I Need?

In order to effectively use this book you need two things: a computer running either Windows 95™ or Windows NT™, because our discussion is mainly focused on the Windows platform, and an Internet connection so that you can download certain utilities or trial software as you proceed through the chapters.

# How to Use This Book

This book contains three parts. If you are already familiar with component technology, JavaBeans, and Enterprise JavaBeans™ architectures, you might want to skip the first part. In the second part most of the chapters are independent, so you can pretty much start off with any chapter you like. But part 3 is based on reusability, and highly depends on the components developed in part 2. So we recommend that you finish part 2 before reading part 3. Within part 2, the only dependency is that you should read chapter 8 (LDAP) before reading chapter 9 (JNDI).

# Code Listings

All of the code samples given in the text are available on the CD-ROM that accompanies this book. Most of our code provides minimal functionality. Feel free to change it and enhance the functionality to build even better applications. Learning is never complete without some independent hacking and finger burning.

# Conventions

We have followed the following conventions in this book:

- Lines of code appear in a special `monospace` typeface
- Variables, class, and method names are set in *italics*
- All directory names are also set in *italics*
- Commands are set in **boldface**
- All the outputs are also set in `Courier`

# Overview

Part 1, "JavaBeans Component Technology Overview," consists of the first four chapters. This introduction discusses the fundamentals of component technology with an emphasis from the JavaBean's perspective.

Chapter 1, "The Need for Component Technology," presents an overview of the current component technologies and the different architectures available today, with an emphasis on COM. At its conclusion, it offers a comparison of these architectures.

Chapter 2, "JavaBeans Architecture," discusses Java's component support in the form of JavaBean APIs. This chapter gives an overall picture but does not go into detail, because we assume that the readers are already familiar with the JavaBeans technology.

Chapter 3, "JavaBeans Framework," will introduce you to existing Java component frameworks and their relationships.

Chapter 4, "Enterprise JavaBeans," discusses the latest server-side component frameworks from JavaSoft.

Part 2, "Developing JavaBeans," contains the lion's share of the book and explores Java's support for developing enterprise solutions. The solutions are also JavaBean-based. There are nine chapters in this part, and each chapter covers one particular technology, with the exception of chapters 8 and 9, which are independent of each other.

Chapter 5, "Using Java Studio™," explores using the tool for wiring the JavaBean components to develop Java applets and applications. It also gives a detailed explanation of converting a JavaBean into a Java Studio component.

Chapter 6, "Java and Electronic Mail," discusses Java's support for email capabilities. Samples and beans to send and receive text-based emails are developed in this chapter.

Chapter 7, "Java Database Connectivity," discusses JDBC™ support and demonstrates code samples using JDBC drivers with the Oracle database. We also develop beans for accessing a database using JDBC.

Chapter 8, "Lightweight Directory Access Protocol," discusses the LDAP protocol and demos searching and updating the LDAP database in the form of code samples and beans.

Chapter 9, "Java Naming Directory Interface," discusses the advantages of using JNDI for directory and naming access. Here we again demonstrate using Netscape's directory server with JNDI to search and update the database in the form of code samples and beans. Readers should read chapter 8 before proceeding with this chapter.

Chapter 10, "Servlets," discusses the advantages of Servlets over traditional CGI programming. We have used Java Web Server for discussing and demonstrating servlets, servlet beans, and using beans in a Servlet. We also discuss developing a bean that will generate HTML files.

Chapter 11, "Internet Security," discusses the security technologies that are associated with the Internet, including symmetric cryptographic algorithms, public key cryptography, digital signatures, digital certificates, and Secured Socket Layer. Many of these topics are supported with code samples.

Chapter 12, "Common Object Request Broker Architecture," discusses the CORBA distributed computing architecture and its advantages. In addition to providing a tutorial on CORBA programming, we develop a CORBA service that accesses a database using the JDBC JavaBean that we developed in chapter 7.

Chapter 13, "Developing Enterprise JavaBeans," teaches you how to develop and test EJB using EJBHome's application server.

Part 3, "Developing Applications Using JavaBeans," is probably the most interesting part of the book and discusses topics that other JavaBean books do not focus on. This section discusses developing enterprise solutions by integrating the beans we developed in part 2.

Chapter 14, "Enterprise Internet Application," gives a brief overview of the types of applications an enterprise may develop—Internet, intranet, and extranet applications. It also briefly goes over Ecommerce-based applications.

Chapter 15, "Email Application," is an ideal example of how to develop applications without coding using Java Studio.

Chapter 16, "Internet Chat Application," demonstrates how to develop a simple chat application using Servlets and JavaBeans.

Chapter 17, "E-Commerce Application," demonstrates developing an e-commerce application using Servlets and CORBA.

Chapter 18, "Project Tracking System," demonstrates a typical extranet application. This application makes use of client digital certificate for verification unlike the traditional user ID and password. This application is developed over SSL.

Chapter 19, "Employee Tracking System," is a typical intranet application which demonstrates using an LDAP server for tracking and modifying employee information. This demo is developed using the Servlets and beans developed in chapters 8 and 9.

Appendix A demonstrates how to use InfoBus technology, Appendix B gives some useful tips that will help you in your Java programming, Appendix C gives some information on how to use jar and serialver utilities, and Appendix D covers code modification and deployment guidelines for projects in chapters 13 and 18 using the new release of the EJBHome server—HomeBase.

This book has a wealth of code samples and demos of real-life applications using JavaBeans. While we have carefully tested the code and included instructions for the reader on how to compile and use it, we realize that no book is completely free from errors. In the interest of making future editions of this book even better, please forward any corrections or suggestions to our editor at simon_yates@mcgraw-hill.com

Component technology is the future of software development. Explore the power of component technology with this book and see where it can take you!

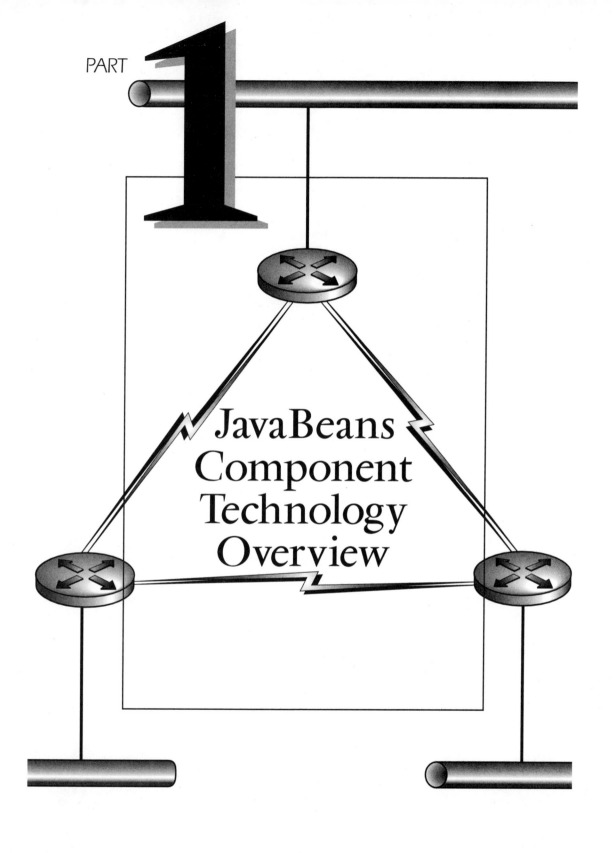

PART

**1**

JavaBeans
Component
Technology
Overview

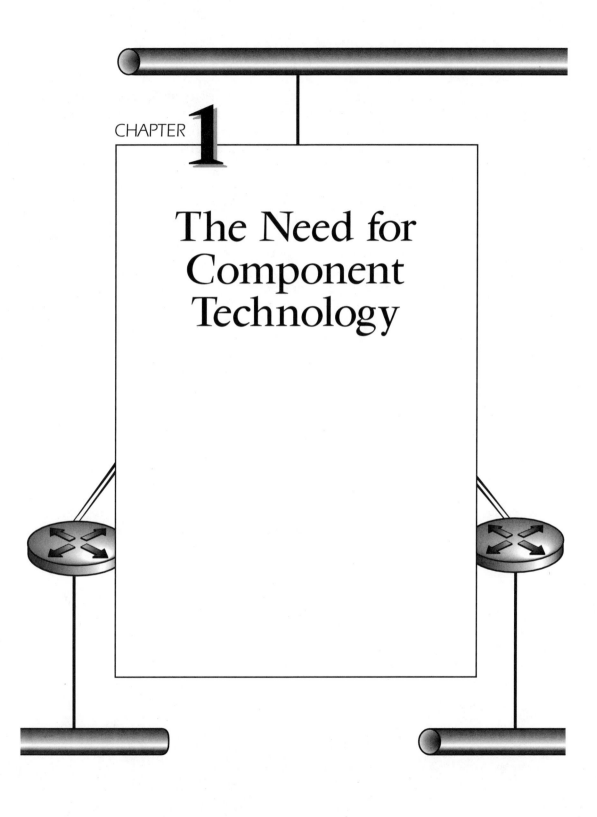

CHAPTER 1

# The Need for Component Technology

# Introduction

The following statement, comparing the auto industry and the computer industry, was misattributed to Bill Gates at a trade show: "If the automobile industry made as much progress as the computer industry has, we would all be driving 10 dollar cars that get 10,000 miles per gallon." The reply from General Motors was: "Right, but who wants to drive a car that crashes twice a day?"

That was a joke that circled widely on the Internet a while ago. In reality, there was no confirmed report that Bill Gates ever made such a statement. The joke, however, does reflect the disparity between the states of hardware and software development. The hardware industry has made vast improvements over the last thirty years, shrinking the power of a room-size mainframe into a notebook PC, meanwhile reducing the price of computers from millions to just thousands of dollars. On the other hand, reliable software systems are still hard to come by.

One of the crucial differences between hardware and software development is that hardware manufacturers have embraced the concept of components. A PC is composed of memory components, a CPU component, and so on, which together are assembled to form a system. Suppose a PC owner wants to extend the functionality of the system to include a CD-ROM, he or she simply buys a CD-ROM device and plugs it into the PC.

Complex hardware systems are built on top of many simpler components, and when the functionality of a single component is enhanced, the whole system often benefits. Complex software systems, however, don't have the same capability. Software applications with millions of lines of code are often built as one large organic program, and the application's developer may very likely write most of the code from the ground up. Such software applications are prone to behave erratically and are hard to debug and extend.

Therefore, the software component model has gradually entered the center stage of software development.

# The Road to Components

The software component model is really about software reuse—the ability to re-use code written by others. This is a fairly complex issue that has attracted a significant amount of research, both in academia and in industry.

The first real answer to increasing software re-usability was object technology. The idea comes from the observation that in large applications, software modules are often very much interrelated. The modification of one module often causes repercussions among many other modules. Such "closeness" among software modules is a big reason why software applications are bug-prone and hard to extend.

Object technology seeks to compartmentalize software by creating a number of self-contained objects and linking those objects into applications. Applications written with object technology in mind are compartmentalized, so that changes within one object do not affect the behavior of other objects. Such software applications are less bug-prone and easier to extend. Object technology also incorporates the notions of *polymorphism* and *inheritance*, which make it easier for programmers to re-use existing code in the programming languages themselves.

The adoption of object technology, however, has not created an object market as many people had hoped. In the realm of hardware manufacturing, component vendors make components that perform different functions, and hardware integrators build more complex systems with components acquired from the market. Object technology has not had the same effect on the software industry. There are many reasons why object technology has fallen short of its promise in this regard. The most important reason is the problem of distributing and integrating third-party software.

Traditionally, a library was the only viable way to distribute software. Libraries are compiled code stored in the form of object files, which are sent to other developers who then link their own code with the libraries. The problem with libraries is that they are very platform-specific. For example, a library built on a Solaris™ 2.5 system may not link with applications built on a Solaris 2.6 system. Even on the exact same platform, because of the peculiarities of each environment, problems often arise when integrators build applications with existing libraries. Because of these problems, libraries today are often distributed with source code so that application integrators may modify them according to their own environment and special needs.

Another problem with libraries is that they are language-dependent. Fortran is known to have a wealth of math libraries. However, in general, these libraries are not available to C++ programmers. Language-dependency limits the market size of potential commercial objects and thus discourages vendors from creating object products.

The biggest problem with libraries is probably that they do not facilitate the notion of re-use of services. All code that comes with a library has to be linked together with the application and distributed to the target machine. This procedure does not take into consideration those cases when a portion of the code is already available locally or remotely on another machine. The inability of an application to re-use services causes large amounts of code to be copied to many machines, thus leading to sky-rocketing maintenance and administration costs. If hardware systems are unable to re-use services, corporations would have to install one printer for every single PC, instead of sharing printers over a network, which is much more efficient.

Object technology, which has breathed life into large application development by creating self-contained modules, still mainly uses libraries as the method of distribution, and thus possesses all the inherent problems of distributing libraries.

The component model, while assimilating many of the advantages of the object technology, builds software applications with a different tool—the interface.

# What is a Component?

Semiconductor chips communicate to the outside world through pins. For example, a chip X may have 100 pins that allow it to connect to other components of an electronic device. The chip vendor publishes manuals that tell developers the functionality of each pin. Table 1-1 gives an example of this type of information.

**Table 1-1**

Some of the pin details for chip X

| Symbol (Pin name) | Type | Name and function |
|---|---|---|
| A0-A16 | I/O | Address bus |
| ACK | O | Acknowledge: Accepted when low |
| D0-D8 | I/O | Data bus |

Hardware system integrators connect pins of chips together according to their functions to build complex electronic devices such as computers.

The software component model takes a very similar approach. In this case, the "pins" of software components are called interfaces. An interface is the set of methods that the component implements. Application integrators examine the interfaces of components and connect them together to form software applications. We'll see such examples in chapters to come.

Component technology is still young, and there isn't even agreement on the definition of its most important element—the component. Paul Harmon of Component Development Strategies probably defined it best in an article for the *Component Development Strategy newsletter* (July 1998): "a component is a software module that publishes or registers its interfaces." Notice that there is no mention of object. Indeed, a component may be implemented in any language as long as all the methods of its interface are implemented.

In addition to being a set of methods, an interface is also seen as the contract between the applications that use the components and the components themselves. When a component publishes its interface, it is telling the world about the services it provides. Client applications only need to call the functions within the interface in order to obtain these services.

Suppose you are writing an application and are in need of a function that calculates the square root of an integer. You may search for the calculator components available on the market. Once you find one, you can examine its interface and see if there is a square root method. If the answer is yes, you will be able to link the calculator code into your application as if it were a library.

The above operation is not much different from what you would do in an object model. However, in the component model, a developer has another choice. Suppose he or she knows that a calculator is a popular component that should be in the target machine already, or at least, that there should be some machine in the neighborhood that has a copy. The developer may distribute the application without linking the calculator, and when the application is in need of a square root function, it searches for a component with a calculator interface on the network. Once a calculator component is found, the application then invokes the square root method, passing the parameter and obtaining the result through inter-process communication. Notice that in this case, the calculator component may or may not reside on the same machine as the application.

The first approach (library linking) is called the in-process model, and the second is called the out-of-process model. Figure 1-1 shows the two approaches.

**The two models of accessing a component**

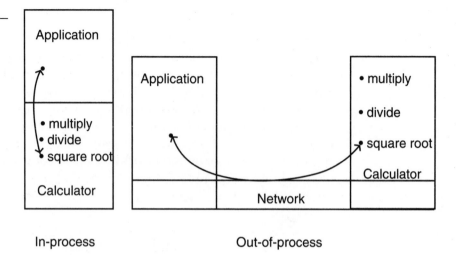

Notice that in the out-of-process model, the component runs in a separate process as the application and does not need to be linked to the application. In this case, the implementation of the calculator interface can be of a different language than that of the application. In the case of the calculator running in a remote host, the target host does not have a copy of the component code. A form of service re-use is thus enabled.

Three component models are competing for developers' loyalty today—Microsoft's Component Object Model (COM), SUN's JavaBean, and OMG's Common Object Request Broker Architecture (CORBA). All these choices support both the in-process and out-of-process models. Both CORBA and COM are language-independent, although in the case of COM, components have to stick to the Windows binary format, making it quite platform-dependent. JavaBean, on the other hand, is platform-independent, although it only supports Java. Whether this is an advantage or disadvantage strongly depends on who's talking.

At this time you may be wondering that if the component model is such a simple and elegant idea, why didn't someone think of it before? The answer points back to the hardware. The power of the component model lies in its out-of-process model, and until recently, the lack of computing power and slow network speeds would lead to noticeable performance degradation for invoking methods over the network. CORBA was deemed too slow for wide deployment at one time. In other words, the performance requirements of the component model made it a deployable technology only in the 1990s.

# The Component Programming Model

It's interesting to notice how the current software component model parallels its hardware counterpart, to the extent that the software model has a new programming model that reminds people how hardware components are connected.

Hardware integrators connect pins of different components with wire, and the connections are carefully constructed according to the I/O functions of each pin. In a similar manner, software integrators connect software components according to the descriptions of the methods within the interface. The process of connecting components is also called "wiring." Figure 1-2 shows both wiring processes.

**Figure 1-2**
Wiring the
components

**Hardware and Software Component Wiring**

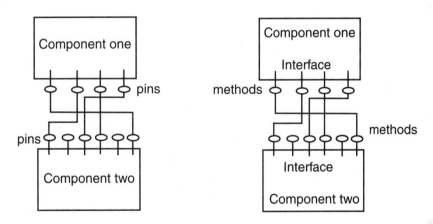

Hardware Component Wiring          Software Component Wiring

## Connection-Oriented Programming Model

The traditional programming model is caller-driven, in the sense that the application calls methods or procedures of a component's interface. The component never calls back. In the component programming model, components are symmetric. Connecting components may call each other much like hardware components interact with each other. Such a programming model is called connection-oriented programming.

There is another way to look at the differences between the two programming models. In the traditional model, information is pulled from the callee as needed. Such a model is inadequate at times. For example, you may want to ask your stock quote component to tell you when a certain company's stock is at a certain price. This would be impossible in the traditional model, where the callee cannot provide information except in response to a specific call. The model that allows a component to push information to another component as some event arises is called the push model. Such an action is also called event notification.

Of course, you can only wire components together when the components are in the same application. How do you wire them in the out-of-process case when the callee components are not present until runtime? We have already discussed the way to invoke methods on the callee component by obtaining its interface. The reverse happens when the caller component pushes its interface to the callee. Such an action is called a callback. Figure 1-3 shows the callback process.

**Figure 1-3**
Callee component
calls back caller
component

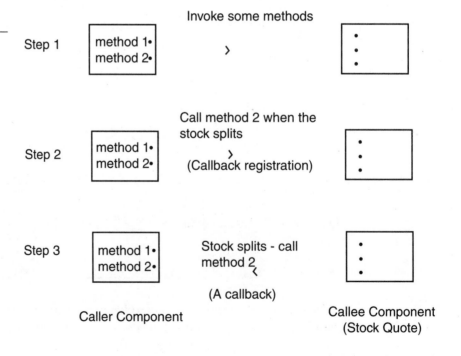

**Callback Registratons - Wiring Components at Runtime**

Step 1 — Invoke some methods

Step 2 — Call method 2 when the stock splits (Callback registration)

Step 3 — Stock splits - call method 2 (A callback)

Caller Component

Callee Component
(Stock Quote)

## The "Wire"

In hardware, the wire conducts electrons and transmits messages between components. In software, the "wiring" material is the communication software between components. Obviously, for the in-process model, no special software is needed to conduct messages between components. For the out-of-process model, the component systems today all use Remote Procedure Call (RPC) as a means of communication.

Remote Procedure Call is a model that allows components to call methods of other components as if they were in-process components, when in fact the other components are out-of-process and may even live on other machines. Such a model allows component integrators to assemble components together easily and transfer the difficulty of communication to component system vendors.

The idea behind Remote Procedure Call is the use of stubs and skeletons. The stub resides on the calling component and intercepts the method invocation. It "flattens" (or "marshalls") the parameters and passes the call and the parameters to the callee components. The skeleton resides on the callee component and intercepts calls from the stub. The skeleton then unpacks (or "unmarshalls") the parameters and passes them to the callee components. Figure 1-4 shows the process.

**Figure 1-4**
Conceptually, the caller calls the callee as if they are on the same machine. In reality, the call goes through the network

**Stubs and Skeleton**

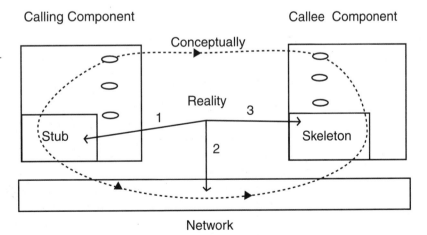

Network

Components talk to each other using RPC. Conceptually, the client thinks it's calling some local methods. In reality, the calls go through the network. Component system vendors provide tools that generate stubs and skeletons. Developers of components don't need to worry about those two modules. What the developers do need to provide is the interfaces of the components. The tools take the interfaces as input and generate stubs and skeletons. Figure 1-5 shows the process.

**Figure 1-5**
Generating stubs and skeletons

**Generating Stubs and Skeletons**

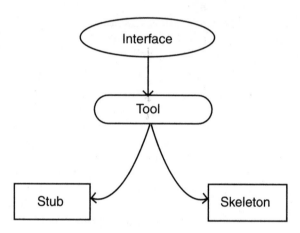

# Component Framework

Before component technology can take off and create a mass market for components, a few problems still need to be addressed. The biggest of these is the problem of fault isolation. When we assemble a large number of components from different vendors, how can we find out what components are at fault when the system fails?

Another problem is the problem of dependencies. Components often depend on the existence of other components in order to function correctly. For example, the stock quote component may depend on a database access component to perform its duty. When we ship the stock component, do we ship a database component also? Where do we draw the line?

Security has always been a concern for both enterprises and consumers. Component systems pose some challenges in this area also. For example, how can you be sure that the third party component you just purchased will not wipe your system out?

And of course, there is the perennial problem of performance. Components often communicate through the network, and stubs and skeletons add further overhead to component-based applications. A lot of work still needs to be done to make sure large scale component-based applications perform up to par with library-based systems.

Many of the above problems can be addressed with a language such as Java, which does strong compile-time and runtime checking and has built-in security. However, the language will not solve all these problems, and in the case of Java, there is still the performance problem.

Researchers have proposed the notion of a framework to deal with those component-specific problems. A framework will impose rules of communication, fault isolation, dependency checking, programming safety checking, security management, and performance enhancement for a component system. It will provide a running environment for components. Microsoft Transaction Server, Enterprise JavaBeans, and Java Embedded Server are all frameworks along that direction, but they still have a long way to go to address the problems associated with the component model.

## The Big Three

In 1987, IBM, HP, and DEC formed a UNIX consortium called the Open Software Foundation, or OSF. The consortium sought to create a common platform for distributed computing that would solve some of the major difficulties in this field (such as interoperability). The resulting specification from OSF is the Distributed Computing Environment (DCE). The Interface Definition Language (IDL) that describes component interfaces was first introduced with DCE.

In 1989, eight U.S. companies formed the Object Management Group (OMG), which was chartered to create a distributed object architecture that is similar to DCE, although from the perspective of object-oriented computing. In 1992, OMG published the first version of the Common Object Request Broker Architecture, or CORBA.

In the early 1990s, Microsoft wanted to improve its Object Linking and Embedding (OLE) technology so that it would embed a spreadsheet inside a word document. It developed the Component Object Model (COM) as the underlying technology to re-implement OLE. Many of COM's features, such as Interface Definition Language and Remote Procedure Call, trace back to the DCE root.

In 1996, JavaSoft announced JavaBeans, a component model for Java. Along with Java's Remote Method Invocation technology, JavaBeans has become a full-blown component architecture comparable to COM and CORBA.

Today, COM, CORBA, and JavaBeans are the three major component systems on the market. We will describe COM in detail later in this chapter, and describe CORBA and JavaBeans briefly in comparison to COM, because entire chapters of this book will describe the latter two technologies in depth (Chapter 2 on JavaBeans and Chapter 12 on CORBA).

# Component Object Model

Microsoft's Component Object Model is the first component system that has created a third party market. It is also the first commercial instantiation of the connection-oriented programming model.

## Compound Document and COM

Microsoft first developed COM to implement compound documents, where a document may contain data from different applications such as Word and a spreadsheet. A question arises naturally—how does a component model have anything to do with the mixing of PC applications? The answer: Interfaces.

Suppose you have a compound document that embeds a spreadsheet in a Word document as in Figure 1-6. When you start editing the spreadsheet, an out-of-process component is already at work—in this case, the spreadsheet application that has registered its interface with the Windows operating system.

**Figure 1-6**
Example of a compound document

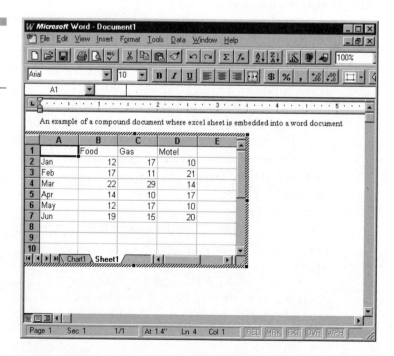

The Word application is the process that handles your request. If you type in the Word area, the Word application handles the edit directly. If you type in the spreadsheet area, however, the Word application detects that this is an area controlled by the spreadsheet application. Therefore, it sends whatever you type to a spreadsheet component, according to the interface that is published in the operating system. The spreadsheet sends the result back and tells the Word application what to display. Figure 1-7 shows the process.

**Figure 1-7**
Communication that happens when an Excel spreadsheet is edited within a Word document

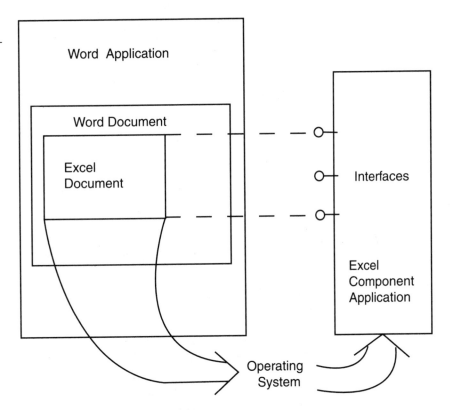

**Compound Document Implemented in COM**

Notice that the communication between the two applications is through the operating system. That is because both the Word and the Excel processes run on the same computer, and some kind of inter-process communication provided by the operating system is used instead of networking software.

Actually, that was a rather simplified explanation of how COM works. The devil is in the details.

## The COM Object

Let's go back to the term interface. An interface is the set of methods that a component tells the outside world that it has. For example, a calculator interface may have methods *add()*, *multiply()*, and *divide()*. It is possible for a component to implement multiple interfaces. For example, a Personal Digital Assistant may support a calendar interface as well as a calculator interface. In fact all COM objects support more than one interface. That is because there is one interface all COM objects have to place in the beginning—the IUnknown interface.

The IUnknown interface is always the first interface of a COM object. The interface includes three methods: *QueryInterface()*, *AddRef()*, and *Release()*. The *QueryInterface()* method returns the other interfaces within the same COM object. The *AddRef()* and *Release()* methods let the COM object keep track of how many clients are currently using its service. The COM object maintains a counter, and whenever the object passes one of its interfaces to a client, it increments it, and whenever a client passes a interface to some other client, it calls *AddRef()*, which causes the counter to be incremented again. When a client finishes its business with an interface, it calls *Release()* to decrement the counter. When the counter becomes zero, the object usually destroys itself.

Reference counting has its drawbacks because it relies on the client application to follow the rules. In reality, the client application may forget to decrement the counter, either because of a bug or a system crash. The net result is that objects may still be alive when no one is using their service. This is usually not a problem for desktop PC applications because users reboot their computers frequently. However, for long-running distributed applications, those clientless objects may accumulate over time and take up a large chunk of the valuable resources of the host machine. Downtime often causes significant financial losses for mission-critical applications. COM's use of reference counting reflects its desktop root. Java's leasing specification, on the other hand, solves the same problems more elegantly in a distributed system.

IUnknown is always the first interface in a COM object, and the first three methods are always *QueryInterface()*, *AddRef()*, and *Release()*, in that order. Order matters in COM because COM is a binary interface. A COM object is in fact the object code of a compiled C++ program.

Figure 1-8 shows a COM object that also includes the Calculator interface.

There is a pointer in the upper-left corner called *vtable* pointer. This pointer is what is handed out as the pointer to the object for the in-process model invocation, when the client calls the component methods. Such an indirect reference of the method table is the distinctive style of C++-type object code.

COM is a binary standard in the sense that COM objects stick to the binary format of C++-style object code. It is language-independent because with the proper tool, components can be compiled into the COM binary format, regardless of the programming language. On the other hand, even though COM is being ported to other operating systems, providing language-independent support for those operating systems is not going to be trivial because of the cost of building the related tools.

**Figure 1-8**
COM object

**A COM Object**

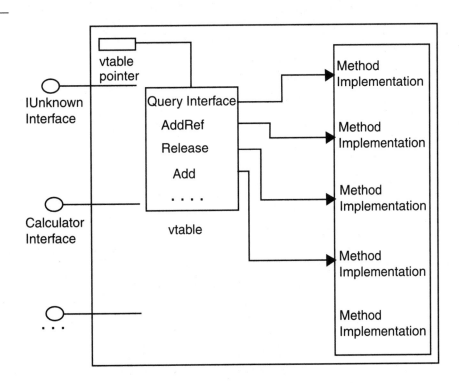

# Object Reuse

Creating new components with existing ones is a great feature for a component model. In this area, COM seems to be more advanced than its competitors. COM's containment and aggregation reuse models are yet to be matched by Java or CORBA.

## Containment

In the containment model, one object, called the inner object, is wrapped by another object, the outer object. Only the outer object's interfaces are exported, and some of those interfaces only point to the inner objects. When a client invokes the methods of the interfaces implemented by the inner object, the outer object only forwards the calls. From the inner object's point of view, it does not know whether the caller is an outer object or a client. On the other hand, the client does not know whether interfaces belong to the outer object or the inner object. In a sense, the outer object "contains" the inner object. Figure 1-9 shows an instance of containment.

**Figure 1-9**
COM's containment

**Containment**

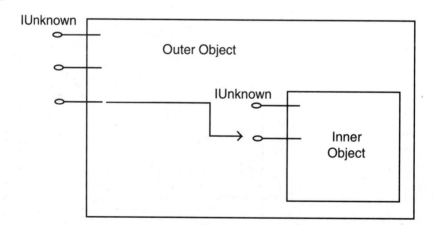

Containment is a nice model for object reuse. However, for each level of containment, there is one more level of indirection. If somehow an object contains deep nesting of containment, performance may suffer. That is why another model for object reuse, aggregation, is needed for such occasions.

## Aggregation

In aggregation, the interfaces of the inner object are exported along with interfaces of the outer object. In this case, there is no more indirection and thus none of the potential performance problems that are associated with containment. The client still does not know whether an interface belongs to the inner object or outer object; however, the inner object itself needs to be aware that it is being aggregated.

Suppose the client calls a QueryInterface of the outer object's IUnknown and searches for interfaces of the inner object. There will be no problem because the outer object is aware of the inner object's interface, since it has a pointer to the inner object. On the other hand, if the client somehow gets hold of the IUnknown of the inner object and queries interfaces of the outer object, the inner object doesn't have an answer. Therefore, during aggregation, the inner object needs to get a pointer to the outer object's IUnknown interface. All method invocations of the inner object's IUnknown interface will be redirected to the outer object's IUnknown interface.

Figure 1-10 shows an example of aggregation.

**Figure 1-10**
COM's aggregation

**Aggregation**

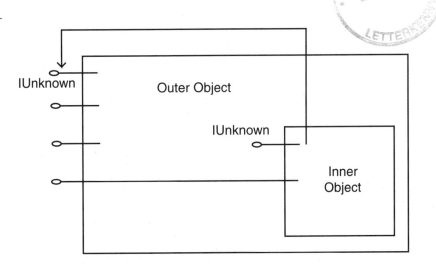

## Inheritance

Inheritance is a common form of object re-use in object-oriented models. In a component model, there are two types of inheritance—interface inheritance and implementation inheritance. Interface inheritance refers to the inheritance of the definition of the object, and implementation inheritance refers to the inheritance of the code of the object.

COM supports interface inheritance but not implementation inheritance. This is a design choice. It is a well known problem that in implementation inheritance, the details of the parent object are exposed to the child object, thus creating the potential that undisciplined programming practices may break the parent object. COM's decision to not support implementation inheritance is a reflection of these concerns.

## The Name Service

A component model needs a name service for clients to find applications' locations. For example, when a user clicks on the spreadsheet portion of a compound document, how does the system locate the Excel program and invoke it? After all, the Excel application program does not always stay at the same place on different machines.

In every Windows system, there is a database called the registry. This is a database that keeps track of all aspects of the system, including hardware configuration. COM's mapping of component names and their physical executable files is also stored in the registry database.

## Component Manager

So far, the components we have discussed are all used in client applications. For large distributed applications, components will need substantial support in terms of transaction, security, and life-cycle management.

One example is a database accessing component. Database base servers require clients to establish a "connection" before being accessed. The connection establishment phase requires user authentication and resource allocation and is a time-consuming process. Suppose we have a Web application that uses a database component to access company information, say, about a product line. In a traditional component model, each client will instantiate a database accessing component, and then destroy it once the client leaves. Each new database component needs to spend time establishing a connection. Wouldn't it be good if we could somehow create a pool of database accessing components, establish the connections, and share them among different clients? Such an approach eliminates the overhead of repeatedly creating and destroying new components and the database connections along with them. Microsoft Transaction Server (MTS) does exactly that. In a way, the name "transaction server" is misleading, because transaction is only a part of what the transaction server does. Component management is probably a more significant usage of the server.

The introduction of MTS is a significant step in enterprise COM—component development. It takes care of the "plumbing" side of the application and allows component developers to concentrate on the business logic instead of spending time on system issues. The comparable technology in Java, the Enterprise JavaBeans, seems to have borrowed quite a few tricks from MTS.

## Distributed COM

In the previous sections, we mentioned that the component object model has two modes of operation—in-process and out-of-process. COM splits the latter into two sub-modes—local process, where the two objects reside on the same machine, and remote process, where the two objects reside on separate machines. Remote process is also called DCOM, which stands for Distributed COM.

The inner working of DCOM is not much different from what's illustrated in Figure 1-4, where client stubs and server skeletons are used to help the components communicate. In addition to the normal COM infrastructure, DCOM is concerned about data representations on different machines. Microsoft has created a platform-independent data format called Network Data Representation to facilitate data exchanges between DCOM components.

COM originates from the desktop PC and is tightly integrated with client Windows operating systems such as Windows 95. By contrast, DCOM is tightly integrated with Windows NT. It leverages the NT's security mechanism, Microsoft Transaction Server, for its distributed application needs. Such dependencies associate DCOM closely to the Microsoft platforms.

# CORBA

While COM grows from the desktop, CORBA comes from the heterogeneous corporate environment, where multiple platforms, from IBM mainframes to PCs, work together over networks. The difference in initial design target of the two architectures has resulted in implementation differences in some important areas. The implementation of language-independence is a good example.

COM's binary standard, while language-neutral, has a strong platform-dependency, because at the time, Windows was the target platform that would run COM. CORBA specifies language mappings from the Interface Definition Language (IDL), and program source is generated for the client and the server in its language of choice.

For example, suppose a developer creates a CORBA system in C++ for both the client and the server component implementation. Now the developer wants to create a Java client. All the developer needs to do is create a Java client stub with the tool provided by the CORBA vendor, and then program her client in Java. The resulting Java client application will have no problem in talking to the C++ server component implementation. Figure 1-11 shows the process.

Because the language mapping generates stubs and skeletons in the source, developers will be able to compile them on different platforms. Therefore the language-independent support in CORBA is a lot more platform-neutral than that of COM.

Another difference between CORBA and COM is that OMG only defines the specifications of CORBA; the implementation of these specifications is left to CORBA vendors. Such an arrangement leaves large gaps between specifications and implementations. For example, CORBA has specified fifteen services for the components, including naming, security, transaction, and so on. But only a small portion of these services is implemented by current CORBA vendors. COM, on the other hand, may utilize a range of services that comes with the Windows family of operating systems.

CORBA components are more object-oriented than COM objects. However, in the component model, the degree of object-orientedness does not matter much any more. What is important is that the interfaces are implemented correctly.

**Figure 1-11**
CORBA architecture

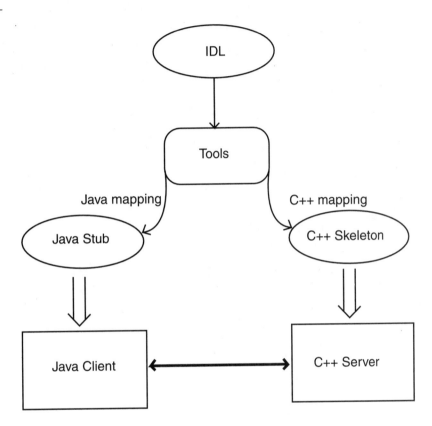

**Language Independence - The CORBA Way**

## JavaBean

Unlike COM and CORBA, JavaBean's interface is not defined explicitly. Instead, the JavaBean specification allows a JavaBean component to export interfaces via method naming patterns. The advantages and disadvantages of such a construct are still hotly debated. But it is definitely convenient, especially for nimble bean applets that don't have much weight.

One of the biggest advantages of JavaBeans is the Java language itself. Java's features—such as not supporting pointers—remove a major hurdle in fault isolation, and its "Write Once, Run Anywhere"™ nature is ideal for creating a mass component market because such a market is no longer segmented by platforms.

Many of the Java supporters are also CORBA backers, and in the face of Microsoft's vigorous push to COM/DCOM, there are political reasons for the gradual merge of Java and CORBA. It so happens that Java and CORBA complement each other nicely. CORBA provides the rich services and language-independence that Java sorely needs in order to access enterprise legacy data. On the other hand, Java provides an ideal means for downloading a CORBA client.

Recent events show that such integration is already happening. For example, OMG has announced that it will support most of Java's RMI technology, which provides "wiring" for Java components. In addition, SUN's Enterprise JavaBeans specification brings tighter integration of CORBA and Java on the server-side.

# Summary

Component technology represents the future of software programming. It is designed to help developers create applications with existing components. It also eases the effort involved in maintaining and extending software applications. All the examples in Part 2 of this book are JavaBean examples, and in Part 3, we demonstrate how to build enterprise Java applications with existing components.

CHAPTER **2**

# JavaBeans
# Architecture

# Introduction

In this chapter we introduce the JavaBean APIs that define a software component model for Java. We assume that readers are already familiar with developing JavaBeans, so we won't go into the details of the archicture. Since the focus of this book is to show you how to use JavaBean components in building enterprise solutions, we will brush you through the JavaBeans architecture, just for the sake of completeness. If you are already familiar with JavaBeans architecture and APIs, you are welcome to skip this chapter.

In Chapter 1 of this book you read about Component technology. In this chapter we will learn how Java supports component technology through JavaBean APIs.

# Basic JavaBean Concepts

In this section we'll discuss some of the JavaBean design rules that every bean must follow, although most of the time we can get away with implementing a minimal set of rules. The rules include persistence, properties, events, customization, and packaging. A bean must at least provide persistence, simple properties, and events, and be packaged into a JAR archive. Customization depends on the complexity of the bean. If you follow the design rules and naming conventions, you may not need customization if the beans are simple. Versioning is not required unless your beans are bound to change.

## Persistence

Every bean should be able to store its information when the application exits. For example, Let's say that we have a Memory bean used in a Calculator application. The bean must be able to store the information in memory, even if the application exits, so that the information can be used later. This persistent storage should be supported by all the beans. To provide persistent storage, it is sufficient to define a class to implement the *Serializable* interface, as shown here:

```
public class MemoryBean implements Serializable{
}
```

Generally, a bean should save all the information except the runtime information. For example, a thread's state should not be saved, because all threads have runtime information in them. In addition, beans should not save references to other external beans. So how does Java virtual machine (JVM) know what to store when a bean exits? This is simple—all those properties whose persistent state should not be saved are marked transient, as shown below:

```
protected transient Thread t;
```

In this case, the information held by $t$ during runtime is not saved, because $t$ is marked transient.

It is very common to release different versions of a bean. Even if a newer release has some newer variables, the older and newer class will still be compatible if the older variable's order is maintained. But when the input stream reads your older version, it will throw an exception because the JVM thinks the classes are incompatible, even though the persistence schema is not changed between the old class and the new class. Fortunately, you can get around this problem by defining a version ID field in your bean class, as shown below

```
static field long SerialVersionUID 123456789012L;
```

If this number matches between different versions of the class, the older class information would still load into the newer version. A *Serial Version UID* for a particular class can be generated using the serialver tool included with the JDK.

To allow the automatic initialization of beans programatically, every bean should have a no-arg constructor, because programmatic initialization will not allow the passing of parameters to the constructor. Even if your bean does not need a no-arg constructor, you have to provide one, as shown below:

```
public MemoryBean(){
    //dummy
}
```

# Properties

A single public attribute is a property. Properties can be either read-only, write-only, or both read and write. There are several types of JavaBean properties:

- Simple
- Indexed
- Bound
- Constrained

The following sections describe each of these properties.

## Simple Properties

Every property will have a pair of *set* and *get* methods. Every pair of *set* and *get* methods will represent a single public attribute and can set or get the attributes value. Simple properties allow the visual manipulation of data. Here's an example:

```
public void setUserName(String name){
   this.name = name;
}

public String getUserName(){
   return name;
}
```

From the code shown here, you can see that the *set* and *get* methods need not manipulate the same variable that they specify in the method. Method *setUserName()* tells you that the UserName is set. This does not mean that the variable name that is being set should also be named as UserName. In our case we have used *name*, but it could just be *x* or even *UserName* for that matter. The method syntax and the variables need not match in the code, though the method syntax should carry sufficient information to convey to the user. To keep things simple, all the samples in this book are simple properties.

## Indexed Properties

Indexed properties represent an array of values. The *set* and *get* methods for indexed properties may take the array index or may take the complete array itself. Here's an example:

```
public void setNumberList(int[] arrNum){
  numbers = arrNum;
}

public int[] getNumberList(){
  return numbers;
}

public void setNumberList(int index, int i){
  numbers[index] = i;
}

public int getNumberList(int index){
  return numbers[index];
}
```

## Bound Properties

If other objects are notified whenever a property's value changes, then that property is a Bound property. The notification of other objects occurs each time the value changes. Every notification carries the property name, old value, and new value along with it. Here's an example:

```
private PropertyChangeSupport pchange = new
PropertyChangeSupport(this);

public void
addPropertyChangeListener(PropertyChangeListener l){
  pchange. addPropertyChangeListener(l);
}

public void
removePropertyChangeListener(PropertyChangeListener l){
  pchange. removePropertyChangeListener(l);
}
```

```
//when property changes in some method you'll call

pchange.firePropertyChange("name", oldval, newval);
```

## Constrained Properties

If other objects are notified whenever a property's value changes, and if this property allows the other objects to veto the change, then such a property is a Constrained property. *PropertyVetoException* is thrown when the Constrained property listeners veto a change. Here's an example:

```
private VetoableChangeSupport vchange = new
VetoableChangeSupport(this);

public void
addVetoableChangeListener(VetoableChangeListener l){
  vchange. addVetoableChangeListener(l);
}

public void
removeVetoableChangeListener(VetoableChangeListener l){
  vchange. removeVetoableChangeListener(l);
}

//when property changes in some method you'll call

vchange.fireVetoableChange("name", oldval, newval);
```

## Events

Events are the means by which one component notifies the other if something interesting has happened. All JavaBeans should follow the delegation event model, which is supported with JDK 1.1.x. In the delegation event model, there is always an event source and an event listener. Any object interested in a particular event must first register itself as an interested party before it can listen to that event. If the object did not register itself for a particular event, then it will not be notified when the event occurs. Every event carries with it an event object that will give more details about the event itself. Listeners can use the event object to learn more about the event.

# Customization

Customization allows you to customize the beans so that they appear the way you intend when used in the builder tools. There are different types of customization, discussed below.

## Customizer Interface

Most of the time the bean properties are displayed by the property sheet. Sometimes you may feel that it's better to expose the properties in your own GUI window. Any changes made in this GUI window will actually be reflected in the bean's property itself. One would implement Customizer interface to provide a customized interface for manipulating properties, as shown here:

```
public MyBeanCustomizer extends Panel implements
Customizer{
```

In your customizer, you should implement *addPropertyChangeListener()* and *removePropertyChangeListener()*, so that the builder tools can register themselves to listen to the property change. However, you'll have to fire the change event every time the property changes. The builder tool will take care of updating the bean properties in turn.

## PropertyEditor Interface

Sometimes you may feel that a particular variable must be restricted to certain specific values. Say, for example, that you have a property called Color. By default you can enter any string, although you want the user to enter either Red, Green, or Blue. If you validate the users' entries, all validation must happen in the bean every time *setColor()* is called. But you can simplify this process by providing a custom property editor for the property color, as shown below:

```
public class ColorEditor extends PropertyEditorSupport{
  public String[] getTags(){
```

```
      String colors={"Red", "Blue", "Green"};
      return colors;
   }
}
```

If you provide a property editor class for a particular property, then this class must be referred to in a *BeanInfo* class.

## BeanInfo Interface

Most bean information is known to the builder tool because it uses the introspection mechanism to find out more about the bean. If a bean is designed adhering to the bean design specifications, then all the builder tools will be able to understand the bean. However, it may be better to have the developer provide all the bean information, including custom display names, an icon that represents the bean, and a short help. In that situation, you'll have to implement the *BeanInfo* interface. A sample of this is shown here:

```
public class MyBeanBeanInfo extends SimpleBeanInfo{
   public propertyDescriptors[]
getPropertyDescriptors(){
     try{
     PropertyDescriptor pd = new
PropertyDescriptor("color", MyBean.class);
     //add your property editor class for color if any
     pd.setPropertyEditorClass(ColorEditor.class)
     PropertyDescriptor[] pdarr = {pd};
     return pdarr;
   }catch{Exception e){}
   }
}
```

## Packaging

JavaBeans are distributed as JAR files. These files contain the bean and all its support classes. Every JAR should also have a MANIFEST file that describes the contents of the JAR. If the MANIFEST file is not present in the JAR, then every class in the JAR is treated as a bean. MANIFEST files allow you to specify the bean classes via an entry: "Java-Bean: True". For example, if I had *MyBeanClass* in JAR, I would have the following entry in my MANIFEST file:

```
Name: MyBeanClass
Java-Bean: True
```

To add "Java-Bean: True" into the MANIFEST, you have to unjar the files, edit the MANIFEST file (Manifest.mf) manually, and then repackage the classes and the MANIFEST file again into a JAR file.

**NOTE**

We did not add the "Java-Bean: True" entry in the MANIFEST files for the beans we develop in this book, because we did not find it necessary. But it may be a good idea for you to do so, especially if you are using a builder tool.

## Can All Java Classes be JavaBeans?

The answer to this question is both yes and no. If your Java class is:

- Reusable
- Easily customized
- Self-sufficient and able to work on its own

then you may want to consider converting this Java class to a JavaBean. Most of the GUI components can be converted to beans; however, it does not make sense to have the libraries or drivers as beans.

Here are some of the qualities of a good bean:

1. Must provide a zero-arg constructor so you can create new instances by calling *Beans.initiantiate()*.
2. Must have the bean class implement Serializable or Externalizable to support persistence.

3. Must have public methods that describe the behavior of the bean. Public methods are exposed by builder tools so that the user can hook it up with other beans.

4. Must have one of the property types described in the previous section.

5. Must fire events to notify other beans. Beans communicate to other beans using delegation event model.

6. May provide an additional information class that would describe more about the bean.

7. Must be delivered in JAR packages.

If you can provide all the above information to your existing Java class, you can convert the class to a JavaBean.

# New Features in JavaBean Component Model

JavaBeans Component provides new features—basically, just a framework to develop better components. All component features available for JavaBeans are discussed in Chapter 3 of this book. (The rules specified earlier in this chapter are for the component model. If you follow the rule shown above and develop a bean, then it can be called as a component.)

# Summary

In this chapter we covered some of the basics of Java's support to the component technology, the JavaBean APIs. It is obvious that JavaBean is an ideal choice for developing platform-neutral software components. This JavaBean model is ideal for GUI-based components, though non–GUI-based components can be developed for use with client applications or on a server. In the chapters to come, we'll develop a bevy of beans and show you how to hook them to develop enterprise solutions.

# JavaBeans
# Framework

# Introduction

"Framework" has become an overloaded word in Java. The latest Java enterprise technology, Enterprise JavaBean, is described as a framework for multitier distributed Java component applications. Java Embedded Server is a "framework" for downloading Java applications. They are both frameworks in the sense that they provide environments for Java components. However, in the case of Enterprise JavaBeans, the framework is more concerned with enterprise computing features such as transactions, security, and so on. By contrast, the framework provided by Java Embedded Server is closer to the component framework we described in Chapter 1, even though Java Embedded Server™ is positioned by JavaSoft as a framework for Java applications rather than JavaBeans.

As we discussed in Chapter 1, a component framework is a set of rules and services that allow components to be plugged-in, and it is an approach to deal with some of the more difficult problems of component technology, such as fault isolation, performance enhancement, and version control.

There are a number of technologies that provide running environments for JavaBeans and Java applications. For convenience, we will call them Java frameworks. None of the Java frameworks deals with all of the issues that a general component framework would deal with. Nonetheless, some of the products, such as Java Embedded Server, contain features that would be included in a general component framework. We expect that JavaSoft may eventually extend and integrate some of the Java frameworks and provide JavaBeans with a general component framework.

This chapter will introduce you to existing Java frameworks and their relationships. Some of them, such as Java Dynamic Management Kit (JDMK) or Java Embedded Server (JES), are targeted for embedded systems. However, the way they are designed does not bind them only to the embedded market, and they may easily be scaled to enterprise servers. We will also describe Jini™, InfoBus, and JavaBeans Activation Framework (JAF). Enterprise JavaBean, the next generation Java framework for enterprise computing, will be covered in Chapter 4 because of its importance and complexity.

Before we introduce the frameworks, let's spend some time on the Java Virtual Machines for embedded systems.

# Java Virtual Machine (JVM)

Since JDMK, JES, and to some degree, Jini, are all targeted for embedded systems, it is necessary to explain the differences between regular Java VMs and the VMs in embedded systems. The original targets of Java are toasters, game devices, thermostats, and so on—the so-called embedded devices. Although Java became popular on desk-top PCs with the help of Netscape, and later found a new home in enterprise servers, the embedded market was too big to be ignored.

JavaSoft released PersonalJava™ and EmbeddedJava™ for embedded systems. The Java VM requirements for embedded systems are different from desktop systems. For one thing, embedded systems generally have stringent memory requirements. PersonalJava targets systems with one megabyte of RAM and one megabyte of ROM, while EmbeddedJava targets devices with half a megabyte of both RAM and ROM. Here ROM represents the maximum code size and RAM represents the size of stack, buffers, and other runtime memory usage.

The target devices for EmbeddedJava are devices that have no graphical user interface, such as a telephone. PersonalJava targets devices that require a graphical user interface, such as a set-top box that may display statistics online on a TV during a baseball game.

An embedded system is sometime also called a real-time system, because the system has to respond to events within certain time constraints. This attribute has ramifications for the Java VMs of PersonalJava and EmbeddedJava. For example, it would be unacceptable for the garbage collector to kick in at any random time and hog the CPU.

Most Java VMs on desktop systems are run inside browsers. Since users may download Java applets from anywhere in the world, security mechanisms must exist to prevent malicious programmers from damaging users' systems. Thus the Java VMs in browsers implement strict restrictions on what an applet can do. Such a running environment is also called a sandbox.

In an enterprise environment, the Java VMs have no security restrictions because it runs in a closed environment.

Figure 3-1 shows the different running environments of Java VMs:

**Figure 3-1**

Different running environments of Java VMs

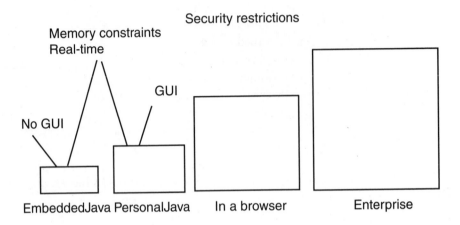

Java VM running environments

Java APIs designed for embedded systems have more restrictions than APIs on the server side. Therefore, it is fairly easy for JavaSoft to move APIs that are designed for embedded systems to the enterprise arena.

# Java Dynamic Management Kit

Java Dynamic Management Kit, or JDMK, is designed to solve a specific problem of networked embedded devices, namely the network management problem.

Network management refers to the task of maintaining, expanding, or troubleshooting a network. The current *de facto* standard in network management is called SNMP—Simple Network Management Protocol—although a lot of proprietary network management protocols still exist in enterprises.

Most network management protocols operate under the assumption that there is a central management station that collects network statistics from and sets state information on the devices. The devices contain a software agent that responds to the management station's requests and reports emergencies if necessary.

Chapter 3: JavaBeans Framework

Although SNMP is a big step forward in network management, it has yet to realize its promise in automating network administrators' tasks of troubleshooting network problems.

One drawback of SNMP is that the agent software is quite passive. Most of the intelligence exists on the server. Ideally, an agent should be able to take a more active role in managing the device, and that is exactly the advantage that JDMK offers.

JDMK is aimed at further automating and simplifying network management tasks. A JDMK agent may download diagnostic software once it finds something wrong with the device. It may also inform other devices of the event. JDMK also comes with JavaBean components that implement HTTP, SNMP, and RMI protocols. Managing stations may use any of these protocols to communicate with the network device. Figure 3-2 shows a somewhat simplified architecture of JDMK.

**Figure 3-2**

Simplified architecture of JDMK

**JMDK Architecture**

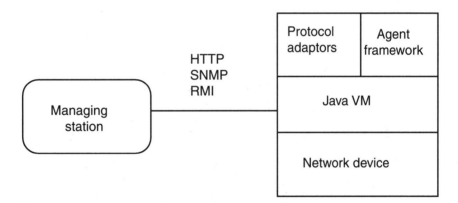

JDMK also comes with some specific network management features for Java. For example, there is a Java Managing Information Base (MIB) compiler, which helps Java programmers deal with SNMP-related development more easily.

# Java Embedded Server

In our discussion of the component technologies in Chapter 1, we discussed the need for a component framework. A framework provides the running environment for components.

One of the biggest drawbacks of component technologies is fault isolation. Namely, when the integrated system fails, how do we find which component caused the problem? There is also the issue of determining the size of a component. Too much self-containment results in large component size. On the other hand, small components sometimes generate many dependencies.

A component framework helps check dependencies of components, activates and deactivates components, and performs fault isolation. Java Embedded Server (JES), in spite of its name, is a framework for Java components. Even though JavaSoft positions it as a tool for embedded system development, there is nothing that is inherently embedded in JES. Such a system would be useful in both desktop systems and enterprise systems. The two components of JES are the ServiceSpace framework and its core services.

## ServiceSpace Framework

The ServiceSpace framework is the running environment of Java components. It offers the following services to Java components:

### Component Deployment

JES has a notion called "bundle," which roughly corresponds to a JavaBean. Bundle is a jar file that may include java classes, data, and a manifest file. The difference between a JavaBean jar and a bundle is that in a JES jar, developers may specify additional information in the manifest file, such as service dependencies.

### Dependency Management

Components may depend on each other. For example, a component that helps customers record a scheduled future TV program may depend on the existence of the scheduler service. The scheduler service allows a service to be run in a future time. You may choose to combine all related services that depend on each other into a bundle and download it to the network device. However, some of the services may already be there and re-downloading them creates waste of network bandwidth and device storage. A better strategy is to only include the core components, and specify the depending services in the manifest file. The ServiceSpace framework will recognize the dependencies and download the necessary services that are not present.

### Service Creation and Registration

The service included in a bundle is registered under service description, which is composed of the name of the Java interface that the service provides and also an identifier string. The inclusion of both the interface name and an identifier string allows multiple sources of the same service to run in a framework.

Bundles that need ServiceSpace assistance include special components called Wizards. Some of the key Wizards are:

- *Wizard,* which tells which services the bundle depends on.
- *Activator Wizard,* which manages the activation and de-activation of the services within a bundle.
- *Updater Wizard,* which tells the ServiceSpace how the implementation of the services may be updated.
- *Installer Wizard,* which controls how the bundle is installed or de-installed.

ServiceSpace has the ability to run multiple instances of the same bundle under difference processes. It is also aided by a sophisticated thread management service, part of the JES core service. The thread service may pool threads or set a limit on the number of threads in the system.

## JES Core Services

JES comes with a set of core services that developers may build on in applications. Those services include:

- *HTTP Service,* which is not intended to create a Web server on the device, but rather, allows the network device to be managed through a browser.
- *Servlet Service,* in which the inclusion Servlets facilitate the management of the device through a browser.
- *SNMP Agent Service,* which allows the device to be managed from an SNMP server.

These services and other services provided by JES form a foundation for higher level applications such as fax and voicemail. Figure 3-3 shows the architecture of JES, including its services:

**Java Embedded Server Architecture**

Applications such as fax, voice mail, and video

HTTP | SNMP | ... | RMI

Service Space

Java VM

Operating System

# Jini

## What is Jini?

Computers have never been easy to use, be it Mainframes or PCs. Despite many software vendors' efforts, PCs remain much less consumer-friendly than stereo systems, where components are plugged together and the whole system starts working like magic. In a PC environment, adding a new device means the system will need a new software module (called a driver) that knows how to interact with the device. Simply plugging in a new printer or disk drive rarely works for ordinary consumers.

An enterprise has the same problem. Acquiring a new device often means a new driver needs to be installed on a user's PC, and with the number and variety of devices within an enterprise, system administrators are fighting a losing battle to bring desktop systems up-to-date with the latest drivers.

Jini is aimed at solving the difficulty of adding new services to an existing computing environment. In a Jini environment, a device will inform its surroundings of its arrival, and will carry software modules that know how to interface with themselves. If a computer on the network wants to interface with the new device, it will download and execute the software modules from the newcomers. The system is made possible by Java's ability to run all byte code. The net effect of Jini is that there is no need to install special drivers for each new device. Jini also allows easier administration of resources in an enterprise network environment. Interestingly, Jini is not an acronym, as many other Java-related products are named. It is simply a new word SUN invented so that it starts with the letter J, and sounds like "genie," as the Jini logo suggests.

Jini achieves its objective by building a federated group of devices and software components into a single distributed system. It is composed of three components: its infrastructure, programming model, and services.

The infrastructure is the set of enabling technologies that build a federation. The services are the entities within the federation, and the programming model is composed of interfaces that allow the construction of the services. We will discuss each of the components in detail in this section.

# Infrastructure

The main communication protocol between two components in Jini is RMI, and the JDK 1.2 security model is extensible to a distributed system. The other two major components of Jini infrastructure are the discovery protocol and the lookup service.

## The Discovery Protocol

This protocol is used for a new device to discover its surroundings and advertise its service. These steps are needed for the new device to become a part of the Jini federation.

## The Lookup Service

This service is essential for the separation of the logical service and the physical device itself. For example, if a computer needs to store a file on a disk, it will query the lookup service for a disk service. The disk service returned by the lookup service may be different on occasion; however, the computer doesn't care which disk is used, as long as it writes the file out. Such a scheme provides a lot of flexibility in the system.

# Programming Model

There are a few programming issues that need to be addressed in the Jini system. For example, once a device or a service enters the federation, how are other members informed? Other issues include how to prevent scenarios where only some of the members are informed of the new service in case of a system crash, and distributed garbage collection.

A Jini programming model is established to address these issues. It is composed of three parts: the leasing interface, the distributed event model, and a two-phase commit transaction model.

## The Leasing Interface

In a distributed environment, the "distributed garbage collection" problem is a notoriously hard one to solve. The term refers to the re-collection of resources no longer needed in a distributed environment.

In a non-distributed environment, software modules have ways to tell the system that a particular object is no longer needed. In many cases, the system knows that an object is no longer needed because no pointer is pointing to the object. The problem becomes substantially more complex in a distributed environment. A machine may crash in the middle of using a service. However, as it boots up, the machine may forget that some service on the network still belongs to it. In this case, the resource must be explicitly released . Other causes of resource lockup include network failure and bugs in distributed applications.

Jini's way of solving this problem is by leasing. When a member is granted a source, there is an expiration time associated with it. If at the end of the granted period the service is still in use, the member needs to renew the lease. If the service is no longer in use, and the member forgets to tell the owner, there will be no lockup, because the granted period will expire and will not be renewed. In this way the owner of the service is constantly updated if the service is still needed.

## The Distributed Event Model

Java has already included an event model that allows an interested party to be informed when a change of state occurs within an object. However, the existing event model is designed for objects within the same Java Virtual Machine. In the Jini environment, events such as new services entering or leaving must be sent across the network. The distributed event model is designed to extend the existing Java event model to the distributed system.

Event notification in a non-distributed system is ordered, timely, and reliable. In addition, we can assume the registering party is the one that needs notification.

However, in a distributed system, event notification may have different orders for different members of the system. Often a third party may act as a notification filter for the registering member. Sometimes, because of various reasons, the registering member is no longer in existence when the event happens.

The Jini distributed event model is designed to deal with these issues. For example, registration is now associated with an expiration time, just like a lease. The interested party must renew the registration if it is still interested at the end of the valid period. In addition, a third party is allowed to receive notifications of events and filter them.

## Transaction

Jini includes a lightweight two-phase commit protocol to coordinate state changes. It is not a full-blown transaction manager, and leaves the details of a full transaction implementation to each object.

Like event and garbage collection, distributed transactions differ from traditional transactions in many ways. For example, one of the characteristics of transactions is durability, which means the result of the transaction should be persistent. However, in a distributed object model, there are cases when a group of transient objects may want to coordinate state change, and the result of the state change does not need to be persistent as transient objects disappear after the operation.

The Jini transaction model leaves the implementation of the transaction to the objects themselves, because objects know best what kind of transaction requirement they need.

In summary, leasing, distributed events, and transactions form the programming model of Jini.

# Services

There are two Jini services at this time of writing—JavaSpace™, and a two-phase commit manager. JavaSpace is a distributed computing environment that is the foundation of Jini. We will discuss JavaSpace in more detail in the next section, because it has ramifications beyond Jini.

In a sense, Jini services also include the lookup service and the discovery protocol in the Jini infrastructure. The lines between the three components of Jini are quite blurred.

## JavaSpace

Microsoft initially developed COM, or Common Object Model, to implement a better version of its Object Linking and Embedding (OLE) technology. Over time, however, COM has become a bigger force than OLE, and has found homes in distributed computing environments beyond desktop PCs.

JavaSpace and Jini have a similar relationship. While JavaSpace provides the underlying technology to Jini, its potential application reaches beyond the realm of Jini.

Distributed systems have the advantage of sharing computing tasks among different machines, thus increasing throughput and resulting in more efficient use of idle computing power. Of course, one of the challenges of this computing model is that coordination among cooperating machines must be maintained. For example, which machine takes which task, or how does a computer obtain the result of another's task? JavaSpace is designed to ease such problems in distributed computing.

In the late eighties, Professor David Gelernter at Yale University developed a system called Linda, in which all computing tasks are posted on a "bulletin board" and cooperating computers look at the bulletin board and find the tasks they are interested in running. The results are then pushed back to the bulletin board. The traditional method before Linda was having a computer assign tasks.

JavaSpace has a very similar approach. Tasks, or in JavaSpace terms, entries, are written to the JavaSpace servers. Other computers in the system may either read, or take, the entries. In the case of read, a copy of the entry is passed to the computer. In the case of take, the entry is read as well as removed from the server. A two-phase commit manager is used to make sure that entries are not lost or duplicated in the transaction because of a network failure or machine crash.

The JavaSpace system is very useful on today's Internet. For example, suppose you want to buy a car and hope to get the best deal. You may write up a description of the car you want and also how much you are willing to pay. You may then submit your request to your JavaSpace server. Your JavaSpace server then pushes copies of the request to the JavaSpace servers of car dealers. The dealers take the entries and submit responses back to your server, and you will then take the responses and select the best deal.

Of course, one day, JavaSpace servers may be everywhere and people will trade, compute, and collaborate on a single, universal, cooperative system. That is JavaSoft's vision for JavaSpace.

# InfoBus

JavaBean's default way of communicating is through events and bound properties, as discussed in Chapter 2. The connection between two beans is made at deploy time when a visual builder is used to examine the data types available through a design pattern. While this is a scalable solution for bean communication, the static nature of the connection has some deficiencies. First of all, some inferences need to be made based on the names of the methods or data. Such inferences become complex while similar names are encountered.

Another drawback of the event model is that the receiver has to know how the data is represented. If a new data type is entered into the system, existing beans cannot easily receive it as data.

Also, in the existing event model, if a receiver wants to receive the same data from multiple beans, it has to make explicit connections to all of them. Over time, the number of connections becomes fairly large.

InfoBus takes a different approach in exchanging data between beans. The idea comes from the hardware bus architecture, where hardware components are connected to a bus rather than creating specific paths for each pair of components. In InfoBus architecture, a software bus is created and beans are attached to the bus just like hardware components, as Figure 3-4 shows.

**Figure 3-4**
InfoBus architecture

**InfoBus**

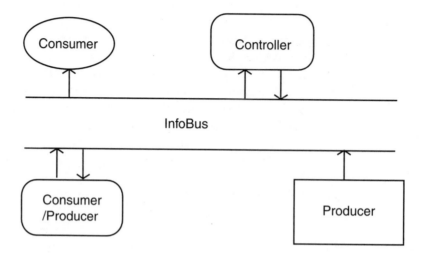

Depending on their roles, beans may connect to the bus either as consumers of data, producers of data, as both producers and consumers, or as controllers who facilitate the data exchange. In addition, the data items passed through the bus are self-describing, so that beans themselves do not need to know the internal representations of the data.

InfoBus is designed to facilitate communications between JavaBeans within the same Java virtual machine. For beans on different virtual machines, RMI or the higher level models such as JavaSpace are used as communication models.

## InfoBus Overview

Any Java object may create an InfoBus and have others join in by creating an InfoBus instance. An InfoBus instance may be created with a string name, or a name calculated based on the DOCBASE of an applet. The latter choice is convenient because all applets downloaded later will be able to join the same InfoBus.

An InfoBus member is either a consumer of data, a producer of data, or both. Another type of membership is the controller type, which distributes events to the appropriate members. If there is no data controller present, the InfoBus itself acts as a data controller.

A bean explicitly joins and leaves the InfoBus and it can join any number of buses. However, some issues may arise when they leave. For example, as a producer leaves, is the data it sends still valid? Or when a consumer leaves, does it still want the data it requested? The InfoBus specification has left such issues to be dealt with by the application developers, since they know best how such issues should be handled.

Central to the InfoBus architecture is the idea of rendezvous, the point where data is exchanged. A producer announces the availability of data when data is present as a result of some operations, such as database access or URL access. The InfoBus, or a data controller if one is present, will send an event to a consumer who is requesting the data. The consumer then decides if it is interested in the data by inspecting the name and the type. If it is interested, it contacts the producer directly and receives the data.

A consumer may request a data item even though no producers of the data are available on the bus. On the other hand, if more than one producer have the requested data, the first one that supplies the data item satisfies the request. However, the consumer has the choice of explicitly requesting data from each of the producers.

Special consideration has been taken to deal with the security issues of the rendezvous. For example, the producers may have a list of the classes that may have access to their data.

## Infobus Data Items

Data items passed on to the InfoBus are self-descriptive, so that consumers have enough information to decide whether or not they want the data. Furthermore, consumers will have the ability to utilize the data without understanding its internal data structure.

A data item may come with an interface for obtaining the source producer and for informing the producer when the consumer is no longer using the data. The latter ability is critical in certain applications. For example, a database application needs to know if a consumer has finished with the data so that it can release the associated database resource.

It may also come with access interfaces that retrieve the data from the data item. The access interface, along with the JDK 1.2 Collection classes, are able to deal with most of the data types in Java. These data types include simple objects such as strings, integers, or array objects, and more complex ones such as database objects, collections of data objects (such as a list), sets, and so on.

The standard access interfaces for data items are crucial to InfoBus's ability to provide data communications between two arbitrary Java components.

# JavaBeans Activation Framework

JDK 1.2 has extended the JavaBean model in three ways under a project code-named Glasgow.

- Extensible Runtime Containment and Service
- Drag and Drop Subsystem
- JavaBeans Activation Framework

The first two parts deal with client-side JavaBean enhancement, which falls outside of the focus of this book. The last item, JavaBeans Activation Framework (JAF), does have some implications on the server-side.

JAF allows Java applications to deal with different data types dynamically. An Internet browser has a standard way of invoking certain applications to process different data types. For example, when a Microsoft Word document is encountered, the browser figures out the data type by the file name extension (.doc), and correctly invokes the Microsoft Word application. JAF will provide the same model for Java applications, and instead of invoking binary applications, JavaBeans are invoked to process data of different types.

Even though JAF is designed with client-side applications, such as browsers or mail clients, in mind, certain server or embedded applications may find it useful. For example, a printer may wish to have a JavaBean present, and depending on the data sent, have the JavaBean do some processing before sending the data to the printer engine. In general, component activation and deactivation are an integral part of a component framework.

## JAF Architecture

An application uses the JAF framework to detect the data type and find the appropriate JavaBean to process the data, as shown in Figure 3-5.. The framework is composed of the following interfaces.

### DataSource

This interface encapsulates the data and outputs the data type, along with an output stream that transfers the data out.

**JAF Architecture**

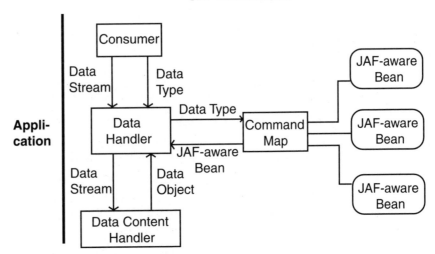

### DataHandler

This interface is the glue of the framework. It queries the DataSource object for the data type, and then finds the list of JAF-aware beans that may process the data.

### CommandMap

This interface stores the map between data types and their commands, or in this case, JAF-enabled beans.

### DataContentHandler

This interface facilitates the operation of DataHandler. It takes a data stream and converts it to an object of that type. DataContentHandler is also discovered using the CommandMap interface.

## JAF-Aware Beans

JavaBeans within the JAF frame should implement the CommandObject interface, which allows the bean to access DataHandler methods.

The DataHandler queries the data type from the DataSource, and then queries the CommandMap for the list of JAF-aware beans that may process the data. The DataHandler then presents the list to the application.

Either the application or the user may select a bean within the list, and the bean will get the data directly from the DataSource and process the data.

# Relationships Among the Frameworks

With so many frameworks, readers may wonder which framework they should use and what the relationship is among the multiple frameworks. Indeed, JDMK sounds a lot like JES, and many people wonder what exactly the difference is between JES lookup and Jini lookup. This section is meant to give readers some idea of where each framework fits.

JDMK is network management—focused. Not only does it come with a framework for application download, it also comes with network management—specific technologies such as a Managing Information Base (MIB) compiler for Java. On the other hand, JES is more focused on managing beans in general. It includes information such as service profiles and dependencies.

JES's dependencies are URL-based. Jini's lookup service, however, is based on package names or object types. Jini is an application that may reside on JES, as Figure 3-6 shows:

**Figure 3-6**

Jini may reside on JES

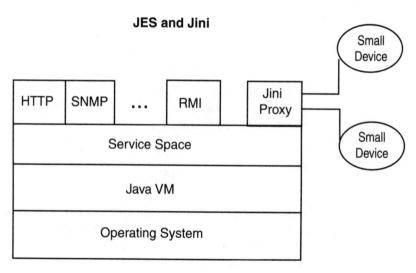

**JES and Jini**

Here, a Jini module resides on a JES framework. This module acts as a Jini proxy for a number of devices. Those devices are so small that no Jini service can reside on them. However, they participate in the Jini environment through the Jini proxy module.

Jini is concerned with communication between beans on different VMs. On the other hand, InfoBus is an elegant solution for beans to communicate on the same VM. JAF is also invoked by beans on the same machine.

# Summary

In this chapter we learned about a number of frameworks that are currently available for Java component technology. We also examined the relationship among these available frameworks. We did not discuss another component framework architecture called Enterprise JavaBeans (EJB), because it is so important we have dedicated the entire next chapter to it.

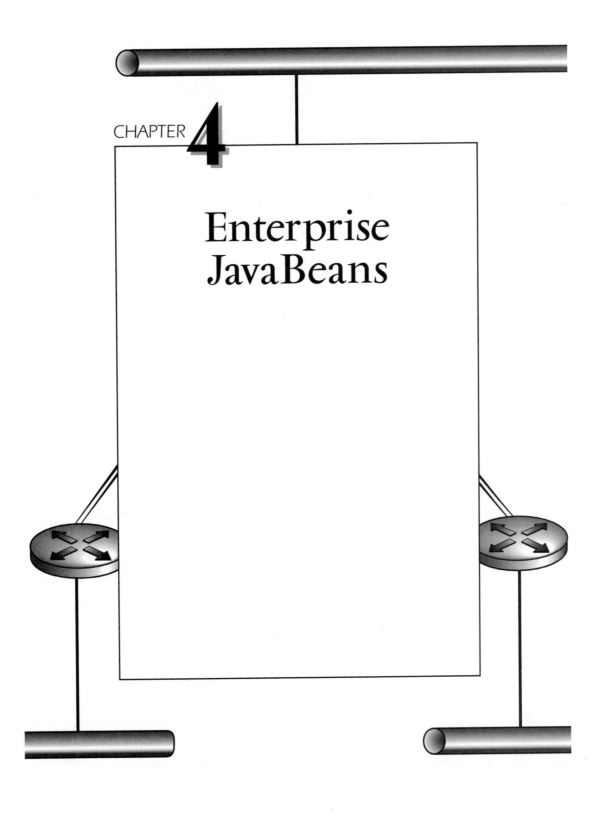

CHAPTER 4

# Enterprise
# JavaBeans

# Introduction

Enterprise JavaBeans, despite the name, are not the same JavaBeans we described in Chapter 2. The JavaBean architecture mainly focuses on connecting beans through visual representation, and has specified an event model for beans to inform each other of events. By contrast, Enterprise JavaBeans specify a complete framework for Java components in the application server environment. The component models for JavaBeans and Enterprise JavaBeans are not the same. Instead of focusing on connecting beans themselves, the Enterprise JavaBeans architecture specifies the communication interface between different components of an application framework.

# The Evolution of Internet Applications

In order to present the advantages of Enterprise JavaBeans, we should start by first describing the evolution of Internet applications.

## The Beginning—Client/Server

The architecture of Internet services has been enhanced significantly since the inception of the World Wide Web. The original Web was designed to help scientists publish papers, and it mainly consisted of Web servers satisfying HTML file requests from users' browsers. The model was a typical client/server model where data was stored on a large server, and the client, in this case a browser, requested service from the Webserver.

Figure 4-1 shows such an architecture.

In this architecture, the Webserver often runs on the same machine where the HTML files are stored. In the early days, the browsers only asked for HTML files, and this architecture worked just fine.

**Figure 4-1**
Client/Server
architecture

**Internet Architecture - I**

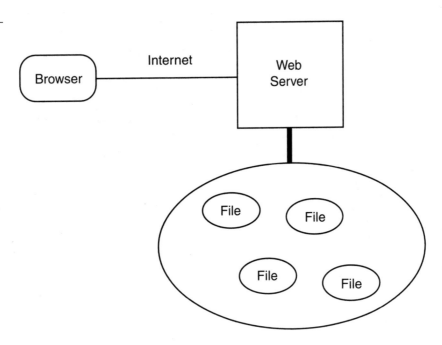

## Three-tier Application

As the Web becomes more popular, however, Web sites often want to collect some user information as part of registration. This requirement extends the needed functionality of a Web server, because the collected user information is often stored in a database, and the Web server now needs to know how to access databases. Furthermore, the content of a Web site has expanded beyond simple HTML files. For example, a company may provide employee information online for internal use, and such information may well be stored in a relational database. The Common Gateway Interface (CGI) has become the most widely used protocol to extend the functionality of a Web server beyond simply serving HTML files.

In a CGI environment, the Web server invokes an application (called a CGI application) to do the actual database accessing. It also passes the parameters needed and obtains the result. The communication between the Web server and the application is through some inter-process communication mechanism provided by the operating system. The application exits after it performs what the Web server asks of it.

Such a model is called a three-tier application model, because we now have three entities in the picture—the browser, the Web server and its CGI application, and the database. Figure 4-2 shows such an architecture.

**Figure 4-2**
Three-tier architecture

**Internet Architecture - II**

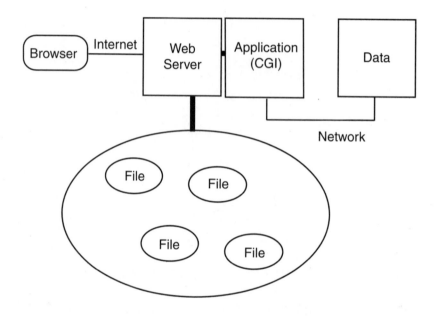

## Transaction Processing Monitor

Today's Internet has more than 100 million users and Internet applications range from electronic commerce to extranet applications to sophisticated intranet applications. These types of applications have placed more demand on Web servers in terms of scalability, security, fault-tolerance, and transaction functionality. For example, Dell Computer sells $6 million worth of equipment on the Internet each day. Such a sales volume requires the careful implementation of financial transaction software that provides a secure infrastructure, together with a scalable application that coordinates all aspects of electronic commerce, including user management, product catalog maintenance, logging, financial transactions, while at the same time, communicating with the Web server.

Obviously, a CGI application will need to be vastly extended to deal with such complex issues. Fortunately, these issues are not new to the computer industry. Financial transactions are common in banking applications, and large online transaction applications routinely deal with thousands of transactions per second. At the core of such applications is the transaction processing monitor, or TP monitor.

The TP monitor coordinates the resource requirements of each client request and makes sure that resources are shared whenever possible. It may also spread workload among different processes that may be running on different machines. It also deals with issues such as fault-tolerance and transaction processing. Some examples of TP monitors include IBM's CICS and BEA's Tuxedo TP monitors.

## Middleware

In addition to the increased complexity of applications, the types of data sources online have also been broadened to include various legacy systems, database systems, and other data sources such as Light Weight Directory Access Protocol (LDAP) servers. The data source access issue is complicated by the fact that many legacy applications are written in languages other than C or C++, and attempts to access these applications through a low level networking protocol results in repetitive programming in different languages. Nowadays, the standard way to access these various data sources is through an application called middleware.

Middleware software, such as the Common Object Request Broker Architecture (CORBA), takes care of the communication issues between distributed applications, even when these applications are written in different programming languages. The programming model is through a remote procedure call, or RPC, where programs make function calls over the network as if they are executed locally. Chapter 12 covers CORBA in more detail.

In addition to CORBA, Java's Remote Method Invocation (RMI) and Microsoft's COM/DCOM architecture are some other examples of the popular middleware software available today. However, in the case of RMI, both applications need to be written in Java, and COM/DCOM is more C/C++-focused.

## Application Server

In today's Internet world, the functionality of a TP monitor and middleware software are combined and result in the Internet application server. This type of software has just become popular recently and its definition varies between different research firms and vendors. ZDNet narrowly defines an application server as a program that runs on a mid-sized machine that handles all application operations between browser-based computers and a company's back-end business applications or databases. On the other hand, Forrester Research defines it more broadly as a program that offloads processing from fat clients and allows developers to create Internet and intranet content and transaction-rich applications.

Of course, both definitions include transaction processing ability and middleware. In addition, Internet application servers need to deal with security issues. Public Key Infrastructure and Internet security protocols such as Secure Socket Layer (SSL) form the cornerstones of future electronic commerce applications. Internet application servers need to be aware of security technologies and deal with any security-related issue. Chapter 11 covers security-related technologies in more detail.

Typical Internet application servers include Netscape's Application Server and SUN's NetDynamics Application Server. Traditional TP monitor vendors have also moved into this market. For example, BEA Systems has announced an application server product built on top of its Tuxedo TP monitor.

Figure 4-3 shows an Internet architecture with an application server handling client requests in the middle.

## Enterprise JavaBeans

Enterprise JavaBeans, or EJB, is the marriage of an Internet application server with a Java component architecture. It specifies a container that is built on top of an application server, and at the same time, acts as a framework for Java components. Because the container is effectively an extension of an application server, it is able to provide transaction and security services, as well as middleware support to Java components.

Furthermore, because the interface between EJB components and their containers is standard, components written for the container and the application from one vendor are able to migrate to other containers and servers effortlessly.

Even though we have introduced EJB in the browser environment, its potential usage includes any type of client applications such as PC client applications, Java applications, and in many cases, Web servers.

Figure 4-4 shows a possible scenario of an EJB implementation.

**Figure 4-3**
Internet architecture
with application
server

**Internet Architecture - III**

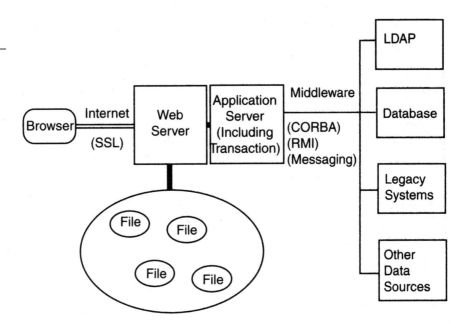

**Enterprise JavaBeans**

**Figure 4-4**
A typical EJB
implementation

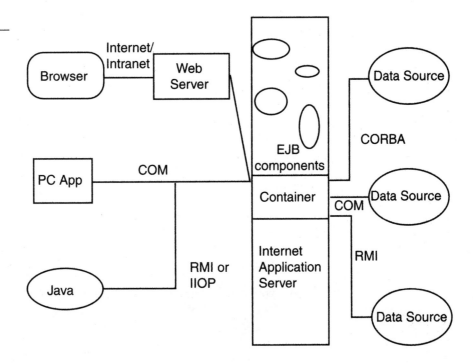

EJB components may communicate with clients and data sources through various middleware protocols, and the details of the protocols are taken care of by the container and the underlying application server. Therefore, the developers of the EJB components don't need to worry about things like how to communicate with a Java client through CORBA. Similarly, services such as transaction and load balancing are transparently handled by the container and the application server. The net result of such an architecture is that developers will be free to focus on application logic itself rather than on system-level programming details. In the Enterprise JavaBeans specification, these Java components are called enterprise beans.

# Enterprise JavaBeans Fundamentals

Suppose you want to write a simple integer calculator program that knows how to calculate multiplication, division, square roots, and logarithms. Now suppose again that you want to place the services of this calculator on the network so everyone may use them.

In a traditional C programming environment, you would first write the calculator program. You would then write some networking code that listens on the network for client requests, gets the input numbers, invokes the calculator, and returns the results to clients. The additional networking code may easily exceed the amount of code in the original calculator. Of course, you still haven't dealt with problems like what happens if two requests arrive at the same time, and so on.

A middleware program like CORBA goes a long way to reduce the amount of networking code you need for such an assignment. Using CORBA, you would write a file that lists the services you want to provide in a calculator. You would then run a tool provided by your CORBA vendor that generates some code for your client and some other code for your server. You would then write your client code utilizing the generated code. After that, you would fill the generated server code with calls to your calculator program. Both the client and the server programs also need to include some CORBA-specific calls. Of course, if they are written in C, the programs will not run on a different hardware platform. Even if they are written in Java, the programs will not run in a different CORBA environment. And you still haven't dealt with issues such as transactions, security, and so on.

In the EJB environment, you would write a file that lists the services of the calculator (the list is called Remote Interface in EJB), write the program in Java, and you would be done! Furthermore, your code works on any hardware platform, any application server, and any EJB container, and if you wanted to store the result of your calculation into a database, you are provided with transaction support if needed.

Too good to be true? Not after you understand how EJB works.

I have a colleague who has been in the computing field for thirty years. He often tells me stories about how he used to program with a stack of cards, and produce another stack of cards after compiling, and another stack of cards after linking with libraries that were themselves stacks of cards. Finally he got to run the program, which was composed of a much larger stack of cards than the original program. I started programming in C. I always feel a bit lucky when he tells me such stories. In the future, young programmers who start with EJB may have the same feeling when I tell them about my C experience in client/server programming.

## How EJB Works

In the EJB architecture, the code you write forms the enterprise bean. There are two types of enterprise beans—a session bean that lasts as long as there is a client associated with it, and an entity bean that represents persistent storage. A more detailed discussion of session beans and entity beans can be found later in this chapter.

In the case of a calculator enterprise bean, it can be considered as a session bean because there is no permanent storage associated with it.

A Java component is a session bean if it implements the *javax.ejb.SessionBean* interface. So your calculator would start with:

```
Public class CalculatorBean implements
javax.ejb.SessionBean
```

On the other hand, an entity bean should implement the *javax.ejb.EntityBean* interface.

You then implement your methods, say *multiply()*, *division()*, *sq_root()*, and *logarithm()*. As in a CORBA environment, you need to list those methods in a file. The list forms the contract between clients and the calculator enterprise bean. The contract is called the Remote Interface and the interface has to extend the *EJBObject* interface.

```
Public interface Calculator extends
javax.ejb.EJBObject{
  public int multiply(int a, int b) throws
RemoteException;
  public double division(int a, int b) throws
RemoteException;
  public double sq_root(int a) throws RemoteException;
  public double logarithm(int a, int b) throws
RemoteException;
}
```

Readers who are familiar with CORBA or RMI may notice that in these types of middleware environments, interfaces between the client and the server do not need to extend a pre-defined interface.

In the EJB environment, the *EJBObject* interface must be extended. In fact, the *EJBObject* interface is the reason why enterprise bean developers may automatically expose the bean's services through CORBA, RMI, COM, or other types of middleware supported by the EJB container vendor.

The *EJBObject* sits in between the client and the enterprise beans and is the object that implements middleware interfaces. For example, in an RMI environment, the *EJBObject* will implement RMI interfaces and allow the client to communicate with the enterprise beans through RMI. In a CORBA environment, the *EJBObject* will implement CORBA interfaces and the communication is done through CORBA. Figure 4-5 shows how *EJBObject* makes a difference.

In the EJB environment, the nitty-gritty of the middleware interface is all taken care of by the *EJBObject*. Method invocations from the client to enterprise beans go to *EJBObject* first, because *EJBObject* knows how to communicate with the client, and the *EJBObject* then invokes the enterprise beans' methods on the client's behalf.

To a client, however, the existence of an *EJBObject* is transparent. The client still thinks it is communicating with the enterprise bean directly. Such a client view is important because it simplifies the programming model.

Experienced middleware programmers may notice that Figure 4-5 is missing an important piece. If the client talks to the *EJBObject* via CORBA, then the client has to be CORBA-aware. Indeed, *EJBObject* is actually divided into a client-side stub and a server-side skeleton. Chapter 12 covers these middleware-related concepts in more detail. Figure 4-6 shows EJBObjects with the stubs and skeletons in the right places.

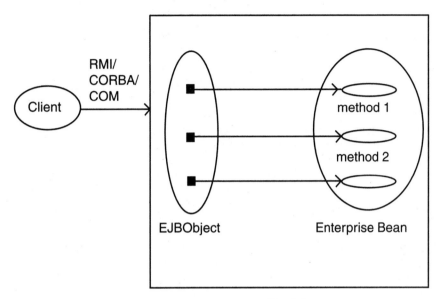

**Figure 4-5**
Client communicat-
ing to EJBObject

**Figure 4-5**
Client communicat-
ing to EJBObject

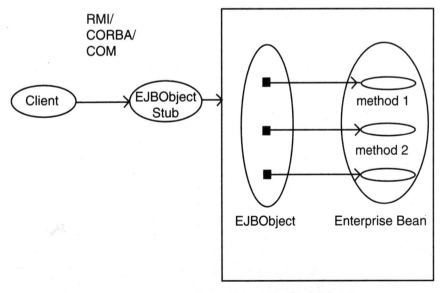

**Figure 4-6**
Complete scenario
with EJBObject

The EJBObjects are generated by a tool provided by the server vendor. Figure 4-7 shows the generation process.

**EJBObject Generation**

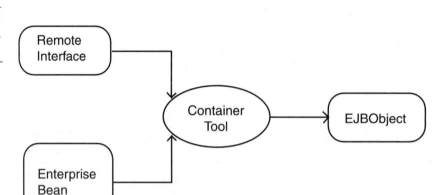

## Home Interface

In the EJB architecture, the container manages the life cycle of the enterprise beans. It has the responsibility of creating and removing objects. Therefore, the client needs to communicate with the container in order to create instances of enterprise beans. The home interface is used by the client to tell the container how to create and remove enterprise bean objects. In the case of entity beans, the home interface also specifies how the client may find them. We'll cover the detail of entity objects later in this chapter.

A home interface needs to extend the *EJBHome* interface. Our calculator may look like this:

```
public interface CalculatorHome extends EJBHome{
   Calculator create() throws CreateException,
RemoteException;
}
```

This interface doesn't specify a *remove()* method. In this case, the default *remove* methods from the container will be used to remove enterprise bean objects.

Analogous to the *EJBObject*, the *EJBHome* stands between the client and the enterprise beans and handles creating and removing the object, and in the case of entity beans, locating the object. Like *EJBObject*, these requests are communicated via some middleware and the *EJBHome* object is generated by the same vendor-provided tool that generates the *EJBObject*. Figure 4-8 shows the different functions of the home interface and the remote interface.

**Figure 4-8**
Functionalities of
EJBObject and
EJBHome objects

**EJB Client Interfaces**

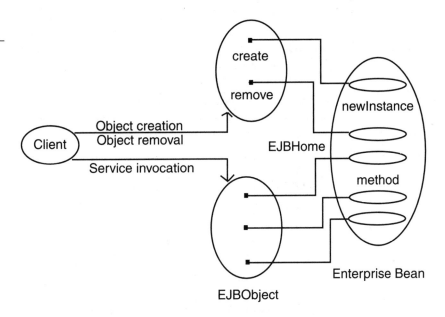

## The Container

In addition to bean creation and removal, the container may also move dormant session beans to secondary storage to clear memory space for other more active beans. Such an operation is called passivating the bean. Of course, it also activates the passivated bean when it is needed again.

The container provides many of the services that are traditionally associated with a transaction manager, including persistence management, transaction management, and security services.

The container is also responsible for advertising the location of the enterprise beans' home object through a naming service, so that a client is able to locate the services through the Java Naming and Directory Interface (JNDI) API. This is covered in detail in Chapter 9 of this book.

# Development and Deployment Workflow

The intent of the Enterprise JavaBeans architecture is to create robust markets for enterprise bean components, containers, and application servers. Any enterprise bean will work within any container, and any container will work on top of any application server. As of this writing, no standard is available for container interaction with the application server.

The specification also distinguishes among the enterprise bean developers, application assemblers, and deployers. All together there are six different roles in the enterprise bean architecture.

## Enterprise Bean Provider and Application Assembler

The object model of Enterprise JavaBeans is very similar to that of the object model of a standard body Object Management Group, or OMG. The OMG's object model specifies the concepts of application domain and business object. Application domains refer to vertically integrated types of applications such as electronic commerce, manufacturing, telecommunication, and so on. Business objects are objects that may be used in multiple application domains. Examples of business objects include credit card transactions and inventory management. If application domains are vertical, then business objects are horizontal.

In the Enterprise JavaBeans architecture, enterprise beans are seen as business objects. These beans may later be assembled into vertical applications. Therefore, the enterprise bean provider creates enterprise beans that implement the business logic of certain tasks or entities such as people, credit, and so on, and application assemblers assemble them into applications such as online banking.

Both the bean providers and the application developers need to understand the domain. The bean provider creates the remote interface, the home interface, and the enterprise beans. The application assemblers create

Enterprise JavaBeans clients with the knowledge of the EJBObject interfaces. The assemblers don't need to understand the details of the enterprise beans' implementation.

The separation of the bean developer and application assembler is needed to create an enterprise bean component market where an application assembler may pick beans from different vendors and assemble them into commercial applications. While this is the ultimate goal of component architecture, so far it has not been realized in any of the existing architectures.

## Deployer and System Administrator

Both the deployers and the system administrators are familiar with the organizations that use the Enterprise JavaBeans application. The deployers adapt the application to specific requirements of the organizations. For example, in the case of an online banking application, the deployer may specify the security needs of the particular organization that deploys it.

Once the application is deployed, the system administrator performs the daily task of maintaining the application.

## Container Provider and Application Server Provider

The application server provides the transaction, security, and middleware support, and the container translates that support into something that enterprise beans can understand. The container provider also provides the tool that generates the home objects and the EJBObject.

The interface between the application server and the container is not included in the Enterprise JavaBeans specification 1.0. Therefore, at this time, application server providers also provide the container. It is expected that future releases of the Enterprise JavaBeans specification will include the interface between the container and the application server, so that any container can plug in to any application server.

# Session Bean

## Introduction

A session bean is created on behalf of a single client. It often does not live long and does not survive a server crash. A session bean must implement the *SessionBean* interface. To a client, the session bean is location-independent. The client uses a naming service to look for a session bean when it is needed.

The following four steps show a typical interaction between a client and a session bean:

1. Look up the location of the session bean using the JNDI API—obtaining the home object.
2. Create the session bean via the home interface.
3. Invoke the session bean's methods via the remote interface.
4. Remove the session bean via the home interface.

If the client forgets to remove the session bean before exiting, the container removes it after some time-out period has passed. Of course, there will be cases when an object is removed by the container when the client has not exited. In this case, the client is expected to create another bean object.

There are two types of session beans—the beans with state and the beans without state. Such a distinction is important for bean passivation.

## Passivation and Activation

For a large Enterprise JavaBeans application, there are often thousands of session beans being created every hour—just imagine some electronic commerce site that has thousands of visitors each hour. In such cases, session beans may occupy a large amount of memory space and cause performance degradation.

The container has the option of moving session beans to some secondary storage if necessary. Such an operation is called bean passivation.

For session beans with states (open file descriptors, open sockets, etc.), the bean developer must make sure the resources are released before the bean is passivated. Such releases are done by a method called *ejbPassivate()*.

This method will be called by the container at the time of passivation. Of course, the resources will need to be reacquired at the time of activation—the reverse of passivation, in the *ejbActivate()* method.

## The Contract Between the Session Bean and the Container

The *ejbPassivate()* and *ejbActivate()* methods are examples of the contract between the session bean and the container, or the *SessionBean* interface.

When the container creates the bean, it first calls the *newInstance()* method to create the bean object. It then calls the *setSessionContext()* method, which allows the container to pass the bean's context to the bean itself. A session bean's context includes its *EJBObject*, home object, environment property list, and identity of the EJB client. The last method that the container calls at bean creation is the *ejbCreate()* method. This method is implemented by the bean developer that initializes the bean.

The container calls the *ejbRemove()* method to signal the bean that it is in the process of being removed. The bean may release the resources it has held in this method.

# Entity Bean

## Introduction

A session bean is always associated with a single client and it keeps states for the client. An entity bean, however, represents some entity in persistent storage, such as a database. In the case of a relational database, the entity bean often represents a row. Unlike a session bean, an entity bean has a long life and survives a server crash, and it does not store client states such as open file descriptors.

While an entity bean only represents one row in a database, the entity bean may be utilized by multiple session beans, and one session bean represents only one remote client. Figure 4-9 shows an online book store where a session bean, the Customer bean, serves a client, and an entity bean, the Book bean, represents a book. A customer may purchase multiple books.

**Figure 4-9**
Interaction of session
and entity beans

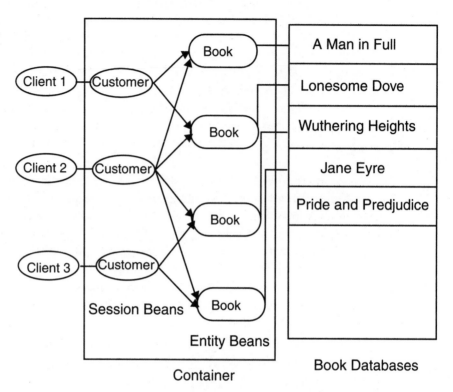

Like a session bean, an entity bean has a remote interface where the business logic is implemented. It also obtains an entity bean through its home interface, like a sessions bean. However, because of the nature of an entity bean, the methods in its home interface perform different functions from those of a session bean.

## Home Interface

The home interface of an entity bean includes *create()* and *remove()*. However, the meaning of these methods is very different from when they are applied to a session bean. Object creation means to insert a row into the underlying database, and removal means removing the row. In fact, direct database manipulation has the same effect as creating and removing entity objects.

The means to obtaining an entity bean is by "finding" it. Each entity object is associated with a unique identifier called the primary key. A client may find the object with its primary key. The method that finds the entity object by its primary key is called *findByPrimaryKey()*. Other find methods may be defined in the home interface. For example, there may be a method called *findByBookSubject()* that returns books within a certain subject.

The effect of invoking a *findBy* method is equivalent to doing a SELECT in a database and returning the rows that match the criteria. In the case of multiple results, an enumeration object consisting of a list of primary keys is returned.

An example of an entity bean home interface looks like this:

```
Public interface BookHome extends EJBHome{
    Book create(String ISBN, String name, String
publisher, float price)throws RemoteException,
CreateException;
    Book findByPrimaryKey(BookPK ISBN) throws
RemoteException, FinderException;
}
```

Here the primary key is represented by a book's ISBN number, and the *remove()* method will be the default method that comes with the container.

## Life Cycle

In a session bean, the client calls the *create()* method of the home interface to create a new instance of a session bean. In an entity bean, the more frequent way of obtaining the bean instance is through the *findBy* method. However, in the case of an entity bean, the *findBy* method does not create a new entity bean instance.

Since entity beans have long lives, creating one instance with each *findBy* method would gradually exhaust system resources. The EJB container creates a pool of anonymous entity beans when the system is initialized. Whenever a *findBy* method is invoked, a bean is selected from the pool and is associated with a client, or an *EJBObject*. As the client calls the *remove()* method, the underlying row of the database is removed, and then the entity bean is returned to the anonymous pool.

When a bean is in the pool, it is in the "pooled" state. When it is associated with an *EJBObject*, it is in the "ready" state.

Of course, a client may use the bean and not call the *remove()* method. In this case, the container may passivate the bean at certain times. Passivating a bean causes it to be put back in the pool, and activating it does the reverse. Passivation and activation of entity beans is therefore quite different from passivation and activation of session beans.

Figure 4-10 shows the state transitions of an entity bean.

**Figure 4-10**
State transitions of an entity bean

**Entity Bean State Transition**

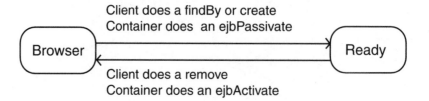

The container may enlarge or shrink the entity bean pool when necessary.

## Persistence

Since an entity bean represents some data in a database, someone has to write the code to access the database itself. For example, when a client invokes a *findBy* method, a SELECT operation will need to be performed on the database. If such an operation is done by the entity enterprise bean developer, then this bean possesses bean-managed persistence. If the container assumes the responsibility of writing to and reading from the database, then the bean possesses container-managed persistence.

The client may cause database access with *findBy, create,* and *remove* operations. In addition, when the container passivates or activates an entity bean, the bean will need to store the data back to the database or load the data from the database, respectively.

The advantage of bean-managed persistence is that the bean is persistent even when the container does not handle database access. The disadvantage is that the code is not portable across databases.

# The Contract Between the Entity Bean and the Container

Like the session bean, the entity enterprise bean runs within the container. The client never directly invokes the methods of the bean itself. Instead, the container, or the container-generated objects, invokes the enterprise Bean's methods on behalf of the client. Furthermore, the container needs to communicate with the bean at the time of passivation or activation. The EntityBean interface contains methods that implement the contract between the bean and the container.

Figure 4-11 shows the corresponding entity enterprise bean's methods of home interface.

**Figure 4-11**
Home interface and corresponding entity bean methods

**Home Interface and corresponding entity bean methods**

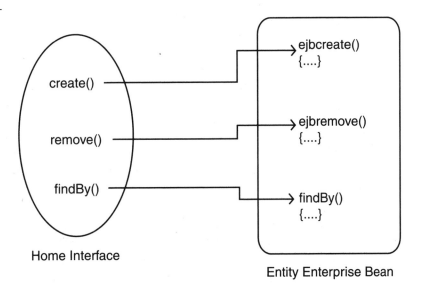

Home Interface

Entity Enterprise Bean

The signatures of the corresponding methods should match. In addition, when a developer wishes to use the default behavior of a container, the method should still be declared in the entity enterprise bean, but the implementation may be left empty.

Some other methods of the entity bean interface include *ejbLoad()* and *ejbStore()*. The *ejbLoad()* method loads the data from the database to the bean, and *ejbStore()* stores the data back to the database. When the container wants to passivate the bean, it calls the *ejbPassivate()* method, and it calls the *ejbActivate()* method when activating the bean.

Like the session bean, the container may pass the context of the bean to the bean itself by calling the *setEntityContext()* method. This method is called during the bean's creation. The reverse of *setEntityContext()* is *unsetEntityContext()*.

# Summary

Enterprise JavaBeans architecture represents the convergence of transaction processing monitors, middleware, component technology, and Java. It allows the developer to develop cross-platform, cross-middleware applications without a detailed knowledge of the middleware programming model, transactions, or security. Enterprise JavaBeans represent the next step in enterprise computing after CORBA, COM, and transaction processing monitors.

There are four components in an Enterprise JavaBeans architecture—the Enterprise JavaBeans client, the enterprise bean, the container, and the application server. Enterprise JavaBeans 1.0 specifies the interface among the client, the container, and the enterprise beans. The next release of the specification will include the interface between the container and the application server.

The Enterprise JavaBeans architecture represents a giant step toward a robust Java component market where application assemblers can assemble off-the-shelf components from different vendors into a single commercial application.

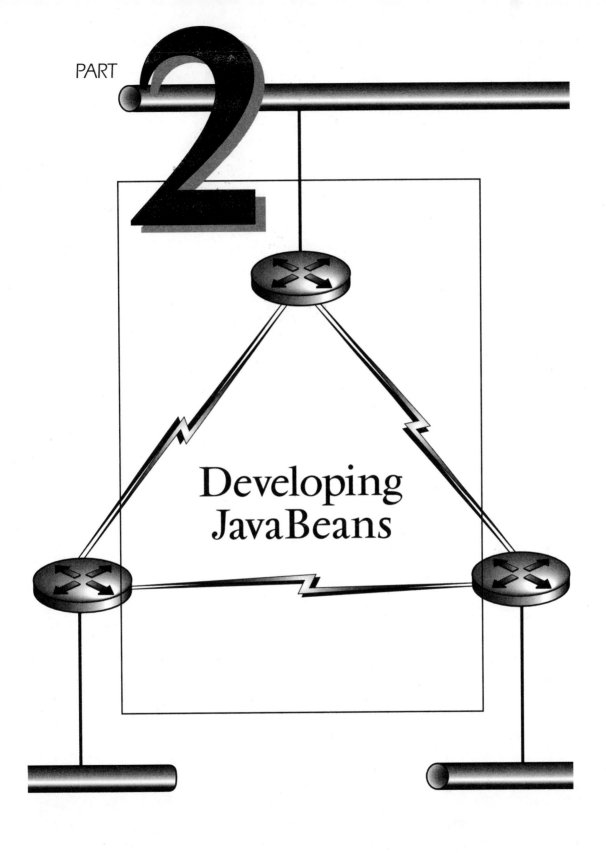

Developing
JavaBeans

# CHAPTER 5

# Using Java Studio

# Introduction

Java Studio is a development tool for developing Java programs rapidly without having to write any pieces of code. One can develop Java applets, application programs, and beans using this tool. No programming knowledge is necessary to use this tool. All one has to do is drag the components, wire up the logic, and save the application. In this chapter we'll see how to install and use the Java Studio tool. One important thing we'll see in this chapter is how to integrate existing JavaBean components into the tool, so that it can be used for developing programs. We will not go into a lot of detail here since there are books already available that are dedicated to Java Studio.

# Installing Java Studio

If you have access to the Internet, you can download the Java Studio 1.0 from *http://www.sun.com/studio*.

To install the product, save the self-extracting executable and execute it.. This will do much of the work for you, except for responding to the installer wizard. After installation, you will be all set to use the tool for developing Java applications rapidly.

Java Studio does not take the CLASSPATH set as the environment variable. We have to set the CLASSPATH in the command line. Here's how to do this:

1. Open the Java Studio program group.
2. Click the right mouse button on the Java Studio 1.0 icon.
3. Select Properties from the floating menu.
4. This will open the Properties dialog for Java Studio.
5. Select Shortcut folder.
6. In the Target field, you'll see *C:\Java-Studio1.0\JS\intel-win32\bin\js.exe*, if your Java Studio is installed in the C: drive.
7. To provide CLASSPATH information, you need to type **CLASSPATH -;.;<complete classpath here>** after *C:\Java-Studio1.0\JS\intel-win32\bin\js.exe* in the Target field. Make sure your CLASSPATH has "-;" as the first two characters. Append the CLASSPATH as and when necessary.
8. Your Java Studio will now search for the classes mentioned in the CLASSPATH.

You can execute the application by double-clicking the icon created after installation. When you double-click the Java Studio program icon, three windows appear:

1. A Main Window—This window contains a series of folders, both default folders and those created by users, which contain components. This window is also called the component palette.

2. A GUI Window—This window will show the actual window look and feel when the program is run, a WYSIWYG (What You See Is What You Get) window. This window is used for placing all the GUI-based components.

3. A Design Window—As the name suggests, this window is the design window where all the logic is built by wiring components. This window can contain both GUI and non-GUI based components that are used in the application development. This is not a WYSIWYG window, because this is available during design time only.

## Using Java Studio

In this section we will use Java Studio to develop the Simplest Arithmetic Calculator and see how to create an application and an applet.

### Design Considerations

We'll use the following components for developing the Simplest Arithmetic Calculator:

■ Three Textfield components, two for input and one to display the result.

■ Two Distributor components to distribute the inputs to memory components.

■ Four Arithmetic components, each responsible for one arithmetic operation (addition, subtraction, multiplication, and division).

■ Four Memory components to store the inputs. Each memory component is associated with one arithmetic component.

■ Four Button components, each for one arithmetic operation. Each button is connected to a respective memory component. When clicked it will trigger the respective memory component, which will output its contents to the arithmetic component.

■ One Merger component for collecting the outputs from the arithmetic component and routing it to the resulting textfield component.

■ Four Label components for labeling the components present in the GUI window.

To create the Simplest Arithmetic Calculator, follow these steps:

1.  To begin, choose File->New.

2.  Place three textfield components and three label components from the GUI folder either in the GUI window or the Design window, as shown in Figure 5-1. Make the resulting textfield non-editable in the customizer window. Name the label components appropriately. To customize any component, you can open the Customizer window by double-clicking the component. By default, when each component is placed, the Customizer window pops up. You can disable this by choosing View->Customizer On Add, which will toggle the command on or off. To place a component, just select the component and click on the Design window or the GUI window.

3.  Place four button components from the GUI folder in the GUI window and label them as +, -, *, and /, which signifies each arithmetic operation. (Refer to Figure 5-1.)

4.  In the Design window, place two distributor components from the Data Flow folder. By default a distributor component has one input and two outputs. Since we need four outputs—one for each memory component—double-click the distributor component. In the Customizer window add two more connectors for each distributor component.

5.  In the Design window place four memory components from the Data Flow folder. Each memory component by default has two inputs and two outputs.

6.  In the Design window place a merger component from the Data Flow folder. Customize it to have four inputs.

7.  In the Design window place four arithmetic components from the Computation folder. Customize each arithmetic component to perform one arithmetic operation by double-clicking on the component and customizing it to perform +, -, *, and /, respectively, for each of the components.

8.  As shown in Figure 5-2, wire the text inputs to the distributor. The output of the first distributor is wired to the first input of every memory component, and the second distributor is wired to the second input. Memory components are triggered by the buttons. Output of the memory is directed to the respective arithmetic components.

For example, say if the – button is pressed, the memory component outputs its contents to the arithmetic component configured to do a subtraction operation. The output of all the arithmetic components is connected to the merger component, which in turn outputs the result to the Result textfield.

**Figure 5-1**
GUI screen for Simple Arithmetic Calculator

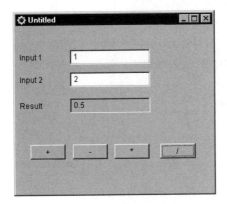

**Figure 5-2**
Wiring diagram for Simple Arithmetic Calculator

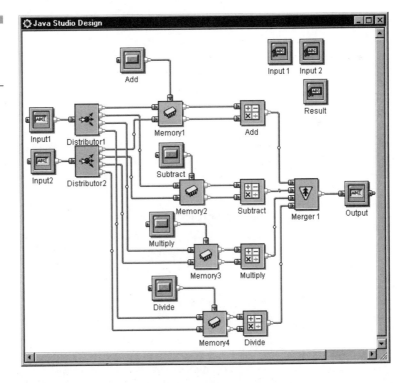

**NOTE**

All the default component names are changed from the Customizer window, but that is not discussed in detail here because it is pretty simple.

To generate an applet of the Simple Arithmetic Calculator, follow these steps:

1. Click on the Generate->Applet menu item. This will bring up the wizard, which asks for more details. Type in the file location and the file name, say **SimpleCalci,** and click Next.
2. Select the display window for viewing the applet. You can choose User Specified Browser. Point to the location where your browser is located by clicking on the Browse button. Click Next.
3. Select In the browser window to view the applet. Click Finish.
4. This will load the applet into the browser you already specified. Now your calculator is ready to use. You can type in number **10** in Input 1, press Enter, and type **10** in Input 2, and press Enter. Now click the buttons to perform different arithmetic operations on the two numbers. You will see the results in the Result textfield.

**NOTE**

The textfields send the event only when Enter is pressed after typing in the values. If you don't press Enter, you will not see any results.

In case the applet does not work in the browser you have selected, make sure that the browser has JDK 1.1 support. Otherwise you can use an applet viewer that supports JDK 1.1 against the HTML file that is generated. In our case it is *SimpleCalci.html.*

You can save the project workspace by selecting File->Save. Type in the Project name, for example Simple Calculator, and select a directory. All the project information is saved for you under *Simple Calculator.vj* file. The next time you need to open the project, just open *Simple Calculator.vj* using File>Open.

Similarly, you can also generate applications or JavaBeans using the Generate menu. In the next section, we will see how to integrate third party components into Java Studio.

Code for this application is available under the *chap5\sample1* subdirectory on the CD-ROM. Use *SimpleCalci.html* in your browser (that supports JDK 1.1) to execute the applet.

# Integrating JavaBean Components into Java Studio

In the previous section you used existing JavaBean components for developing applications. In this section we'll see how to create components from existing JavaBeans to use with Java Studio by adding necessary connectors. Components that are written using JDK™ 1.1 and above can be directly integrated into Java Studio. However, beans not written using JDK 1.0.2 can be wrapped using the Transitional APIs to support JDK 1.0.2 environment also. In this section we'll only see how to wrap a JDK 1.1-compliant JavaBean into Java Studio. For more information on "transitional" JavaBean components, see the Java Studio online help.

We'll use a *SimpleBooleanSwitch* bean developed for the purposes of demonstration. *SimpleBooleanSwitch* is a very simple Boolean switch that can be set on and off. We'll wrap this component so that it can be used with Java Studio. Since we won't discuss the *SimpleBooleanSwitch* bean's code here, it would be a good idea for you to take a look at the source for this *SimpleBooleanSwitch* before continuing to read this section. You can find the example and the source under the *chap5/sample2* subdirectory on the CD-ROM.

To create a Java Studio component from an existing bean component, we have to write some code.

Decide the functionality you want to expose. We'll expose *toggleSwitch()*, *switchOn()*, and *switchOff()* methods for the input connectors, and two output connectors that will send "Switch On" and "Switch Off" for the two events generated depending on the switch state by the enclosed bean class. To provide the output connectors, the component must implement the enclosed bean's listener class.

To create an end-user bean component for Java Studio you have to subclass the *VJComponent* class provided with Java Studio library. Note that it must implement events of the bean's listener class in order to provide respective output connectors in case the output connectors are mapped to the events of the enclosed bean.

```
public class VJBooleanButton extends VJComponent
implements SimpleBooleanListener
```

Here *VJBooleanButton* is the component name that extends *VJComponent* and implements *SimpleBooleanListener*.

Override *VJComponentInit()* as shown below. The parameter passed is a string that is the display name used for the component instance. However, we are not interested in this parameter. Connectors are created in this method.

```
public void VJComponentInit(String nm){
```

Create the enclosed bean.

```
SimpleBooleanSwitch bb = new SimpleBooleanSwitch();
```

We'll create an instance of *SimpleBooleanSwitch* because this is the bean we want to wrap up into a Java Studio component.

Create data transfer objects that implement the *OutputDataTransfer* interface. See Java Studio online help for all the supported data transfer objects.

```
ObjectInputTransfer objectIn = new
ObjectInputTransfer();
StringToBasicOutputTransfer stringOut = new
StringToBasicOutputTransfer();
```

Since our input connectors for *switchOn()*, *switchOff()*, and *toggleSwitch()* don't require any parameters, it is sufficient to just create *ObjectInputTransfer*. For the output connectors, we need to create *StringToBasicOutputTransfer*.

We'll expose *switchOn()*, *switchOff()*, and *toggleSwitch()* methods for the input connectors

```
Method inMethod1 = boolClass.getMethod("switchOn", new
Class[0]);
Method inMethod2 = boolClass.getMethod("switchOff", new
Class[0]);
Method inMethod3 = boolClass.getMethod("toggleSwitch",
new Class[0]);
```

Bind input connectors to methods. Whenever any connector receives the message, it invokes that method to which it is bound.

```
inPort1 = new VJBoundPort(this, inMethod1, objectIn);
inPort2 = new VJBoundPort(this, inMethod2, objectIn);
inPort3 = new VJBoundPort(this, inMethod3, booleanIn);
```

In our case, either *switchOn()*, *switchOff()*, or *toggleSwitch()* will be invoked, depending which of the input connectors gets the message.

```
Class outargs[] =
{Class.forName("SimpleBooleanEvent")};
Method outMethod1 = myClass.getMethod("switchOn",
outargs);
Method outMethod2 = myClass.getMethod("switchOff",
outargs);
outPort1 = new VJBoundPort(this, outMethod1,
stringOut);
outPort2 = new VJBoundPort(this, outMethod2,
stringOut);
```

Similarly, bind the output connector to a method. In our case we bind the events generated by *SimpleBooleanButton* to the output connectors. For this reason *VJBooleanButton* implements *SimpleBooleanListener*.

Messages to the output connector from the methods are bound to the events generated by the enclosed bean. Whenever the enclosed bean fires an event, messages are sent to the output connector from *VJBooleanButton* class, as shown below.

```
public void switchOn(SimpleBooleanEvent be){
  try{
    outPort1.sendMessage("Switch On");
  }catch(Exception
e1){System.out.println(e1.getMessage());}
}

public void switchOff(SimpleBooleanEvent be){
  try{
    outPort2.sendMessage("Switch Off");
  }catch(Exception
e2){System.out.println(e2.getMessage());}
}
```

Create a list of connectors. Register the connectors and the enclosed bean by calling the *super.VJInitComponent()* method, as shown below.

```
VJPort[] connectorList = {(VJPort)inPort1,
(VJPort)inPort2, (VJPort) inPort3, (VJPort)outPort1,
(VJPort)outPort2};
super.VJComponentInit((Object)bb, connectorList);
```

Listing 5-1 shows the complete code that creates a *VJBooleanButton* component for Java Studio.

**Listing 5-1**

Code to convert SimpleBooleanSwitch bean to a Java Studio component

**VJBooleanButton.java**

```
import com.sun.jpropub.vj.vjcomp.*;
import com.sun.jpropub.vj.vjcomp.util.*;
import java.lang.reflect.*;

public class VJBooleanButton extends VJComponent
implements SimpleBooleanListener{

  VJBoundPort outPort1, outPort2, inPort1, inPort2,
inPort3;

  public VJBooleanButton(){
    super();
  }

  public void VJComponentInit(String nm){
    SimpleBooleanSwitch bb = new SimpleBooleanSwitch();

    StringToBasicOutputTransfer stringOut = new
StringToBasicOutputTransfer();
    ObjectInputTransfer objectIn = new
ObjectInputTransfer();

    Class boolClass = bb.getClass();
    Class myClass = this.getClass();

    try{
      Class outargs[] =
{Class.forName("SimpleBooleanEvent")};
```

```
        Method outMethod1 = myClass.getMethod("switchOn",
outargs);
        Method outMethod2 =
myClass.getMethod("switchOff", outargs);


        Method inMethod1 =
boolClass.getMethod("switchOn", new Class[0]);
        Method inMethod2 =
boolClass.getMethod("switchOff", new Class[0]);
        Method inMethod3 =
boolClass.getMethod("toggleSwitch", new Class[0]);

        outPort1 = new VJBoundPort(this, outMethod1,
stringOut);
        outPort2 = new VJBoundPort(this, outMethod2,
stringOut);

        inPort1 = new VJBoundPort(this, inMethod1,
objectIn);
        inPort2 = new VJBoundPort(this, inMethod2,
objectIn);
        inPort3 = new VJBoundPort(this, inMethod3,
objectIn);

        VJPort[] connectorList = {(VJPort)inPort1,
(VJPort)inPort2, (VJPort) inPort3, (VJPort)outPort1,
(VJPort)outPort2};
        super.VJComponentInit((Object)bb, connectorList);
        bb.addBoolListener(this);

    }catch(Exception
e){System.out.println(e.getMessage());
e.printStackTrace();}
    }

  public void switchOn(SimpleBooleanEvent be){
    try{
      outPort1.sendMessage("Switch On");
    }catch(Exception
e1){System.out.println(e1.getMessage());}
    }
```

```
public void switchOff(SimpleBooleanEvent be){
  try{
    outPort2.sendMessage("Switch Off");
  }catch(Exception
e2){System.out.println(e2.getMessage());}
  }
}
```

Compile *VJBooleanButton.java*. Make sure to include jws.zip under the *js\lib* subdirectory under your Java Studio installed directory in your CLASSPATH.

**NOTE**

If you are using some other bean that is already in a JAR file, you should unjar the contents. Later JAR all the bean classes and the wrapper classes into a single JAR because Java Studio components needs all the information in a single JAR.

# Creating Design Time Information

Sometimes it is useful to provide a design time information class, which gives more information about the bean itself to the user. In this section let us see how to provide design time information to the *VJBooleanButton* component.

We can make use of *VJComponentInfo* class to provide design time information to our bean component. *SimpleVJComponentInfo* is a dummy class that implements *VJComponentInfo*. We can subclass *SimpleVJComponentInfo* to provide more information about the bean component.

**NOTE**

Java Studio maintains a registry of component manufacturers and a unique ID for each manufacturer. If you want to distribute or sell your components, you should register your component with Sun. Since we are only going to use it for testing purposes, we can get away with not registering.

To provide design time information, follow the steps below.

To provide additional information about the *VJBooleanButton* component, subclass *SimpleVJComponentInfo* as shown below.

```
public class VJBooleanButtonVJComponentInfo extends
SimpleVJComponentInfo{
```

Define the *getVJComponentDescriptor()* method, which returns the *VJComponentDescriptor*.

```
public VJComponentDescriptor
getVJComponentDescriptor(){
```

Create an instance of *VJComponentDescriptor* to provide information on the *VJComponent* class, enclosed bean, optional customizer class, and the manufacturer's details.

```
Class vjcompClass = Class.forName("VJBooleanButton");
Class enclClass = Class.forName("SimpleBooleanSwitch");
VJComponentDescriptor c = new
VJComponentDescriptor(vjcompClass, enclClass, null);
```

*VJComponentDescriptor* will provide information on *VJBooleanButton* and *SimpleBooleanSwitch*. Since we do not have any customizer class, a *null* is passed as the third parameter as shown above.

You can use *setManufacturerName()* of *VJComponentDescriptor* to set the Manufacturer's Name.

```
c.setManufacturerName("Tester");
```

Since we are not manufacturers, we will just put the manufacturer's name as Tester.

Method *setDisplayName()* provides localized display name and *setShortDescription()* provides a short description of the component.

```
c.setDisplayName("Simple Boolean Switch");
c.setShortDescription("This is a simple boolean
switch");
```

Method *getVJPortDescriptors()* returns an array of connector descriptors corresponding to an array of connectors provided when creating the component. Each and every connector descriptor should contain the display name, a short description, location of the connector, and whether it's an input connector or output connector or both, as shown below.

```
public VJPortDescriptor[] getVJPortDescriptors(){
  try{
    Class vjcompClass =
Class.forName("VJBooleanButton");
    VJPortDescriptor i1Desc = new
VJPortDescriptor("Switch On", "Puts switch to On
position", VJPortDescriptor.IN_ONLY,
VJPortDescriptor.WEST_CENTER, vjcompClass);
    VJPortDescriptor i2Desc = new
VJPortDescriptor("Switch Off", "Puts switch to Off
position", VJPortDescriptor.IN_ONLY,
VJPortDescriptor.WEST_CENTER, vjcompClass);
    VJPortDescriptor i3Desc = new
VJPortDescriptor("Toggle's the Switch", "On if Off, Off
if On", VJPortDescriptor.IN_ONLY,
VJPortDescriptor.WEST_CENTER, vjcompClass);
    VJPortDescriptor o1Desc = new
VJPortDescriptor("Switch On", "Outputs 'Switch On'
string", VJPortDescriptor.OUT_ONLY,
VJPortDescriptor.EAST_CENTER, vjcompClass);
    VJPortDescriptor o2Desc = new
VJPortDescriptor("Switch Off", "Outputs 'Switch Off'
string", VJPortDescriptor.OUT_ONLY,
VJPortDescriptor.EAST_CENTER, vjcompClass);
    VJPortDescriptor[] desc = {i1Desc, i2Desc, i3Desc,
o1Desc, o2Desc};
    return desc;
  }catch(Exception e1){e1.printStackTrace(); return
null;}
}
```

There are some more useful methods, such as *getComponentID()*, that will return the component ID *getSmallImage()*, *getMediumImage()*, and *getLargeImage()* for loading the icon images and so on, which we won't discuss here. You may want to use them to provide more detailed information about your component.

Here's the complete code for the *VJBooleanButton VJComponent* class:

**`VJBooleanButtonVJComponent.java`**

```
import com.sun.jpropub.vj.vjcomp.*;
import com.sun.jpropub.vj.vjcomp.util.*;
import java.lang.reflect.*;

public class VJBooleanButtonVJComponentInfo extends
SimpleVJComponentInfo{

  public VJComponentDescriptor getVJComponentDescriptor(){
    try{
      Class vjcompClass = Class.forName("VJBooleanButton");
      Class enclClass = Class.forName("SimpleBooleanSwitch");

      VJComponentDescriptor c = new
VJComponentDescriptor(vjcompClass, enclClass, null);

      c.setManufacturerName("Tester");
      c.setDisplayName("Simple Boolean Switch");
      c.setShortDescription("This is a simple boolean
switch");

      return c;
    }catch(Exception e){e.printStackTrace(); return
null;}
  }

  public VJPortDescriptor[] getVJPortDescriptors(){
    try{
      Class vjcompClass = Class.forName("VJBooleanButton");

      VJPortDescriptor i1Desc = new
VJPortDescriptor("Switch On", "Puts switch to On
position", VJPortDescriptor.IN_ONLY,
VJPortDescriptor.WEST_CENTER, vjcompClass);
      VJPortDescriptor i2Desc = new
VJPortDescriptor("Switch Off", "Puts switch to Off
position", VJPortDescriptor.IN_ONLY,
VJPortDescriptor.WEST_CENTER, vjcompClass);
      VJPortDescriptor i3Desc = new
```

```
VJPortDescriptor("Toggle's the Switch", "On if Off, Off
if On", VJPortDescriptor.IN_ONLY,
VJPortDescriptor.WEST_CENTER, vjcompClass);

     VJPortDescriptor o1Desc = new
VJPortDescriptor("Switch On", "Outputs 'Switch On'
string", VJPortDescriptor.OUT_ONLY,
VJPortDescriptor.EAST_CENTER, vjcompClass);
     VJPortDescriptor o2Desc = new
VJPortDescriptor("Switch Off", "Outputs 'Switch Off'
string", VJPortDescriptor.OUT_ONLY,
VJPortDescriptor.EAST_CENTER, vjcompClass);

     VJPortDescriptor[] desc = {i1Desc, i2Desc,
i3Desc, o1Desc, o2Desc};

     return desc;
   }catch(Exception e1){e1.printStackTrace(); return
null;}
  }
}
```

# Compile VJBoolean-ButtonVJComponentInfo.java.

Here are the steps to integrate the *VJBooleanButton* component to Java Studio:

1. Copy all the source files present under the *chap5\sample2* subdirectory from the CD-ROM to some temporary directory, for example *C:\temp\chap5\sample2*.
2. Change the directory to where the source files are located.
3. Make sure your CLASSPATH also includes *jws.zip*.
4. Compile all the java files.
5. Create the JAR archive *VJBooleanButton.jar*.
6. Extract the information from the *VJBooleanButton.jar* you just created.

7. Edit the META-INF/MANIFEST.MF. For *VJBooleanButton.class* add **VJComponent: True** and for *SimpleBooleanSwitch.class* add **Java-Bean:True.**
8. Delete *VJBooleanButton.jar.*
9. Recreate the JAR archive using the manifest information you just edited.
10. Import the *VJBooleanButton.jar* in Java Studio.

You are now all set to use the component you just created.

In the next section, let's see how to use the component to generate the application without coding.

# Importing and Using the Simple Boolean Switch Component

Let us first see how to import the Simple Boolean Switch component we just created in the previous section. Using this component, we'll develop an animator whose animation will be controlled by the switch.

Follow these steps to import the component:

1. Start Java Studio 1.0. When the complete application comes up, select Import->JavaBeans...
2. The Wizard will pop up asking you to locate the component you want to import. Click the Browse button and point to *VJBooleanButton.jar*, whereever you saved it. Click Next.
3. All beans in the JAR file will be listed. Since we have only "Simple Boolean Switch" packaged in our JAR file, it is the only item listed. Select Simple Boolean Switch and click Add>>. Click Next.
4. It will ask you if you need the component to be visible under the User category. If this is acceptable, click on Finish. For now let us retain the component under the User folder.
5. Select the User folder to make sure the component is there. By pointing the mouse onto the component, you'll get a brief description of the component in the status bar of the Main Window. This will be the same information that you provided in the *VJBooleanButton-VJComponentInfo* class.

Place the Boolean switch from the User folder, a slider from the GUI folder to control animation speed, and an animator component from the Multimedia folder, as shown in Figure 5-3. Add some labels to spice up the GUI.

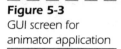

**Figure 5-3**
GUI screen for
animator application

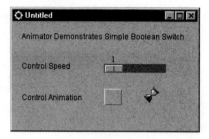

Wire up the components as shown in Figure 5-4.

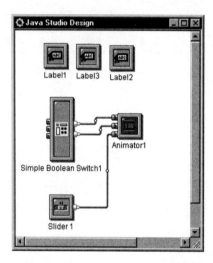

**Figure 5-4**
Wiring diagram for
animator application

You can now test the application. The switch should now control the animation and the slider should control the speed. Isn't that a great way to create applets?

# Summary

In this chapter we learned how to use Java Studio to develop applets without coding. Similar techniques can be employed to develop applications too. We also learned how to integrate existing JavaBean components into Java Studio, and how to use them. Unfortunately, Java Studio can be used to create client applications only. As of this writing, there is no tool available to import Servlet Beans. In the next chapter we'll discuss JavaMail APIs and how to use them to send and read emails. We'll also discuss how to use the JavaMail APIs to develop the Email bean.

# CHAPTER 6

# Java and Electronic Mail

Java has gained popularity in the three years since its first release. Developers started using Java more as a platform than as a language. Java's support to networking, threading, and distributed computing was all built into the language. Now Java also supports email capabilities, built as a Java extension. Without the JavaMail APIs, if you had to write an email application using Java, you'd have to implement the complete low-level protocol using Java. But JavaMail APIs provide a rich set of APIs for programmers to develop email applications.

JavaMail APIs provide a set of abstract classes that define a mail system. Classes like *Message, Store, Transport,* and so on, can be extended to support newer protocols and functionality.

In this chapter we'll examine the architecture of JavaMail and describe some of the major components of the JavaMail system. Later in this chapter we'll develop some sample applications and beans to send and receive email.

# JavaMail Architecture

JavaMail provides several classes that implement RFC822 and the MIME Internet Messaging Standard. These classes are delivered as part of the JavaMail extension package. JavaMail API provides layered architecture, as shown in Figure 6-1. It contains the following components:

1. Abstract Layer: This layer declares classes, interfaces, and methods that form a complete mail system. These abstract layer classes and interfaces need to be extended and sub-classed as necessary to add functionality to support mail system.

2. Implementation Layer: This layer implements part of the Abstract Layer to support RFC822 and MIME.

3. Java Activation Framework (JAF): JavaMail uses JAF to handle particular data types that are not supported by JavaMail API.

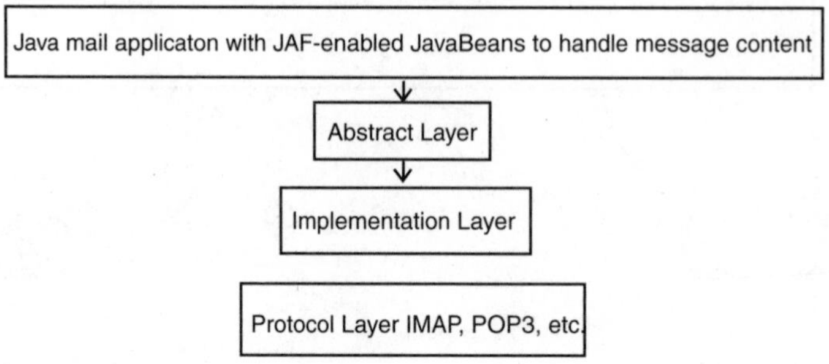

**Figure 6-1**
Layered architecture

| Java mail applicaton with JAF-enabled JavaBeans to handle message content |
| Abstract Layer |
| Implementation Layer |
| Protocol Layer IMAP, POP3, etc. |

For a typical mail client application, JavaMail APIs are intended to perform the following functions, as shown in Figure 6-2:

1. Create a mail message consisting of data and header fields. Data type is specified in the *Content-Type* header field.
2. Send the message to the intended recipients.
3. Retrieve the message from a message store, the server. A *Session* object authenticates the User and controls access to the mail system.
4. Data handling is accomplished using JAF-aware JavaBeans.

The above steps will be more clear when we develop some samples.

**Figure 6-2**
JavaMail framework

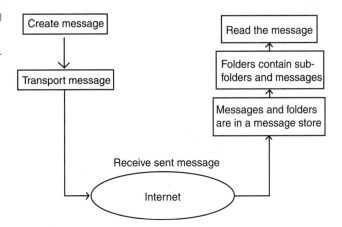

# Major JavaMail API Components

In this section we will review some of the major components of the JavaMail System.

## The Message Class

*Message* is an abstract class that models an email message. Subclasses of the *Message* class provide the actual implementation. Message contains sets of attributes like From, Subject, To, Reply-To, and so on. A collection of bytes is encapsulated with a Message object that forms the data, and the recipient handles the data using JAF-enabled JavaBeans. Messages within a folder have a set of flags that describe the message's state in the folder. *Message* also supports multiple-part message objects.

## Storage and Retrieval of Messages

A *Folder* object stores messages. *Folder* is an abstract class, subclasses of which can implement protocol-specific folders. *Folders* can contain *Messages* or *Folders* themselves or sometimes both. JavaMail provides APIs to create, delete, or open a *Folder*.

A *Store* object holds the folder hierarchy (folders and subfolders) along with its messages. *Store* is subclassed to provide message access protocols such as IMAP, POP3, and similar protocols.

## Message Composition and Transport

A new message is created by instantiating an appropriate *Message* subclass; for example, the *MimeMessage* class. All the relevant attributes are set, such as From, To, Date, and so on. The body of the message is encapsulated into the *Message* object. The resulting *Message* object is sent using *Transport.send()*.

Subclasses of *Transport* provide actual implementation of a transport agent that will be responsible for routing the message to the intended recipient.

## Session Class

The *Session* class is a final class, whose instance represents a mail session.

## JavaMail Event Model

JavaMail supports and understands JDK 1.1 delegation event model. JavaMail clients can throw events that are subclassed from *MailEvent*. All clients interested in a particular event register themselves to listen to that event. During a session, components may generate events and notify all the registered clients about the type of event generated.

# Sending an Email

In this section we will learn how to use the JavaMail APIs to send an email to an intended recipient. We'll develop two examples: one that just sends a text message, and another that sends a multipart message that will contain plain text and html.

## Sending a Simple Message

This example will send "Sending a test email message using JavaMail APIs." as the message body and "Test Message" as the subject of the message. You'll have to supply the From, To, and SMTP hostname, though. Let's look at some of the code snippets:

First set the SMTP host responsible for sending email to intended recipients.

```
Properties props = new Properties();
props.put("mail.smtp.host", args[2]);
```

Property *mail.smtp.host* specifies the protocol-specific SMTP mail server. Obtain a *Session* instance for this mail session.

```
Session session = Session.getDefaultInstance(props,
null);
```

The above code sets some properties and gets the default *Session* instance.

*MimeMessage* implements a *Message* class that completely supports MIME-style email messages. Clients wanting to create new MIME messages will instantiate *MimeMessage* and fill in the appropriate attributes and contents before sending. Examples are shown below.

```
Message msg = new MimeMessage(session);
InternetAddress from = new InternetAddress(args[0]);
msg.setFrom(from);
```

A new *InternetAddress* object is created using the first argument passed by the user, the from address. If the address is not in the right format, then an *AddressException* is thrown if the parse failed. The From header is then set using the *setFrom()* method of the *MimeMessage* class.

Similarly the recipient addresses are set using *setRecipients()*.

```
InternetAddress[] address = {new
InternetAddress(args[1])};
msg.setRecipients(Message.RecipientType.TO, address);
```

We set the To address by specifying *Message.RecipientType.TO*. The Cc and Bcc addresses can also be specified similarly. The recipient address can be an array of addresses.

```
msg.setSubject("Test Message");
```

Method *setSubject()* of *Message* class sets the Subject of the Email message.

```
msg.setContent(msgText, "text/plain");
```

This code sets the *ContentType* header field in the email header. The snippet indicates that it is sending a plain text message. The data content is wrapped in *msgText,* which is just a string.

```
Transport.send(msg);
```

This code snippet sends the message to the intended recipients.

The complete code for sending plain text messages is listed under Listing 6-1.

**Listing 6-1**
Complete code to
send plain text
messages

**SendEmailMessage.java**

```
import java.util.*;
import javax.mail.*;
import javax.mail.internet.*;

public class SendEmailMessage {

  public static void main(String args[]){

    if(args.length < 3){
      System.out.println("Send Email: <from> <to>
<smtphost>");
      System.exit(0);
    }

    String msgText = "Sending a test email message
using JavaMail APIs.";
```

```
    Properties props = new Properties();
    props.put("mail.smtp.host", args[2]);

    Session session = Session.getDefaultInstance(props,
null);
    try {
      Message msg = new MimeMessage(session);

      InternetAddress from = new InternetAddress(args[0]);
      msg.setFrom(from);

      InternetAddress[] address = {new
InternetAddress(args[1])};
      msg.setRecipients(Message.RecipientType.TO,
address);

      msg.setSubject("Test Message");
      msg.setContent(msgText, "text/plain");

      Transport.send(msg);
    } catch (MessagingException mex)
{mex.printStackTrace();}
  }
}
```

To compile and run this example you must download JavaMail SDK from *http://java.sun.com/products*. You can unzip the contents to a directory you wish to install; for example, in the *C:* drive root directory. You'll find mail.jar under the installed directory. Change your CLASSPATH to include mail.jar before you compile this program. Once the compilation is successful, you can execute by typing the command shown below.

**java SendMailMessage fromAddress toAddress smtphostName**

You can use your mail client to read the delivered message.

The complete source code for this example is available under the *chap6\sample1* subdirectory on the CD-ROM.

## Sending a Multi-part Message

In the next example, we will learn how to send a multipart email message. This email message will contain both *text/plain* and *text/html* mime types.

To create a Multipart mime message, follow these steps:

1. Create *MimeBodyPart* for each part of the body, and set its content type.
2. Create an instance of *MimeMultiPart.*
3. Add the body part.
4. Send the message.

The following code snippet shows these steps:

```
MimeBodyPart mbp1 = new MimeBodyPart();
mbp1.setContent(msgText, "text/plain");

MimeBodyPart mbp2 = new MimeBodyPart();
FileDataSource fds = new FileDataSource("test.html");
mbp2.setDataHandler(new DataHandler(fds));
mbp2.setFileName("test.html");

Multipart mp = new MimeMultipart();
mp.addBodyPart(mbp1);
mp.addBodyPart(mbp2);

msg.setContent(mp);
```

**NOTE**

You may have noticed that there is something unusual in the code—some of it is in boldface. You may be wondering why are we not doing something like:

```
mbp2.setContent("<HTML><BODY>Test</BODY></HTML>",
"text/html");
```

If you set *mbp2* as shown above, the code will throw an *UnsupportedDataTypeException* when executing because the MimeType "text/html" is not supported in JAF. So we need to make the modifications that are shown in bold.

Listing 6-2 gives the complete code for sending a multipart email message.

**Listing 6-2**
Complete code to
send multipart
messages

**SendMultipartMessage.java**

```java
import java.util.*;
import javax.mail.*;
import javax.mail.internet.*;
import javax.activation.*;

public class SendMultipartMessage{
  public static void main(String args[]){
    if(args.length != 3){
      System.out.println("Send multipart email message:
<from> <to> <smtp host>");
      System.exit(0);
    }

    String msgText = "This time testing multipart email
message using JavaMail APIs";

    Properties prop = new Properties();
    prop.put("mail.smtp.host", args[2]);

    Session session = Session.getDefaultInstance(prop,
null);

    try{
      Message msg = new MimeMessage(session);

      InternetAddress from = new InternetAddress(args[0]);
      msg.setFrom(from);

      InternetAddress[] to = {new
InternetAddress(args[1])};
      msg.setRecipients(Message.RecipientType.TO, to);

      msg.setSubject("Testing multipart email with
JavaMail APIs");

      MimeBodyPart mbp1 = new MimeBodyPart();
      mbp1.setContent(msgText, "text/plain");
```

```
        MimeBodyPart mbp2 = new MimeBodyPart();
        FileDataSource fds = new
FileDataSource("test.html");
        mbp2.setDataHandler(new DataHandler(fds));
        mbp2.setFileName("test.html");

        Multipart mp = new MimeMultipart();
        mp.addBodyPart(mbp1);
        mp.addBodyPart(mbp2);

        msg.setContent(mp);

        Transport.send(msg);
    }catch(MessagingException
me){me.printStackTrace();}
  }
}
```

To compile this code you'll need to install JAF support on your machine. For Windows, you can download jaf10.zip from *http://java.sun.com/products/*, and unzip it to a directory on your local machine. You'll see activation.jar under the installed directory. Make sure to point the activation.jar file in your CLASSPATH. To execute this sample, see the steps in the first sample above.

The complete source code for this example is available under the *chap6\sample2* subdirectory on the CD-ROM.

# Building an Email Bean for Sending Text-Based Email Messages

Now we will design and build an email bean that can be used for emailing text-based messages. The bean should support multiple recipients. Multiple recipients are input as a comma-separated string (for example, test1@foo.com, test2@foo.com, etc.). To, Cc, and Bcc should support multiple recipients. The bean should also be capable of displaying the message status, such as mail sent, recipient information not available, and the like. This bean will not support multipart body content. This bean should also return the recipient information as a comma-separated string when requested.

The email bean listed below is very simple, so only some of the code snippets are explained. You can find the complete source code for this example bean under the *chap6\sample3* subdirectory on the CD-ROM. To compile the source, refer to previous examples.

**Listing 6-3**
Email bean to send
text-based messages

**SendEmailBean.java**

```java
import java.util.*;
import javax.mail.*;
import javax.mail.internet.*;
import java.io.*;

public class SendEmailBean implements Serializable{
   protected String smtphost;
   protected transient String subject, body;
   private transient InternetAddress[] toAddress,
ccAddress, bccAddress;
   private InternetAddress fromAddress;

   public SendEmailBean(){
      smtphost = subject = null;
      body = null;
      toAddress = ccAddress = bccAddress = null;
      fromAddress = null;
   }

   public String getSMTPHostName(){
      return smtphost;
   }

   public void setSMTPHostName(String smtphost){
      this.smtphost = smtphost;
   }

   public String getFromAddress(){
      return fromAddress.getAddress();
   }

   public void setFromAddress(String from){
      fromAddress = new InternetAddress();
      fromAddress.setAddress(from);
   }
```

```
public String getToAddress(){
  return concatenate(toAddress);
}

public void setToAddress(String address){
  toAddress = split(address);
}

public String getCcAddress(){
  return concatenate(ccAddress);
}

public void setCcAddress(String address){
  ccAddress = split(address);
}

public String getBccAddress(){
  return concatenate(bccAddress);
}

public void setBccAddress(String address){
  bccAddress = split(address);
}

public String getSubject(){
  return subject;
}

public void setSubject(String subject){
  this.subject = subject;
}

public String getMessage(){
  return body;
}

public void setMessage(String body){
  this.body = body;
}

public void send(String temp){
  Properties prop = new Properties();
```

```
    if(smtphost != null && !smtphost.equals("")){
      prop.put("mail.smtp.host", this.smtphost);
    }
    else{
      fireEmailEvent("No SMTP host set. Can't send
email");
      return;
    }

    if(fromAddress == null && !fromAddress.equals("")){
      fireEmailEvent("From Address not specified");
      return;
    }

    if(toAddress == null && !toAddress.equals("")){
      fireEmailEvent("Recipient(s) information not
available");
      return;
    }

    Session session = Session.getDefaultInstance(prop,
null);

    try{
      Message msg = new MimeMessage(session);
      msg.setFrom(fromAddress);
      msg.setRecipients(Message.RecipientType.TO,
toAddress);
      if(ccAddress != null){
        msg.setRecipients(Message.RecipientType.CC,
ccAddress);
      }
      if(bccAddress != null){
        msg.setRecipients(Message.RecipientType.BCC,
bccAddress);
      }
      if(subject != null){
        msg.setSubject(subject);
      }
      msg.setContent(body, "text/plain");
      Transport.send(msg);
    }catch(MessagingException me){me.printStackTrace();
fireEmailEvent("Messaging Exception thrown");}
```

```java
        fireEmailEvent("Email sent successfully");
    }

    protected Vector listeners = new Vector();

    public synchronized void
addEmailListener(EmailListener l){
        listeners.addElement(l);
    }

    public synchronized void
removeEmailListener(EmailListener l){
        listeners.removeElement(l);
    }

    protected void fireEmailEvent(String msg){
        EmailEvent ee = new EmailEvent(this);
        ee.setEventMessage(msg);

        Vector listeners = (Vector) this.listeners.clone
();
        for (int i = 0; i < listeners.size (); ++ i){
            ((EmailListener) listeners.elementAt
(i)).emailBeanMessage(ee);
        }
    }

    private String concatenate(InternetAddress[]
addressArray){
        String tempAddress = "";

        if(addressArray == null){
            return tempAddress;
        }

        for(int index = 0; index < addressArray.length;
index ++){
            tempAddress += addressArray[index].getAddress();
            if(index < addressArray.length - 1){
                tempAddress += ", ";
            }
        }
        return tempAddress;
    }
```

```
    private InternetAddress[] split(String address){
       StringTokenizer st = new StringTokenizer(address,
", ");
       InternetAddress[] addressArray = new
InternetAddress[st.countTokens()];
       int i = 0;


       while (st.hasMoreTokens()) {
         try{
           addressArray[i] = new
InternetAddress(st.nextToken());
         }catch(AddressException ae){ae.printStackTrace();
fireEmailEvent("Address Exception thrown");}

         i++;
       }

       return addressArray;
    }
}
```

Most of the code is written along similar lines to Listing 6-1, shown above. Here the recipient information (to, cc, bcc, subject, and body) is all marked transient, because it is runtime information and we do not want to serialize this information when the application exits.

The *split()* method is responsible for converting the comma-separated recipient information into an array of InternetAddress.

```
private InternetAddress[] split(String address){
   StringTokenizer st = new StringTokenizer(address, ",
");
   InternetAddress[] addressArray = new
InternetAddress[st.countTokens()];
   int i = 0;

   while (st.hasMoreToken s()) {
     try{
       addressArray[i] = new
InternetAddress(st.nextToken());
     }catch(AddressExceptionae){ .printStackTrace();}
```

```
      i++;
   }


   return addressArray;
}
```

We assume that the email addresses that are comma-separated may or may not have spaces before or after every comma.

The *concatenate()* method does the reverse of split.

```
private String concatenate(InternetAddress[]
addressArray){
   String tempAddress = "";

   if(addressArray == null){
     return tempAddress;
   }

   for(int index = 0; index < addressArray.length; index
++){
     tempAddress += addressArray[index].getAddress();
     if(index < addressArray.length - 1){
       tempAddress += ", ";
     }
   }
   return tempAddress;
}
```

It converts the array of Internet addresses to a string of comma-separated values.

The *SendEmailBean* also fires events when there is insufficient information for success. You will find the code for *Event* classes in Listings 6-4 and 6-5, below. Since they are developed according to the JavaBean specifications, no further explanation is needed.

**Listing 6-4**
Listener class used in
SendEmailBean

**EmailListener.java**

```
import java.util.*;

public interface EmailListener extends EventListener{
   public void emailBeanMessage(EmailEvent e);
}
```

**EmailEvent.java**

```java
import java.util.*;

public class EmailEvent extends EventObject{
  protected String message;

  public EmailEvent(SendEmailBean source){
    super(source);
    message = "";
  }

  public void setEventMessage(String message){
    this.message = message;
  }

  public String getEventMessage(){
    return message;
  }
}
```

In Chapter 15, we will use this bean to develop a Java client application for sending email using Java Studio.

In the next section we will learn how to display messages using JavaMail APIs.

# Receiving an Email

In this section we will learn how JavaMail APIs can be used to read and display email messages. We'll only try to read textual email messages, since email messages with special content types need JAF-aware beans to handle such content.

Let's look at the code snippets first:

```java
public class FetchEmailMessage implements
ConnectionListener{
```

The *FetchEmailMessage* class implements *ConnectionListener.Store*, which models a message storage and its access protocol, and can listen to connection events. When the event occurs, we'll keep track of whether a valid user is connected. Otherwise, we won't proceed.

Perform some initializations first, i.e setting default properties and obtaining the *Session* object.

```
FetchEmailMessage(String protocol) throws
NoSuchProviderException{
  props = System.getProperties();
  session = Session.getDefaultInstance(props, null);
  store = session.getStore(protocol);
  store.addConnectionListener(this);
  loggedin = false;
}
```

In the constructor, we get the *Session* object. As mentioned earlier, an instance of a *Session* object represents a mail session. The constructor also specifies that this class will listen to connection events. The variable *loggedin* will keep track of whether the user has logged in or not, which is initialized to false.

The *login()* method will try to connect to the specified host with the given username and password.

```
public void login(String host, String user, String
password) throws MessagingException{
  store.connect(host, user, password);
}
```

The *connect()* method of the *Store* class provides a simple authentication scheme.

If the connection is successful, an "opened" connection event is delivered to the listeners.

```
public void opened(ConnectionEvent e){
  if(e.getType() == ConnectionEvent.OPENED){
    loggedin = true;
  }
}
```

We get an "opened" connection event, as shown above. Similarly, when the connection is closed or disconnected, we set the logged-in variable to false.

```
public void logout() throws MessagingException{
  store.close();
}

public void closed(ConnectionEvent e){
  if(e.getType() == ConnectionEvent.CLOSED){
    loggedin = false;
  }
}
```

The *logout()* method closes the connection already made to the earlier specified host. This will fire a "closed" event to all listeners. In the closed method that we implemented, we set the logged-in variable to false.

```
public void displayMessage(String mailbox, int
messageNum) throws MessagingException, IOException{
  for (int i = 0; i < 10; i++){
    if(!loggedin){
      try{
        Thread.sleep(1000);
      }catch(InterruptedException ie){}
    }
    else{
      break;
    }
  }
  if(!loggedin)
    System.out.println("Could not connect to the
server");
    System.exit(0);
  }

  Folder folder = store.getDefaultFolder();

  if(folder == null){
    System.out.println("No Default folder");
    return;
  }
```

```
    folder = folder.getFolder(mailbox);

    if(folder == null){
      System.out.println("Invalid mail box");
      return;
    }

    folder.open(Folder.READ_WRITE);
    Message msg = folder.getMessage(messageNum);
    printHeaderInfo(msg);
    printMsgContent(msg);
}
```

The *displayMessage()* method is responsible for displaying the message header and content only if it is a string. In *displayMessage()* we loop for ten seconds to wait for the "opened" event to occur so that the connection is established. If no connection is established after 10 seconds, we just exit out of the application. If the connection is successful, we open the specified folder and display the header and message (if the message content is a String). Other codes are pretty much self-explanatory.

Listing 6-6 contains the complete code for fetching and displaying an email message.

**Listing 6-6**
Complete code to
fetch email message

**FetchEmailMessage.java**

```java
import java.util.*;
import javax.mail.*;
import javax.mail.internet.*;
import java.io.*;
import javax.mail.event.*;

public class FetchEmailMessage implements
ConnectionListener{
  protected Session session;
  protected Store store;
  protected Properties props;
  boolean loggedin;

  FetchEmailMessage(String protocol) throws
NoSuchProviderException{
    props = System.getProperties();
```

```
        session = Session.getDefaultInstance(props, null);
        store = session.getStore(protocol);
        store.addConnectionListener(this);
        loggedin = false;
    }

    public void login(String host, String user, String
password) throws MessagingException{
        store.connect(host, user, password);
    }

    public void logout() throws MessagingException{
        store.close();
    }

    public void displayMessage(String mailbox, int
messageNum) throws MessagingException, IOException{
        for (int i = 0; i < 10; i++){
            if(!loggedin){
                try{
                    Thread.sleep(1000);
                }catch(InterruptedException ie){}
            }
            else{
                break;
            }
        }

        if(!loggedin){
            System.out.println("Could not connect to the
server");
            System.exit(0);
        }

        Folder folder = store.getDefaultFolder();

        if(folder == null){
            System.out.println("No Default folder");
            return;
        }

        folder = folder.getFolder(mailbox);
```

```java
    if(folder == null){
      System.out.println("Invalid mail box");
      return;
    }

    folder.open(Folder.READ_WRITE);
    Message msg = folder.getMessage(messageNum);
    printHeaderInfo(msg);
    printMsgContent(msg);
  }


  private void printHeaderInfo(Message msg) throws
MessagingException{
    Address[] a;

    a = msg.getFrom();

    if(a != null){
      System.out.print("From: ");
      for (int i = 0; i < a.length; i++){
        System.out.println(a[i].toString());
      }
    }

    a = msg.getRecipients(Message.RecipientType.TO);

    if(a != null){
      System.out.print("To: ");
      for (int i = 0; i < a.length; i++){
        System.out.println(a[i].toString());
      }
    }

    a = msg.getRecipients(Message.RecipientType.CC);

    if(a != null){
      System.out.print("Cc: ");
      for (int i = 0; i < a.length; i++){
        System.out.println(a[i].toString());
      }
    }
```

```java
        System.out.println("Subject: " + msg.getSubject());

        Date sentDate = msg.getSentDate();
        System.out.println("Date: " + (sentDate != null ?
sentDate.toString() : "Unknown"));
    }

    private void printMsgContent(Message msg) throws
MessagingException, IOException{
        Object o = msg.getContent();
        if(o instanceof String){
            System.out.println((String)o);
        }
        else{
            System.out.println("Can't display content");
        }
    }

    public void opened(ConnectionEvent e){
        if(e.getType() == ConnectionEvent.OPENED){
            loggedin = true;
        }
    }

    public void disconnected(ConnectionEvent e){
        if(e.getType() == ConnectionEvent.DISCONNECTED){
            loggedin = false;
        }
    }

    public void closed(ConnectionEvent e){
        if(e.getType() == ConnectionEvent.CLOSED){
            loggedin = false;
        }
    }

    public static void main(String[] args){
        if(args.length != 6){
            System.out.println("Fetches email message:
FetchEmailMessage  <host> <protocol> <username>
<password> <mailbox> <messagenumber>");
            System.exit(0);
        }
```

```
    try{
      FetchEmailMessage fe = new
FetchEmailMessage(args[1]);
      fe.login(args[0], args[2], args[3]);
      fe.displayMessage(args[4],
Integer.parseInt(args[5]));
      fe.logout();
    }catch(Exception e){e.printStackTrace();}
  }
}
```

Compile FetchEmailMessage.java and run it by giving the required command line parameters.

In the next section, we'll develop a bean that reads text-based email.

# Building an Email Bean for Reading Text-Based Email Messages

In this section, we'll design and build an email bean that can be used for reading text-based messages. This email bean, which is intended to read email messages, should be capable of reading text-based email messages only. Messages containing other contents are not displayed. This bean has the capability of getting lists of emails from the specified mailbox and sending out a header string for each message. It also has the capability of reading the message and displaying the body text.

Most of the code is straightforward and resembles Listing 6-6. Let's take a closer look at some of the important code snippets:

```
for(int x = 0; x < a.length; x++){
  int index = a[x].toString().indexOf("<");
  if(index > 0){
    header = a[x].toString().substring(0, index -1);
  }
  else if(index == -1){
    header = a[x].toString();
  }
}
```

The above code snippet extracts the "Sender Name" if the Sender information is of the form "Sender Name <sendername@foo.com>"; otherwise it is retained as sendername@foo.com.

```
String subject = "";

if((subject = allMessages[i].getSubject()) != null){
   if(subject.length() > 20){
      header += "       " + subject.substring(0, 20);
   }
   else{
      header += "       " + subject;
   }
} else{
   header += "<no subject>       ";
}
```

Similarly, if the "Subject" is greater than 20 characters, then the extra characters are snipped off. If there is no subject, we add "<no subject>" as the default message.

```
for(Enumeration e =
messageHeaderHolder.elements();e.hasMoreElements(); ){
   fireEvent((String)e.nextElement());
}
```

For all the messages in the specified mailbox, an event is fired.

```
for (msgnum = 0; msgnum < messageHeaderHolder.size();
msgnum++){

if(((String)messageHeaderHolder.elementAt(msgnum)).equals(header)){
      msgnum++;
      matchfound = true;
      break;
   }
}
```

The above code snippet in *getMessageBody()* determines which message to retrieve by matching the input string with the string passed as the parameter. This should ideally be one of the strings returned by the *getAllMessageHeader()* method. Once a match is found we know the message number that needs to be retrieved. Once the message is retrieved, the body is created and an event is fired.

Listing 6-7 lists the complete code for *ShowMessageBean*.

**Listing 6-7**

Email bean to display text-based messages

**ShowMessageBean.java**

```java
import java.util.*;
import java.io.*;
import javax.mail.*;
import javax.mail.internet.*;

import java.util.*;
import java.io.*;
import javax.mail.*;
import javax.mail.internet.*;

public class ShowMessageBean implements Serializable{
  protected String hostname, protocol, username;
  protected transient String password, mailbox;
  protected transient Properties props;
  protected transient Session session;
  protected transient Store store;
  protected transient Vector messageHeaderHolder;

  ShowMessageBean(){
    this(null, null, null, null, null);
  }

  ShowMessageBean(String hostname,
      String protocol,
      String username,
      String password,
      String mailbox){
    this.hostname = hostname;
    this.protocol = protocol;
    this.username = username;
    this.password = password;
    this.mailbox = mailbox;
  }
```

```java
public void setHostname(String hostname){
  this.hostname = hostname;
}

public String getHostname(){
  return hostname;
}

public void setProtocol(String protocol){
  this.protocol = protocol;
}

public String getProtocol(){
  return protocol;
}

public void setUsername(String username){
  this.username = username;
}

public String getUsername(){
  return username;
}

public void setPassword(String password){
  this.password = password;
}

public String getPassword(){
  return password;
}

public void setMailbox(String mailbox){
  this.mailbox = mailbox;
}

public String getMailbox(){
  return mailbox;
}

public Vector getAllMessageHeader(){
  if(hostname == null || hostname.equals("")
```

```
     || protocol == null || protocol.equals("")
     || username == null || username.equals("")
     || mailbox == null || mailbox.equals("")){
       fireEvent("Insufficient information to get messages",
2);

       return null;
   }

   try{
     props = System.getProperties();
     session = Session.getDefaultInstance(props, null);
     store = session.getStore(protocol);
     store.connect(hostname, username, password);

     Folder folder = store.getDefaultFolder();
     if (folder == null) {
       fireEvent("No default folder available", 2);
       return null;
     }

     folder = folder.getFolder(mailbox);
     if (folder == null) {
       fireEvent("Folder " + mailbox + " does not exist", 2);
       return null;
     }

     folder.open(Folder.READ_WRITE);
     int totalMessages = folder.getMessageCount();

     Message[] allMessages = folder.getMessages();

     messageHeaderHolder = null;

     messageHeaderHolder = new Vector();

     for (int i = 0; i < totalMessages; i++) {
       String header = "";
       Address a[];
       a = allMessages[i].getFrom();

       for(int x = 0; x < a.length; x++){
         int index = a[x].toString().indexOf("<");
```

```
            if(index > 0){
               header = a[x].toString().substring(0, index - 1);
            }
            else if(index == -1){
               header = a[x].toString();
            }
         }

         String subject = "";

         if((subject = allMessages[i].getSubject()) !=
null){
            if(subject.length() > 20){
               header += "      " + subject.substring(0, 20);
            }
            else{
               header += "      " + subject;
            }
         }
         else{
            header += "<no subject>          ";
         }

         header += "      " +
allMessages[i].getSentDate().toString();

            messageHeaderHolder.addElement(header);
         }

         for(Enumeration e =
messageHeaderHolder.elements();e.hasMoreElements(); ){
            fireEvent((String)e.nextElement(), 1);
         }

         return messageHeaderHolder;
      }catch(Exception e){e.printStackTrace(); return
null;}
   }

   public String getMessageBody(String header){
      int msgnum;
      String body = "";
```

```
    boolean matchfound = false;

    try{
      if(messageHeaderHolder == null ||
messageHeaderHolder.size() <= 0
         || hostname == null || hostname.equals("")
         || protocol == null || protocol.equals("")
         || username == null || username.equals("")
         || mailbox == null || mailbox.equals("")){
          fireEvent("Insufficient information to get
messages", 2);
          return null;
       }

      for (msgnum = 0; msgnum <
messageHeaderHolder.size(); msgnum++){

if(((String)messageHeaderHolder.elementAt(msgnum)).
equals(header)){
          msgnum++;
          matchfound = true;
          break;
        }
      }

      if(matchfound == false){
        fireEvent("Cannot find the message: " + header,
2);
        return null;
      }

      props = System.getProperties();
      session = Session.getDefaultInstance(props,
null);
      Store store = session.getStore(protocol);
      store.connect(hostname, username, password);
      Folder folder = store.getDefaultFolder();

      if(folder == null){
        fireEvent("No Default folder", 2);
        return null;
      }
```

```java
folder = folder.getFolder(mailbox);

if(folder == null){
  fireEvent("Invalid mailbox", 2);
  return null;
}

folder.open(Folder.READ_WRITE);

Message msg = folder.getMessage(msgnum);

Address[] a;

a = msg.getFrom();

if(a != null){
  body = "From: ";
  for (int i = 0; i < a.length; i++){
    body += a[i].toString() + "\n";
  }
}

a = msg.getRecipients(Message.RecipientType.TO);

if(a != null){
  body += "To: ";
  for (int i = 0; i < a.length; i++){
    body += a[i].toString() + "\n";
  }
}

a = msg.getRecipients(Message.RecipientType.CC);

if(a != null){
  body += "Cc: ";
  for (int i = 0; i < a.length; i++){
    body += a[i].toString() + "\n";
  }
}

body += "Subject: " + msg.getSubject() + "\n";
```

```
      Date sentDate = msg.getSentDate();
      body += "Date: " + sentDate.toString() + "\n\n";

      Object o = msg.getContent();
      if(o instanceof String){
        body += (String) o;
      }
      else{
        body += "Can't display content";
      }

      fireEvent(body, 2);

      return body;
    }catch(Exception e){e.printStackTrace(); return
null;}
  }

  protected Vector listeners = new Vector();

  public synchronized void
addShowMessageBeanListener(ShowMessageBeanListener l){
      listeners.addElement(l);
  }

  public synchronized void
removeShowMessageBeanListener(ShowMessageBeanListener l){
      listeners.removeElement(l);
  }

  private synchronized void fireEvent(String header,
int msgNo){
      ShowMessageBeanEvent e = new
ShowMessageBeanEvent(this);
      e.setMessage(header);

      Vector currentListeners =
(Vector)listeners.clone();

      for(int i = 0; i < currentListeners.size(); i++){
        if(msgNo == 1){
```

```
((ShowMessageBeanListener)currentListeners.elementAt(i)).
messageHeaderReceived(e);
      }
      else if(msgNo == 2){

((ShowMessageBeanListener)currentListeners.elementAt(i)).
messageBodyReceived(e);
      }
    }
  }
}
```

Listings 6-8 and 6-9 contain the complete code listings for the *Event* and *Listener* classes.

**Listing 6-8**
Event class used in
ShowMessageBean

**ShowMessageBeanEvent.java**

```
import java.util.*;

public class ShowMessageBeanEvent extends EventObject{
  protected String message = "";

  public ShowMessageBeanEvent(ShowMessageBean source){
    super(source);
  }

  public void setMessage(String message){
    this.message = message;
  }

  public String getMessage(){
    return message;
  }
}
```

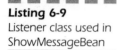

**ShowMessageBeanListener.java**

```
import java.util.*;

public interface ShowMessageBeanListener extends
EventListener{
  public void
messageHeaderReceived(ShowMessageBeanEvent e);
  public void messageBodyReceived(ShowMessageBeanEvent
e);
}
```

You can also find the complete source code in the *chap6\sample5* subdirectory on the CD-ROM. To compile the source code, refer to the previous examples.

# Summary

In this chapter we learned how to use the JavaMail APIs to build cross-platform Java-based email applications. We also built two useful beans for reading and sending text-based emails. Later, in Chapter 15, we'll see how to build two other email applications using JavaStudio, one that sends text-based email and another that receives email using the beans that we developed in this chapter.

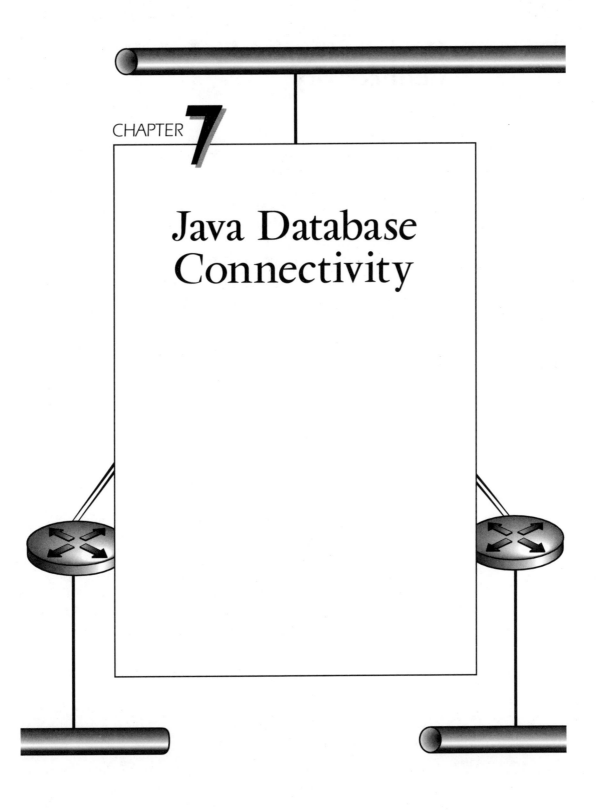

CHAPTER **7**

# Java Database
# Connectivity

# Introduction to the Java Database Connectivity

As everyone knows, Java is a robust, secure, easy-to-use cross-platform language. Programmers need to build Java applications that allow the same program to access a variety of databases. JDBC, which stands for Java Database Connectivity, is the solution.

JDBC consists of a variety of classes and interfaces written in Java that developers can use to write a pure Java program for accessing virtually any relational database. The combination of Java and JDBC lets programmers "write once, access anywhere."

Using JDBC, you can do the following:

■ Establish a database connection with virtually any relational database
■ Send SQL statements to the database
■ Process the query results

In this chapter we'll discuss JDBC in brief; that is, just enough to meet the needs of this book. Since databases are a huge topic to cover in a single chapter, we'll just discuss some simple operations like creating tables and updating and retrieving table values. If you're interested in learning about JDBC's more powerful features, such as cursors, transactions, and stored procedures, we recommend you explore other available books.

## JDBC and Open DataBase Connectivity

JDBC APIs execute the SQL commands directly. These APIs can be used to provide high-level user-friendly APIs. Before the release of the JDBC APIs, Microsoft's ODBC (Open DataBase Connectivity) was the most widely used API for accessing relational databases. JDBC provides a bridge that allows programmers to use ODBC from within Java. Despite this bridge, there is still a need for pure Java APIs to connect to relational databases. Here are the reasons why pure Java APIs are preferred over the ODBC APIs:

1. ODBC is a "C" interface that lacks in robustness, security, portability, etc.

2. Because of pointers and other features of "C," a literal translation of the ODBC API to Java is not desirable.

3. ODBC is not simple to use like JDBC.

4. Database applications using JDBC are cross-platform.

5. When the JDBC-ODBC bridge is used, the bridge driver must be copied to the client machines in order to run the applications. When JDBC APIs are used, pure Java driver classes are downloaded automatically.

## The JDBC Framework

The JDBC framework consists of three important components:

1. The *DriverManager* is the most important component. All Java programs get connected to the right JDBC drivers via *DriverManager.*

2. The JDBC drivers can be of different types, depending on the specific database being accessed. Setting up these drivers is simple.

3. The JDBC-ODBC Bridge is packaged in JDK 1.x. Setting up this driver is not as straightforward as setting up the JDBC drivers.

A simple JDBC framework is shown in Figure 7-1.

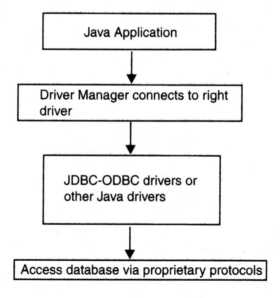

**Figure 7-1**
Simple JDBC
framework

Java Application

Driver Manager connects to right driver

JDBC-ODBC drivers or other Java drivers

Access database via proprietary protocols

## JDBC Driver Types

There are four types of JDBC Driver:

1. JDBC-ODBC Bridge (Type 1). This driver is provided by Javasoft to allow access to databases via most ODBC drivers. The client code and the native ODBC driver should be on the client that uses this driver.
2. A native-API driver (Type 2). This driver converts JDBC calls into their respective database's client API.
3. A net-protocol driver (Type 3). With this type of driver, JDBC calls are translated to a DBMS independent network protocol. The calls are then translated into a DBMS-specific protocol by a server that receives them.
4. A native-protocol driver (Type 4). With this driver, a direct call to the DBMS server is possible from the client.

# Installing Personal Oracle

In the following sections we'll write some generic programs that can be used to create, update, and retrieve tables. To write these programs, we'll use Personal Oracle Version 8.0 and access it via JDBC. We'll use the type 4 driver for Oracle 8 for JDBC access. Here are the steps to follow to install and set up Personal Oracle on Windows NT:

1. Download the latest version of Personal Oracle from *http://www.oracle.com/products/trial/html/trial.html#personalo8multi* (these files are also available on the accompanying CD-ROM).
2. Run the program files *po8mle1.exe, po8mle2.exe,* and *po8mle3.exe.*
3. After the extraction process is complete, you'll find an executable called *Setup.exe.*
4. Double-click this application file to do a complete install of Oracle database.
5. Download the latest version of JDBC thin driver and patch from *http://www.oracle.com/products/free_software/index.html#jdbc8* and follow the instructions there to install the driver and the patch. (These files are also available on the accompanying CD-ROM.)
6. Open Oracle 8 Navigator from the Personal Oracle 8 for Windows NT Program Group.
7. Expand the Local Database tree. Double-click on User.
8. Select the File->New->New User menu item.

9. In the New User Properties dialog, type **admin** as your username and password.

10. In the Role/Privilege tab, grant Connect and Resource Roles. Click on OK. This is the user ID we'll use throughout this book.

11. Make sure your CLASSPATH also points to the classes111.zip (if using JDK 1.1.x), which is present under the *lib* subdirectory, where the driver contents were unzipped.

**NOTE**

When distributing a client application, you'll need to package classes111.zip of the JDBC driver along with your application to access the Oracle database. For applets, the JDBC driver can be downloaded to the client's machine using the ARCHIVE attribute.

Also, in the Oracle installed directory, you'll find the *Tnsnames.ora* file under the *Net80/Admin* subdirectory. Before doing any database access, Oracle's TNS Listener will query *Tnsnames.ora* file to find out the database-specific information like the hostname or port number for a specific SID. We use the SID as ORCL for our samples. When you open this file in notepad, you can append the entry as shown below:

```
test.world =
  (DESCRIPTION =
    (ADDRESS_LIST =
        (ADDRESS =
          (PROTOCOL = TCP)
          (Host = yourhostname)
          (Port = 1521)
        )
    )
    (CONNECT_DATA = (SID = ORCL)
    )
  )
```

The *Host* entry will point to the host where your database is installed. If it's local, it will be 127.0.0.1.

That's pretty much it. In the next few sections we will write some generic programs to access Oracle database.

**NOTE**

Since Oracle is a heavyweight database and needs huge disk space to install the software, you may want to reuse the existing database in your enterprise. Otherwise you may want to consider installing a lightweight database for testing purposes. The code sample, however, should work for all other databases as long as the drivers are available.

# Creating a Table

Let us see how to create a table called *BOOKS* that has the columns TITLE (which can store a SQL type *VARCHAR* up to a maximum of 32 characters), RATE of SQL type *FLOAT*, and INSTOCK of SQL type *INTEGER*. When we execute SQL statements to create a table, it will look something like this:

```
CREATE TABLE BOOKS (TITLE VARCHAR(32), RATE FLOAT,
INSTOCK INTEGER)
```

This SQL statement will create a table called *BOOKS* with three columns to store Title, Rate, and Instock information.

```
import java.sql.*;
import java.io.*;
```

These two statements import the Java IO and the SQL package. SQL package is part of the JDK 1.1.x download.

The following code asks the user to enter the URL where the database is installed.

```
System.out.print("Enter database URL: ");
String url = readFromStdin();
```

Since you have installed Oracle thin JDBC driver, your URL will look something like this:

```
jdbc:oracle:thin:@<database>
```

<database> is a string of the form <host>:<port>:<sid>. Host, Port, and Sid values for <database> can be found in your *Tnsnames.ora* file (refer to the note on an earlier page). In our case we would enter a URL that looks something like this:

```
jdbc:oracle:thin:@127.0.0.1:1521:ORCL
```

The following code asks the user to enter the username, password, and table name. Type **admin** for both the username and the password.

```
System.out.print("Enter userid: ");
String userid = readFromStdin();

System.out.print("Enter password: ");
String password = readFromStdin();

System.out.print("Enter Table name: ");
String tableName = readFromStdin();
```

In the following code, the user is asked to enter the number of columns in the table, the column names, and column types.

```
System.out.print("Number of columns in table: ");
String cols = readFromStdin();

for(i = 0; i < noOfCols; i++){
  System.out.print("Column Name " + i + ":");
  columnName[i] = readFromStdin();

  System.out.print("Column Type " + i + ":");
  columnType[i] = readFromStdin();
}
```

With all the information provided by you, a SQL query is assembled to create a table as specified in *tableName*. For a table called *BOOKS*, the SQL statement for creating the table may have the form "CREATE TABLE BOOKS (TITLE VARCHAR(32), RATE FLOAT, INSTOCK INTEGER." Here's the code snippet that creates the SQL statement programmatically:

```
String query = "CREATE TABLE " + tableName;
query = query + "(";

for(i = 0; i < noOfCols - 1; i++){
  query += (columnName[i] + " " + columnType[i] + ",");
}

query += (columnName[i] + " " + columnType[i] +")");
```

The statement below registers the Oracle driver before being able to use it. This statement must be the first statement executed before we can access any database:

```
DriverManager.registerDriver(new
oracle.jdbc.drivracleDriver());
```

**NOTE**

The program statement shown above is specific to the Oracle's JDBC thin driver. If you have some other database, see your vendor's documentation for your program to register your vendor's database driver.

Next step is to establish the connection to database.

```
Connection conn = DriverManager.getConnection (url,
userid, password);
```

The statement shown above establishes a connection with the DBMS specified in the URL parameter.

The following code fragment creates a *Statement* object. It is with the *Statement* object we'll be able to execute the SQL statement and obtain the result. This object will be used to pass the SQL query.

```
Statement stmt = conn.createStatement ();
```

The method *executeUpdate()* will pass the query constructed by us to the DBMS specified in the URL (jdbc:oracle:thin:@127.0.0.1:1521:ORCL) discussed earlier in this section.

```
stmt.executeUpdate(query);
```

In many cases, it is desirable to immediately release a statement's and connection's database and JDBC resources instead of waiting for this to happen when it is automatically closed; the *close()* method provides this immediate release.

```
stmt.close();
conn.close();
```

**NOTE**

There are two methods usually used to manipulate a table, *executeUpdate()* and *executeQuery()*. If you are wondering which one to use when, this sidebar can help.

Method *executeUpdate()* is usually used for data definition commands like *CREATE* table, *DROP* table, and *ALTER* table. This method is also used to update a table, though *UPDATE* is a data manipulation command .

Method *executeQuery()* is usually used to execute SELECT statements.

Now, let's put it all together to create tables in a database.

**Listing 7-1**
Program for creating tables

**CreateTable.java**

```java
import java.sql.*;
import java.io.*;

public class CreateTable{
  public static void main(String args[]){
    try{
      System.out.print("Enter database URL: ");
      String url = readFromStdin();

      System.out.print("Enter userid: ");
      String userid = readFromStdin();

      System.out.print("Enter password: ");
      String password = readFromStdin();

      System.out.print("Enter Table name: ");
```

```
        String tableName = readFromStdin();

        System.out.print("Number of columns in table: ");
        String cols = readFromStdin();

        int noOfCols = Integer.parseInt(cols);
        int i = 0;

        String columnName[];
        String columnType[];

        columnName = new String[noOfCols];
        columnType = new String[noOfCols];

        for(i = 0; i < noOfCols; i++){
          System.out.print("Column Name " + i + ":");
          columnName[i] = readFromStdin();

          System.out.print("Column Type " + i + ":");
          columnType[i] = readFromStdin();
        }

        String query = "CREATE TABLE " + tableName;
        query = query + "(";

        for(i = 0; i < noOfCols - 1; i++){
            query += (columnName[i] + " " + columnType[i] +
",");
        }

        query += (columnName[i] + " " + columnType[i] +")");


        DriverManager.registerDriver(new
oracle.jdbc.driver.OracleDriver());
        Connection conn = DriverManager.getConnection
(url, userid, password);
        Statement stmt = conn.createStatement();
        stmt.executeUpdate(query);
        stmt.close();
        conn.close();
```

```
        }catch(IOException e){e.printStackTrace();}
        catch(SQLException se){se.printStackTrace();}
    }

    protected static String readFromStdin()throws
IOException{
        String nextLine  = "";
        char x;
        while((x = (char)System.in.read()) != '\n'){
          nextLine += String.valueOf(x);
        }

        return nextLine.trim();
    }
}
```

Complete source code for Listing 7-1 can be found under the
*chap7\sample1* subdirectory on the CD-ROM. Compile the code and execute
it to create tables that fit your needs. Make sure that the classes111.zip provided with the Oracle JDBC thin driver is in your CLASSPATH for proper
compilation and execution. You'll also need the core JDK classes for
compilation.

When executing the sample if your client is on a different machine
than the server, make sure you have the database driver in your CLASSPATH.

**NOTE**

If you have problems obtaining a database connection while executing
the program make sure the URL parameter is right. Also make sure the
Oracle services are all up and running. If not, you need to start these
services before executing your program.

To start the services, open Control Panel and double-click the Services
icon. You'll see OracleStartORCL, OracleServiceORCL, and Oracle-
TNSListener80. Select each one of them and click Start.

# Entering Data Into a Table

Once you have created a table in your database, the next thing you'll want to do is populate the table.

When we execute SQL statements to populate the *BOOKS* table that we described in the beginning of the last section, they look something like this:

```
INSERT INTO BOOKS VALUES('Developing JavaBeans Vol1',
51.99, 2)
INSERT INTO BOOKS VALUES('Developing JavaBeans Vol2',
49.99, 3)
INSERT INTO BOOKS VALUES('Developing JavaBeans Vol3',
52.99, 1)
```

These SQL statements will add three entries into the *BOOKS* table. When the first statement is executed it will enter "Developing JavaBeans Vol1" in the Title column; 51.99, which is a float, in the Rate column; and 2, which is an integer, in the Instock column.

**NOTE**

Values are inserted into the columns in the same order that the columns were declared when the table was created.

If there is a mismatch in the values entered and in the SQL type declared for that column, a *SQLException* is thrown.

Here's the complete source code that you'll need to update the database. Since the code is very simple, we won't explain it further.

**Listing 7-2**
Program for populating tables

**PopulateTable.java**

```java
import java.sql.*;
import java.io.*;

public class PopulateTable{
  public static void main(String args[]){
    try{
      System.out.print("Enter database URL: ");
      String url = readFromStdin();

      System.out.print("Enter userid: ");
```

```
        String userid = readFromStdin();

        System.out.print("Enter password: ");
        String password = readFromStdin();

        System.out.print("Enter Table name: ");
        String tableName = readFromStdin();

        System.out.print("Number of columns in table: ");
        int noOfCols = Integer.parseInt(readFromStdin());

        System.out.print("Number of entries you want
insert: ");
        int entries = Integer.parseInt(readFromStdin());

        int i = 0;

        String columnValue[][];

        columnValue = new String[entries][noOfCols];

        for(int j = 0; j < entries; j++){
          for(i = 0; i < noOfCols; i++){
            System.out.print("Entry " + (j + 1 )+ "
Column Value " + (i + 1) + " :");
            columnValue[j][i] = readFromStdin();
          }
        }

        String query[];
        query = new String[entries];

        for(int j = 0; j < entries; j++){
          query[j] = "INSERT INTO " + tableName + "
VALUES (" ;
          for(i = 0; i < noOfCols - 1; i++){
            query[j] += columnValue[j][i] + ",";
          }
          query[j] += columnValue[j][i] + ")";
        }

        DriverManager.registerDriver(new
```

```
oracle.jdbc.driver.OracleDriver());
     Connection conn = DriverManager.getConnection
(url, userid, password);
     Statement stmt = conn.createStatement();

     for(i = 0; i < entries; i++){
       stmt.executeUpdate(query[i]);
     }

     stmt.close();
     conn.close();
    }catch(IOException e){e.printStackTrace();}
    catch(SQLException se){se.printStackTrace();}
  }

  protected static String readFromStdin()throws
IOException{
    String nextLine  = "";
    char x;
    while((x = (char)System.in.read()) != '\n'){
      nextLine  += String.valueOf(x);
    }

    return nextLine.trim();
  }
}
```

Complete source code for Listing 7-2 can be found under the *chap7\sample2* subdirectory on the CD-ROM. To compile and test the program instructions are the same as in previous example.

**NOTE**

When you execute this program, remember to enclose all the strings for VARCHAR SQL types with single quotes. For example, when you are prompted to enter:

*Entry 1 Column Value 1*

You'll have to enter:

*'Developing JavaBeans Vol1'*

# Getting Data From a Table

Now that we know how to create and update tables, we'll see how to retrieve the values that were entered into the table. We can use the SQL SELECT statement to read back the values. When executing the SELECT statement, we can use an asterisk (*) to select all the data, or we can specify specific columns we want to select. We can also retrieve all the records, or we can retrieve a subset of records by using the WHERE clause to match a specified condition.

Again using our *BOOKS* table, we can execute the following statements:

```
SELECT * FROM BOOKS
```

This statement returns all the entries in the *BOOKS* table. The output may look like this, if the INSERT statements in the previous section were executed:

**Table 7-1**

Result of SELECT *
FROM BOOKS

| Title | Rate | Instock |
|---|---|---|
| Developing JavaBeans Vol1 | 51.99 | 2 |
| Developing JavaBeans Vol2 | 49.99 | 3 |
| Developing JavaBeans Vol3 | 52.99 | 1 |

Instead of getting all the books, let's suppose we are only interested in those books whose rates are greater than 50.00. Then our SQL would look like this:

```
SELECT * FROM BOOKS WHERE RATE > 50.00
```

This SQL statement produces the following result:

**Table 7-2**

Result of SELECT *
FROM BOOKS
WHERE RATE
> 50.00

| Title | Rate | Instock |
|---|---|---|
| Developing JavaBeans Vol1 | 51.99 | 2 |
| Developing JavaBeans Vol3 | 52.99 | 1 |

If we are just interested in the titles of those books whose rate is greater than 50.00, then the SQL would be:

```
SELECT TITLE FROM BOOKS WHERE RATE > 50.00
```

This SQL statement produces the following result when executed:

**Table 7-3**

Result of SELECT
TITLE FROM BOOKS
WHERE RATE
> 50.00

| Title |
|-------|
| Developing JavaBeans Vol1 |
| Developing JavaBeans Vol3 |

Here's the complete code for retrieving values from a database. Since the code is very simple, no further explanation is given.

**Listing 7-3**
Program for getting
table contents

**ReadTable.java**

```java
import java.sql.*;
import java.io.*;

public class ReadTable{
  public static void main(String args[]){
    try{
      System.out.print("Enter database URL: ");
      String url = readFromStdin();

      System.out.print("Enter userid: ");
      String userid = readFromStdin();

      System.out.print("Enter password: ");
      String password = readFromStdin();

      System.out.print("Enter Table name: ");
      String tableName = readFromStdin();

      System.out.print("Number of columns to read (* for
all): ");
      String cols = readFromStdin();

      int actualCols = 0;

      if(cols.equals("*")){
        System.out.print("Number of actual columns in "
+ tableName + ": ");
```

```
        actualCols = Integer.parseInt(readFromStdin());
}

int i = 0;
int noOfCols = 0;
String columnName[] = null;

if(!cols.equals("*")){
  noOfCols = Integer.parseInt(cols);

  columnName = new String[noOfCols];

  for(i = 0; i < noOfCols; i++){
    System.out.print("Column Name :");
    columnName[i] = readFromStdin();
  }
}

System.out.print("Any conditions Y for Yes? :");
String condn = readFromStdin();
String condnStr = "";

if(condn.equals("Y") || condn.equals("y")){
  System.out.print("Enter condition: ");
  condnStr = readFromStdin();
}

String query = "SELECT ";

if(cols.equals("*")){
  query += "* FROM " + tableName;
}
else{
  for(i = 0; i < noOfCols - 1; i++){
    query += columnName[i] + " ,";
  }

  query += columnName[i] + " FROM " + tableName;
}

if(condn.equals("Y") || condn.equals("y")){
  query += " WHERE " + condnStr;
}
```

```java
        DriverManager.registerDriver(new
oracle.jdbc.driver.OracleDriver());
        Connection conn = DriverManager.getConnection
(url, userid, password);
        Statement stmt = conn.createStatement();
        ResultSet rs = stmt.executeQuery(query);

        i = 0;

        while(rs.next()){
          if(cols.equals("*")){
            for(i = 1; i <= actualCols; i++){
              System.out.print(rs.getString(i) + "    ");
            }
            System.out.println();
          }
          else{
            for(i = 0; i < noOfCols; i++){
              System.out.print(columnName[i] + "    " +
rs.getString(columnName[i]) + "      ");
            }
            System.out.println();
          }
        }

        stmt.close();
        conn.close();
      }catch(IOException e){e.printStackTrace();}
      catch(SQLException se){se.printStackTrace();}
    }

  protected static String readFromStdin()throws
IOException{
    String nextLine = "";
    char x;
    while((x = (char)System.in.read()) != '\n'){
      nextLine += String.valueOf(x);
    }

    return nextLine.trim();
  }
}
```

Complete source code for Listing 7-3 can be found under the *chap7\sample3* subdirectory on the CD-ROM. To compile and test the program instructions are the same as in previous examples.

# Performing a Meta-Data Query

In the ReadTable.java example we developed in the previous section a problem arises if the user wants to select all the columns with or without any condition, as shown below. In this case, we don't know how long to loop and display the columns, because we don't know how many columns the table contains.

```
if(cols.equals("*")){
    System.out.print("Number of actual columns in " +
tableName + ": ");
    actualCols = Integer.parseInt(readFromStdin());
}
```

The code shown above overcomes the problem, by asking the user for the number of columns in the table. However, the user may find this solution annoying at times, especially if the user does not have access to the table statistics.

Using the meta-data classes provided in the JDK will help to dynamically discover the database tables. *ResultSetMetaData* and *DatabaseMetaData* are the two meta-data classes provided to obtain information dynamically. The *ResultSetMetaData* class provides information about columns in a *ResultSet* like the types and properties of the columns. *DatabaseMetaData* provides information about the database that we are not concerned with here.

Let's change the ReadTable.java example to use *ResultSetMetaData* to get more information about the columns dynamically. Instead of asking the user for the number of columns in the table, we'll do it dynamically using *ResultSetMetaData* class:

The *ResultSet rs* can invoke the *getMetaData()* method to obtain an instance of *ResultSetMetaData*. The method *getColumnCount()* will give the number of columns in the result set.

```
ResultSetMetaData rsmd = rs.getMetaData();
int actualCols = rsmd.getColumnCount();
```

**NOTE**

All methods of *ResultSetMetaData* will return information about an individual column, except *getColumnCount()*, which will give the number of columns in the result set.

```
System.out.print(rsmd.getColumnLabel(i));
```

The method *getColumnLabel()* will return the column label as entered when the database was created.

Here's the complete code that will read the table information using meta-data, which is pretty straightforward.

**Listing 7-4**
Program for getting table contents using meta-data

**ReadTableUsingMetaData.java**

```java
import java.sql.*;
import java.io.*;

public class ReadTableUsingMetaData{
  public static void main(String args[]){
    try{
      System.out.print("Enter database URL: ");
      String url = readFromStdin();

      System.out.print("Enter userid: ");
      String userid = readFromStdin();

      System.out.print("Enter password: ");
      String password = readFromStdin();

      System.out.print("Enter Table name: ");
      String tableName = readFromStdin();

      System.out.print("Number of columns to read (* for
all): ");
      String cols = readFromStdin();

      int i = 0;
      int noOfCols = 0;
      String columnName[] = null;

      if(!cols.equals("*")){
        noOfCols = Integer.parseInt(cols);
```

```
      columnName = new String[noOfCols];

      for(i = 0; i < noOfCols; i++){
        System.out.print("Column Name :");
        columnName[i] = readFromStdin();
      }
    }

    System.out.print("Any conditions Y for Yes? :");
    String condn = readFromStdin();
    String condnStr = "";

    if(condn.equals("Y") || condn.equals("y")){
      System.out.print("Enter condition: ");
      condnStr = readFromStdin();
    }

    String query = "SELECT ";

    if(cols.equals("*")){
      query += "* FROM " + tableName;
    }
    else{
      for(i = 0; i < noOfCols - 1; i++){
        query += columnName[i] + " ,";
      }

      query += columnName[i] + " FROM " + tableName;
    }

    if(condn.equals("Y") || condn.equals("y")){
      query += " WHERE " + condnStr;
    }

    DriverManager.registerDriver(new
oracle.jdbc.driver.OracleDriver());
    Connection conn = DriverManager.getConnection
(url, userid, password);
    Statement stmt = conn.createStatement();
    ResultSet rs = stmt.executeQuery(query);
    ResultSetMetaData rsmd = rs.getMetaData();
```

```
        i = 0;
        int actualCols = rsmd.getColumnCount();

        for(i = 1; i <= actualCols; i++){
          if(i > 1){
            System.out.print("        ");
          }
          System.out.print(rsmd.getColumnLabel(i));
        }

        System.out.println("\n");

        while(rs.next()){
          for(i = 1; i <= actualCols; i++){
            if(i > 1){
              System.out.print("        ");
            }
            System.out.print(rs.getString(i));
          }
          System.out.println();
        }

      stmt.close();
      conn.close();

      }catch(IOException e){e.printStackTrace();}
      catch(SQLException se){se.printStackTrace();}
    }

  protected static String readFromStdin()throws
IOException{
      String nextLine = "";
      char x;
      while((x = (char)System.in.read()) != '\n'){
        nextLine += String.valueOf(x);
      }

      return nextLine.trim();
    }
  }
```

Complete source code for Listing 7-4 can be found under the *chap7\sample4* subdirectory on the CD-ROM. Again to compile and test the program instructions are the same as in previous examples.

We have shown a very simple way to use meta-data. *DatabaseMetaData* has more than a hundred methods that can be used for getting information about the database itself. You can do much more with it than we have covered here, but further discussion of this topic is beyond the scope of this book.

In the next section we will write a JDBC Bean for database access.

# Developing a JDBC Bean

In this section we'll develop a JDBC bean that will create, update, and retrieve table values in a given database. To keep things simple we will just focus on simple database operations. All table information is passed or retrieved from the bean as a vector of strings that will represent one row of the table.

Our JDBC bean will also fire an event every time a table retrieve is completed. This event will be used by the listeners to obtain the latest database information.

Here's the complete code for the JDBC bean. Since everything in this code has been covered in previous sections, no further explanation will be given here.

**JDBCBean.java**

**Listing 7-5**
JDBC Bean

```java
import java.sql.*;
import java.io.*;
import java.util.*;

public class JDBCBean implements Serializable{
    protected transient String tableName;
    protected transient Vector columnNames, columnTypes,
columnValues;
    protected String url;
    protected transient String query;
    private transient Connection conn;
    private transient String userid, password;
```

```java
public JDBCBean(){
  tableName = null;
  columnNames = null;
  columnTypes = null;
  columnValues = null;
  query = null;
  conn = null;
  userid = null;
  password = null;
}

public void setTableName(String tableName){
  this.tableName = tableName;
}

public String getTableName(){
  return tableName;
}

public void setURL(String url){
  this.url = url;
}

public String getURL(){
  return url;
}

public void setUserid(String userid){
  this.userid = userid;
}

public String getUserid(){
  return userid;
}

public void setPassword(String password){
  this.password = password;
}

public String getPassword(){
  return password;
}
```

```java
public void setColumnNames(Vector columnNames){
  this.columnNames = null;
  this.columnNames = columnNames;
}

public Vector getColumnNames(){
  return columnNames;
}

public void setColumnValues(Vector columnValues){
  this.columnValues = null;
  this.columnValues = columnValues;
}

public Vector getColumnValues(){
  return columnValues;
}

public void setColumnTypes(Vector columnTypes){
  this.columnTypes = null;
  this.columnTypes = columnTypes;
}

public Vector getColumnTypes(){
  return columnTypes;
}

public void createTable(){
  int i = 0;

  if((columnNames == null) || (columnTypes == null)){
    fireErrorEvent("Column information not set
properly");
    return;
  }

  query = new String("CREATE TABLE " + tableName +
"(");

  for(i = 0; i < columnNames.size() - 1; i++){
    query += (String)columnNames.elementAt(i) + " " +
columnTypes.elementAt(i) + ",";
  }
```

```
      query += (String)columnNames.elementAt(i) + " " +
columnTypes.elementAt(i) + ")";

      executeUpdate(query);
   }

   public void populateTable(){
      int i = 0;

      if(columnValues == null){
         fireErrorEvent("Column information not set
properly");
         return;
      }

      for(i = 0; i < columnValues.size(); i++){
         query = "INSERT INTO " + tableName + " VALUES (";
         query += (String)columnValues.elementAt(i) + ")";
         executeUpdate(query);
      }
   }

   public void readTable(String condn){
      int i = 0;
      String condition = "";

      if(columnNames == null){
         fireErrorEvent("Column information not set
properly");
         return;
      }

      if(condn == null){
         condition = "";
      }
      else{
         condition = " WHERE " + condn;
      }

      query = "SELECT ";

      if(((String)columnNames.elementAt(0)).equals("*")){
         query += "* FROM " + tableName;
```

```
      }
      else{
        for(i = 0; i < columnNames.size() - 1; i++){
          query += columnNames.elementAt(i) + ",";
        }
        query += columnNames.elementAt(i) + " FROM " +
tableName;
      }

      if((!condition.equals(""))){
        query += condition;
      }
      executeQuery(query);
    }

  private void executeUpdate(String query){
    if(conn == null){
      initialize();
    }

    try{
      Statement stmt = conn.createStatement();
      stmt.executeUpdate(query);
      stmt.close();
    }catch(SQLException se){se.printStackTrace();}
  }

  private void executeQuery(String query){
    if(conn == null){
      initialize();
    }

    try{
      Statement stmt = conn.createStatement();
      ResultSet rs = stmt.executeQuery(query);
      ResultSetMetaData rsmd = rs.getMetaData();

      int actualCols = rsmd.getColumnCount();
      int i = 0;
      int columnType;

      columnNames = null;
      columnValues = null;
```

```java
      columnNames = new Vector();
      columnValues = new Vector();

      for(i = 1; i <= actualCols; i++){
        columnNames.addElement(rsmd.getColumnLabel(i));
      }

      while(rs.next()){
        String result = "";
        for(i = 1; i <= actualCols - 1; i++){
          result += (String)rs.getString(i) + ", ";
        }

        result += (String)rs.getString(i);
        columnValues.addElement(result);
      }

      fireResultEvent();
      stmt.close();

    }catch(SQLException se){se.printStackTrace();}
  }

  private void initialize(){
    try{
      DriverManager.registerDriver(new
oracle.jdbc.driver.OracleDriver());
      conn = DriverManager.getConnection (url, userid,
password);
    }catch(SQLException se){se.printStackTrace();}
  }

  public void done(){
    if(conn != null){
      try{
        conn.close();
      }catch(SQLException se){se.printStackTrace();}
    }
  }

  protected Vector listeners = new Vector();
```

```
    public synchronized void addJDBCListener(JDBCListener l){
      listeners.addElement(l);
    }

    public synchronized void
  removeJDBCListener(JDBCListener l){
      listeners.removeElement(l);
    }

    protected void fireResultEvent(){
      Vector l = (Vector)listeners.clone();

      JDBCEvent e = new JDBCEvent(this);
      e.setColumnNames(columnNames);
      e.setColumnValues(columnValues);
      e.setErrorMessage("");

      for(int i = 0; i < l.size(); i++){
        ((JDBCListener)l.elementAt(i)).result(e);
      }
    }

    protected void fireErrorEvent(String error){
      Vector l = (Vector)listeners.clone();

      JDBCEvent e = new JDBCEvent(this);
      e.setColumnNames(columnNames);
      e.setColumnValues(columnValues);
      e.setErrorMessage(error);

      for(int i = 0; i < l.size(); i++){
        ((JDBCListener)l.elementAt(i)).error(e);
      }
    }
  }
```

This next sample code shows the *Listener* and *Event* classes:

**Listing 7-6**
JDBC Event class

**JDBCEvent.java**

```java
import java.util.*;

public class JDBCEvent extends EventObject{
  protected Vector columnNames;
  protected Vector columnValues;
  protected String message;

  public JDBCEvent(Object o){
    super(o);
  }

  public Vector getColumnNames(){
    return columnNames;
  }

  public void setColumnNames(Vector columnNames){
    this.columnNames = columnNames;
  }

  public Vector getColumnValues(){
    return columnValues;
  }

  public void setColumnValues(Vector columnValues){
    this.columnValues = columnValues;
  }

  public void setErrorMessage(String message){
    this.message = message;
  }

  public String getErrorMessage(){
    return message;
  }
}
```

**JDBCListener.java**

```
import java.util.*;

public interface JDBCListener extends EventListener{
    public void result(JDBCEvent e);
    public void error(JDBCEvent e);
}
```

Complete source code for these samples can be found under the *chap7\sample5* subdirectory on the CD-ROM.

**NOTE**

Our JDBC bean is very simple and creates a new database connection for every instance. Since database connections are very costly, you may want to modify the bean so that the connection is reused. We have not implemented these things to keep code simple.

Also make sure that the application that uses the modified bean reuses the connection and is thread safe.

■ ■ ■ ■ # Summary

In this chapter, we built the groundwork for using the very basics of the databases and JDBC. If you already had some database expertise, this chapter was sufficient to jumpstart you on JDBC. In Chapter 17 of this book we'll use the JDBCBean we developed in this chapter as one of the components to develop an electronic commerce application.

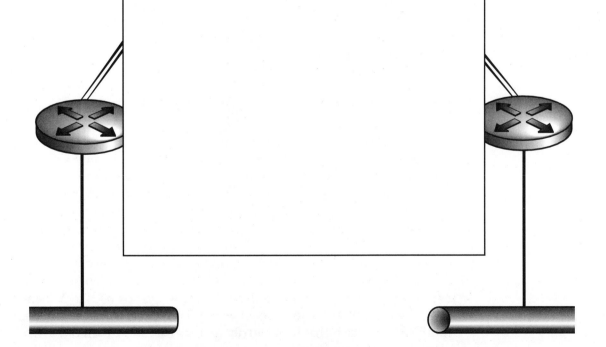

CHAPTER **8**

# Lightweight
# Directory
# Access Protocol

# Introduction to LDAP

## What is LDAP?

For those of us who have had more than one job, the experience of the first few days at a new job is probably quite similar. Your phone works but your email does not. You have a UNIX account but you can't access the printers. Your voicemail starts working in about three days and you are able to dial-in from your home in about three weeks. The reason for the disparity is that each of these conveniences is enabled by some software application, and each application has its own name listing, or a directory of names. Your name has to be inserted into each directory for that application to work for you. Your system administrator most likely inserts your name into each application manually, and the task takes time.

Wouldn't it be nice if all your system administrator had to do was insert your name into a master directory and all these applications would be informed at once? That is exactly what Lightweight Directory Access Protocol (LDAP) allows you to do. Once an LDAP service is introduced to a company, employee names and employee information are maintained in an LDAP directory. All other applications query and update the LDAP directory through the LDAP API. Not only does LDAP maintain a synchronized directory for all applications, it saves software developers time because they don't have to write code to maintain a separate directory.

## The Need for LDAP Model

Readers familiar with relational databases may think that this sort of information may well be handled by a relational database. Why do we need a new model to access directory information? The answer lies in the characteristics of directory information, which is searched much more frequently than it is updated. We only get the new yellow pages once a year.

There is also no need for sophisticated transaction capabilities in directory information manipulation. Because of those differences, the LDAP server is optimized for very fast access and much slower updates.

There are some other differences between a relational database and an LDAP server. For example, LDAP defines a feature called *referral*. A client may ask an LDAP server to refer other servers if the entry is not found. Another difference is that LDAP attributes may have more than one value, and that is hard to map into the relational model.

# How Information is Organized in LDAP

Information in LDAP is maintained through names and entries, and the entries are organized in a hierarchical tree. The top level entries represent countries, the next level represents states or provinces within a country, and the next level represents organizations such as companies or universities. In practice, some of the levels may be omitted.

Figure 8-1 shows an example of an LDAP tree. Each node within the tree is an entry. An entry is comprised of a list of attribute names and their values. Each attribute can have more than one value. For example, a person may have more than one email address.

**Figure 8-1**
LDAP structure

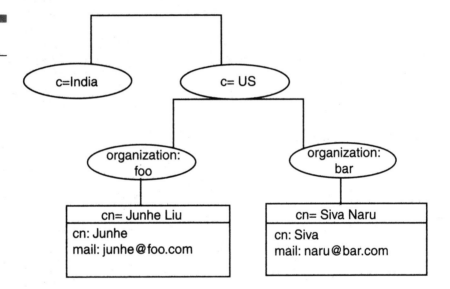

Figure 8-2 shows how an entry is organized. Each entry has a name; for example, my entry in a directory server may have the attribute: "name=Junhe Liu". However the name alone may not be enough to uniquely identify an entry, because two entries may have the same name just like two people may have exactly the same name. To solve this problem, LDAP uses distinguished names (DN) to identify an entry. Distinguished names are the concatenation of an entry's name and the names of its ancestor entries. For example, the DN of my entry could be "name=Junhe Liu, ou=Partner and Developer Relations, o=Netscape Communications Corp., c=US".

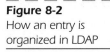
**Figure 8-2**
How an entry is
organized in LDAP

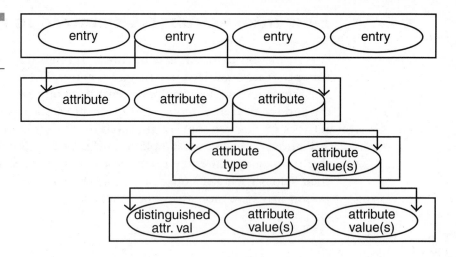

## Entry and Object Classes

The information in an entry is defined by object classes. Object classes allow users to know what attributes are most likely to appear in an entry. The reason we say "most likely" is that some attributes are mandatory for an object class and some attributes are optional. The following table shows examples of some of the object classes:

**Table 8-1**

Object Classes

| Object class | Entry it describes | Abbreviation |
|---|---|---|
| Top | All entries | |
| Country | Country entries | c |
| Locality | Locality entries— state, province, etc. | l |
| Organization | Organization entries | o |
| Organization Unit | Organization unit entries— division, department, etc. | ou |

We have now described everything in an entry, and here is an example of what a real world entry might look like:

```
dn: cn=Kurt Jensen, ou=Product Development,
o=Ace Industry, c=US
cn: Kurt Jensen
sn: Jensen
givenname: Kurt
```

```
objectclass: top
objectclass: person
objectclass: organizationalPerson
objectclass: inetOrgPerson
ou: Product Development
l: Santa Clara
uid: kjensen
mail: kjensen@aceindustry.com
telephonenumber: +1 408 555 6127
facsimiletelephonenumber: +1 408 555 8721
roomnumber: 1944
userpassword: regulatory
```

# The LDAP Architecture

The need for a global directory service was noted in the early 1980s. CCITT and ISO started working on this area in 1984. In 1988, they released a standard called X.500. The X.500 directory service runs on top of the OSI environment, and even though it has rich features, its performance is often slow. LDAP was designed to run most features of X.500 in a TCP/IP environment, thus the word "lightweight."

Like X.500, LDAP operates in a client/server model. All the information is stored in an LDAP server, and software applications that utilize LDAP act as clients and invoke operations on the server. The operations include search, update, and authentication.

# Objects LDAP Describes

Although describing people is the main goal of LDAP, it is designed to describe almost all kinds of objects. For example, the current Internet standard to describe a computer is the Domain Name Service, which translates the name of a computer to its IP address. However, in a corporate environment, much more information about a computer is needed at various times. We need to know the physical location of the machine, its manufacturer, its model, and so on. LDAP is an ideal tool to store such information.

Another example of entities that LDAP suits well is a printer. LDAP may store its IP address, its type, maker, physical location, and so on. In the real world, LDAP servers are already being used to store information about printers and machines.

Even when describing a person, LDAP offers software developers interesting options that they didn't have before. For example, most people customize their favorite software applications to a certain degree. They may bookmark some URLs for their browsers, or create some aliases for their email clients. However if they log-on from some other machine, they no longer have their customizations available to them. It's possible for an application to store users' preferences within an LDAP so that when they log-in from other computers, they can still fetch their customization from an LDAP server and be able to function in a familiar environment. As LDAP grows in popularity, more and more classes of applications will benefit from its flexibility.

# Introduction to LDAP API

An LDAP server comes with an API for C to access information within an LDAP server. The API is not part of the LDAP specification, but since it is the most widely used API for LDAP, it has become the *de facto* standard. The picture is quite similar with the LDAP Java API.

## Introduction to Netscape LDAP Java API

Netscape has released a Java library that allows programmers to access directory information in Java. So far, Netscape's Java API is the most widely used and is JavaSoft's LDAP hook for its JNDI service. Netscape has also submitted the Java API as a standard to the Internet Engineering Task Force (IETF). In this chapter we will discuss how to search and update information in an LDAP server with the Netscape LDAP Java API. This library is freely downloadable from Netscape's developer site, along with an LDAP server. In the "Netscape LDAP Server section," we will tell you how to download the software and configure it.

## Overview of Netscape LDAP Classes

The first class you'll need in LDAP programming is the *LDAPConnection* class. This class forms the abstraction of a connection with the LDAP server. Once we have obtained such a connection, we will be able to search, modify, and provide authentication information to the LDAP server. *LDAPConnection* also contains methods for us to set the characteristics of the connection. For example, we can specify whether we want the LDAP client to follow referrals automatically, or the maximum number of search results returned.

The result of an LDAP search is an object of *LDAPSearchResults* class. Assume you want to search all employees who are managers in your company; the *LDAPSearchResults* object returned will contain entries which represent managers. Those entries are embodied in *LDAPEntry* objects. Each *LDAPEntry* contains a distinguished name (DN) and an *LDAPAttributeSet*. An *LDAPAttributeSet* contains a number of *LDAPAttributes,* which contain the name of the attribute as well as its values. While the data structures seem a bit complicated, the model actually maps exactly the way information is organized in an LDAP entry. Please refer to Figure 8-2 to see how an entry is organized.

There is an *LDAPSearchConstraint* class that lets you set how you want to do your search. For example, you can set how much time you want to wait before results come back, or how many hops you want to follow for referrals.

If you want to update some entries, you will need to use the *LDAPModification* and the *LDAPModificationSet* classes. If something unexpected happens during an LDAP operation, you will be thrown an LDAPException. We will describe in detail how these classes are used in later sections.

# Searching Netscape LDAP Server

Central to an LDAP server is the search operation. A lot of searching and very little updating is the central characteristic of LDAP. Not surprisingly, the LDAP Java API has provided programmers with a rich set of features for doing searches. The first step is to create an *LDAPConnection*.

```
String host = "phonebook";
int port = 389;
LDAPConnection ldc = new LDAPConnection();
try {
  ldc.connect(host, port);
}catch (LDAPException e){
  e.printStackTrace();
}
```

To establish a connection with an LDAP server, you will need the hostname of where the server resides, as well as the port number on which it is listening. The default port number for LDAP is 389. Notice that you'll need to catch the *LDAPException*.

Once you have obtained an *LDAPConnection*, you can then launch a search operation. The following code will return entries for people whose given name is Jeff. You need to specify a search base that specifies the top-level DN of your search, and also a filter that specifies the criteria of your search:

```
String searchBase = "o=Airius.com";
String filter = "givenname=Jeff";
String[] attrs = null;
boolean attrsOnly = false;
LDAPSearchResults res = null;
try{
  res = ldc.search(searchBase, ldc.SCOPE_SUB, filter,
  attrs, attrsOnly);
}catch (LDAPException e){
  e.printStackTrace();
}
```

The string array attrs specifies what attributes you are interested in. For example, if you are only interested in phone numbers, you may want to assign attrs to *{"phone"}* as in the following statement, and then set the Boolean *attrsOnly* to true. The search operation then returns the names but not the values of the attributes found. If set false, it returns both the names and values for attributes found.

```
String[] attrs ={"phone"};
```

The filter string is a regular expression that is capable of specifying complicated search criteria. If you want to search for all managers, you will assign the filter string as follows:

```
String filter = "title=*manager*";
```

This filter will return entries of people whose title contains manager. Here are a few examples of how you can specify the filter string to achieve different kinds of searches.

| **Table 8-2** | Filter StringFilter | Types of search |
|---|---|---|
| Examples of the filter string | (objectclass=*) | Search for all entries |
| | (cn~=Dave) | Entries whose common name is not Dave |
| | (&(title="manager")(ou=marketing)) | All managers in marketing organization unit |
| | (\|(ou=engineering)(ou=sales)) | All entries in engineering or sales organization unit. |

## Extracting the Search Results

The result of the search operation is returned in an object that belongs to the *LDAPSearchResults* class. This class implements the Enumeration interface, allowing us to loop through the search results and extract the information from each entry:

```
while (res.hasMoreElements()){
  LDAPEntry entry = (LDAPEntry)res.nextElement();
  // extract information from entry
}
```

Each entry in the search results is an instance of *LDAPEntry*. The two main methods of this class are *getDN()*, which returns the distinguished name of the entry, and *getAttributeSet()*, which returns the set of attributes for the entry. The following code extracts the distinguished name of the entry and then gets the attribute set:

```
String nextDN = entry.getDN();
System.out.println("\nDN: " + nextDN + "\n");
LDAPAttributeSet entryAttrs = entry.getAttributeSet();
```

Class *LDAPAttributeSet* represents the set of attributes. The method *getAttributes()* returns an enumeration of attributes of type *LDAPAttribute*. Once we get the enumeration, we can iterate over the values to process each attribute for a given entry.

```
Enumeration attrsInSet = entryAttrs.getAttributes();
while (attrsInSet.hasMoreElements()){ LDAPAttribute
```

```
nextAttr = (LDAPAttribute)attrsInSet.nextElement();
  //do something with the LDAPAttribute for this entry...
}
```

*LDAPAttribute* represents one attribute of an entry. Because an attribute may have more than one value, this class has methods that allow a programmer to add and remove values to the attribute. The method *getName()* returns the name of the attribute, and the methods *getStringValues()* and *getByteValues()* return an enumeration of values associated with the attribute.

```
Enumeration valsInAttr;
valsInAttr = nextAttr.getStringValues();

if (valsInAttr == null) {
  valsInAttr = nextAttr.getByteValues();
}

while(valsInAttr.hasMoreElements()) {
  String nextValue = (String)valsInAttr.nextElement();
  System.out.println("\t " + attrName + ": " +
  nextValue);
}
```

An example of binary values is the personal certificate associated with the entry. If we use *getStringValues()* to extract binary data, we will be thrown a *NullPointerException*. Here is some sample code that prints the values of a certificate. Chapter 11 gives greater details on the subject of certificates.

```
Object nextValue = valsInAttr.nextElement();
if (nextValue instanceof String){
  System.out.println(attrName + ": " + nextValue);
}
else{
  X509Cert cert = new X509Cert((byte [])nextValue);
  System.out.println(attrName + ": " +
cert.toString());
  }
```

# Putting it All Together for Search

Here is a complete program that queries all entries in the LDAP server and then prints out all the attribute names and their values.

■ ■ ■ ■ ■ ■
**Listing 8-1**
Code for searching
all entries of a
directory database

**SearchAll.java**

```java
import java.io.*;
import java.net.*;
import java.util.*;
import netscape.ldap.*;
import netscape.ldap.util.*;
import netscape.ldap.controls.*;

public class SearchAll{

  SearchAll(){}

  public static void main(String args[]){

    String searchBase = "o=Airius.com";
    String host = "localhost";
    int port = 389;
    String filter = "(objectclass=*)";
    String[] attrs = null;
    boolean attrsOnly = false;

    LDAPConnection ldc = new LDAPConnection();

    try{
      ldc.connect(host, port);
      LDAPSearchResults res = ldc.search(searchBase,
ldc.SCOPE_SUB, filter,attrs, attrsOnly);
      showResults(res);
      ldc.disconnect();
    }catch (LDAPException e){
      e.printStackTrace();
    }
  }
```

```
   public static void showResults(LDAPSearchResults
res){
    while (res.hasMoreElements())
    {
      LDAPEntry entry = (LDAPEntry)res.nextElement();
      String nextDN = entry.getDN();
      System.out.println("\nDN: " + nextDN + "\n");

      LDAPAttributeSet entryAttrs = entry.getAttributeSet();
      Enumeration attrsInSet = entryAttrs.getAttributes();

      while (attrsInSet.hasMoreElements()){
        LDAPAttribute nextAttr =
LDAPAttribute)attrsInSet.nextElement();
        String attrName = nextAttr.getName();
        Enumeration valsInAttr ;
        valsInAttr = nextAttr.getStringValues();

        if (valsInAttr == null){
          valsInAttr = nextAttr.getByteValues();
        }

        while ( valsInAttr.hasMoreElements() ){
          String nextValue =
(String)valsInAttr.nextElement();
          System.out.println("\t " + attrName + ": " +
nextValue);
        }
      }
    }
  }
}
```

You can find the complete code for Listing 8-1 under the *chap8\sample1* subdirectory on the CD-ROM. You can compile the program and execute it. Make sure to point to ldap10.jar in your CLASSPATH. You'll find ldap10.jar when you install Netscape Communicator under *<netscape installed directory>\communicator\program\java\classes.* The Java SDK described in the Netscape LDAP Server section also contains the same jar file.

# Update Netscape LDAP Server

## Regular Update

Updating an entry is not as mind-boggling as traversing attribute values in an entry. All you need to specify is the distinguished name, the attribute name you want to modify, and its new value. The only catch is that in most cases, you will need to be authenticated with the LDAP server before you do the modification. Most LDAP servers in the real world allow anonymous users to make queries, but only allow a certain group of users to modify their contents.

There are two types of authentication—the traditional username-and-password scheme, and authentication based on certificate technology. Chapter 11 is devoted to certificate-based security, so we will only cover the username-and-password part here. The *authenticate()* method of the *LDAPConnection* class does the actual authentication. If anything goes wrong with the authentication process, an *LDAPException* is thrown. You can use the *getLDAPResultCode()* method of *LDAPException* class to check the error code. The code piece shown below does the authentication.

```
LDAPConnection ldc;

// initialize ldc ...

String adminDN = "cn=Directory Manager";

String DN = " uid=rdaugherty, ou=People, o=airius.com
";
String password = "secret99";
    try {
  ldc.authenticate(adminDN, password);
    }catch(LDAPException e){
  switch(e.getLDAPResultCode()) {
    case
e.INVALID_CREDENTIALS:System.out.println("Invalid pass-
word.");
            break;
    default:System.out.println("Error number: " +
e.getLDAPResultCode());
            e.printStackTrace();
            break;
}
```

In order to modify some attributes of an entry, you need to call the *modify()* method of *LDAPConnection* class. Method *modify()* takes an object of either *LDAPModification* or *LDAPModificationSet* as a parameter. If you want to make changes to more than one attribute, you want to use *LDAPModificationSet.* For our purposes, let's just make one change to Kurt Jenson, and change his user ID from "kjensen" to "kurtj".

```
LDAPAttribute newAttr = new LDAPAttribute("uid", "kurtj");
LDAPModification singleChange = new
LDAPModification(LDAPModifcation.REPLACE, newAttr);
try{
  ldc.modify(DN, singleChange);
}catch(LDAPException e){
  switch(e.getLDAPResultCode()){
    case e.NO_SUCH_OBJECT:System.out.println("The
specified use does not exist." );
    break;
  default:System.out.println("Error number: " +
e.getLDAPResultCode());
    e.printStackTrace();
    break;
  }
}
```

# Dealing With Referrals

In a geographically dispersed corporation, it is often necessary to have multiple LDAP servers. Some of them serve as masters and others as slaves. In such cases, referral becomes a necessity. In the case of modification, you need to reauthenticate yourself against a different LDAP server. The reauthentication process is embodied in the *LDAPRebind* interface. First you develop a generic class that implements *LDAPRebind*, such as:

```
String DN;
String password;
public Rebind(String DN, String password){
  this.DN = DN;
  this.password = password;
}
```

```
public LDAPRebindAuth getRebindAuthentication(String
host, int port){
   return new LDAPRebindAuth(DN, password);
}
```

Then, before you call the *authenticate()* and *modify()* methods, you set
some options for your *LDAPConnection* object so that it does referrals and
also uses the above class to do the rebind.

```
ldc.setOption(LDAPv2.REFERRALS, new Boolean(true));
ldc.setOption(ldc.REFERRALS_REBIND_PROC, new Rebind(DN,
args[0]));
```

## Put it All Together for Update

The following program updates the user ID attribute of an entry, and the
update follows referrals, too.

**Listing 8-2**
Modify an LDAP entry

**Modification.java**

```
import java.io.*;
import java.net.*;
import java.util.*;
import netscape.ldap.*;
import netscape.ldap.util.*;
import netscape.ldap.controls.*;

class Rebind implements netscape.ldap.LDAPRebind{

   public Rebind (String DN, String password){
      this.DN = DN;
      this.password = password;
   }

   public LDAPRebindAuth getRebindAuthentication(String
host, int port){
      return new LDAPRebindAuth(DN, password);
   }
```

```
    String DN;
    String password;
}

public class Modification{

  Modification(){}

  public static void main(String args[]){

  if (args.length == 0){
    System.out.println("usage: Java Modification passwd");
    return;
  }

    String DN = "uid=rdaugherty, ou=People,
o=airius.com";
    String host = "localhost";
    int port = 389;
    String adminDN = "cn=Directory Manager";
    LDAPAttribute newAttr = new LDAPAttribute("ou", "Hu-
man Resources");
    LDAPModification singleChange = new
LDAPModification(LDAPModification.REPLACE, newAttr);

    LDAPConnection ldc = new LDAPConnection();

    try{
      ldc.connect(host, port);
      ldc.setOption(LDAPv2.REFERRALS, new Boolean(true));
      ldc.setOption(ldc.REFERRALS_REBIND_PROC, new
Rebind(DN, args[0]));
      ldc.authenticate(adminDN, args[0]);
      System.out.println("Authenticated ... ");
      ldc.modify(DN, singleChange);
      System.out.println("modified");
      ldc.disconnect();
    }catch (LDAPException e){
      switch(e.getLDAPResultCode()){
        case e.NO_SUCH_OBJECT: System.out.println("The
specified user does not exist.");
              break;
        case e.INVALID_CREDENTIALS:
```

```
System.out.println("Invalid password.");
          break;
     default:System.out.println("Error number: " +
e.getLDAPResultCode());
          e.printStackTrace();
          break;
   }
   return;
   }
   finally{
     System.exit(0);
   }
   }
}
```

You can find the complete source code to the example under the *chap8\sample2* subdirectory on the CD-ROM. When running this example, make sure you pass the password as a command line parameter. For example, *java Modification admintest.*

# Netscape LDAP Server

In this section, we'll learn how to download and test the Netscape Directory Server 3.1.

Netscape has put both the LDAP server and the LDAP Java SDK on the Web, and they are freely downloadable for evaluation purposes. The URL for the software download is: *http://developer.netscape.com/software/index.html.* You can also use the evaluation copy bundled in the CD-ROM. Copy the executable to a temporary location on your local hard drive and double-click the self-extracting executable "d31eiu.exe" for Windows NT. During the installation, you'll be prompted to enter an administrator's log-in ID and password. You can type **admin** as the log-in ID and **admin** as the password. You'll also be prompted to choose the admin port that should be selected per your requirement, for example, 13346. At the end of installation, you will be prompted whether you want to connect to the admin page. Click on OK. You'll be prompted for a user ID and password for the administrator. Type in **admin** and **admin**.

**NOTE**

When you access the site *http://developer.netscape.com/software/index.html*, the directory server is under the server software category and the Java SDK is under the tools category.

Installation is based on SmartUpdate and you'll need communicator 4.x for installation. When installed ldap10.jar under *<netscape installed directory>\communicator\program\java\classes* is updated to ldap3x.jar. Your CLASSPATH should now point to ldap3x.jar instead of ldap10.jar. But in this book we usually refers to ldap10.jar.

After the installation, there are a few more things you need to do before the LDAP server is fully configured and ready for use. Below are the few steps you need to follow to set up the server:

1. In the administrator page, click the link that says "Create New Netscape Directory Server 3.1."
2. Fill in the configuration details. Leave everything at the default.
3. Type in the admin password as **admin** and the Unrestricted user password as **admintest**. Click on OK.
4. After the successful installation, it returns to the administration page automatically.
5. The directory server account you just created is listed in the admin page. Start the server by clicking the ON icon.
6. Click on the button that displays your server name to enter the server management page.
7. Click the database management button on the top frame
8. Click Import link on the left frame to import the database; this will shut down your server. Once the server is shut down successfully, click Import link again.
9. Airius.ldif is selected by default; click on OK.
10. Once your database is imported, select Server Preferences from the top frame and start the server.

To learn more about access control and directory server configuration, please check Netscape's online documentation at *http://developer.netscape.com/docs/manuals/index.html?content=directory.html.*

**NOTE**

Once you have installed the sample database, you can test the Search and Update sample programs that we developed earlier in this chapter. Our examples all assume that they are run on the local host where the LDAP server is installed. We also assume that LDAP is installed on its default port 389. If your settings vary, you'll have to change the sample programs accordingly. Also make sure your CLASSPATH is pointing to ldap10.jar, which contains all the LDAP Java classes needed for your samples to run. The Java LDAP SDK contains the same jar file.

# Developing LDAP Bean

In this section we will develop an LDAP bean that will search and update an LDAP database. Updates will require authentication, but searches will not. First we will develop an *LDAPUtility* class that will search and update the LDAP database. Then we'll develop a bean wrapper over it. The *LDAPUtility* class will have search, update, authenticate, and log-out methods.

Our LDAP bean will also fire an event every time a search or an update is completed. This event will be used by listeners to obtain the latest database information. Whenever update is called we'll do a search again on the database to get the latest information.

## LDAPUtility

This class is straightforward. Since all the code has been explained earlier, we won't get into the details again here.

**Listing 8-3**
LDAPUtility class that searches and updates an LDAP directory

**LDAPUtility.java**

```
import java.io.*;
import java.net.*;
import java.util.*;
import netscape.ldap.*;
import netscape.ldap.util.*;
import netscape.ldap.controls.*;

class Rebind implements netscape.ldap.LDAPRebind{
  String DN;
  String password;
```

```
    public Rebind (String DN, String password){
      this.DN = DN;
      this.password = password;
    }
    public LDAPRebindAuth getRebindAuthentication(String
host, int port){
       return new LDAPRebindAuth(DN, password);
    }
}

public class LDAPUtility
{
  String organization = null;
  String organizationUnit = null;
  String commonName = null;
  String searchBase = null;

  String host;
  int port;

  LDAPConnection ldc;

  LDAPUtility(){}

  LDAPUtility(String organization, String
organizationUnit, String host, int port){
      this.organization = organization;
      this.organizationUnit = organizationUnit;
      searchBase = organization;
      this.host = host;
      this.port = port;

      ldc = new LDAPConnection();

      try{
        ldc.connect(host, port);
      }catch (LDAPException e){
        System.err.println ("Can't connect to " + host);
        e.printStackTrace();
      }
    }
```

```java
    private String getSearchBase(){
      String searchBase;

      searchBase = "o=" + organization;

      if (!organizationUnit.equals(""))
        searchBase = "ou=" + organizationUnit + ", " +
searchBase;
      return searchBase;
    }

    private String getDN(String cn){
      commonName = cn;
      return ("cn=" + cn + ", ou=" + organizationUnit +
", o=" + organization);
    }

    public Vector search(String filterString){
      String searchBase = getSearchBase();
      String filter = filterString;
      String[] attrs = null;
      boolean attrsOnly = false;

      LDAPSearchResults res = null;

      try{
        res = ldc.search(searchBase, ldc.SCOPE_SUB, fil-
ter, attrs, attrsOnly);
      }catch(LDAPException e){
        System.err.println("Search failed");
        e.printStackTrace();
      }


      if (res != null)
        return (extractResults(res));
      else
        return (null);
    }

    private Vector extractResults(LDAPSearchResults res){
      Vector resultVec = new Vector();
```

```
    while (res.hasMoreElements()){
      LDAPEntry entry = (LDAPEntry)res.nextElement();
      String nextDN = entry.getDN();
      resultVec.addElement ("DN=" + nextDN);

      LDAPAttributeSet entryAttrs =
entry.getAttributeSet();
      Enumeration attrsInSet =
entryAttrs.getAttributes();

      while (attrsInSet.hasMoreElements()){
        LDAPAttribute nextAttr =
LDAPAttribute)attrsInSet.nextElement();
        String attrName = nextAttr.getName();

        Enumeration valsInAttr = null;

        try{
          valsInAttr = nextAttr.getStringValues();
        }catch (NullPointerException e){
          valsInAttr = null;
        }

        if (valsInAttr == null)
          valsInAttr = nextAttr.getByteValues();

        while (valsInAttr.hasMoreElements()){
          try{
    String nextValue =
(String)valsInAttr.nextElement();
            resultVec.addElement(attrName + "=" +
nextValue);
          }catch(NullPointerException e){}
        }
      }
    }
    return (resultVec);
  }

  public boolean authenticate(String dn, String
passwd){
    try{
```

```
        ldc.setOption(LDAPv2.REFERRALS, new
Boolean(true));
        ldc.setOption(ldc.REFERRALS_REBIND_PROC, new
Rebind(dn, passwd));
      ldc.authenticate(dn, passwd);
      System.out.println("Authenticated");
    }catch(LDAPException e){
      switch(e.getLDAPResultCode()){
        case e.INVALID_CREDENTIALS:
System.err.println("Invalid password.");
          return false;
        default: System.err.println("Error number: " +
e.getLDAPResultCode());
          e.printStackTrace();
          return false;
      }
    }
    return true;
  }

  void update (String dn, String attributeName, String
attributeValue){
      LDAPAttribute newAttr = new
LDAPAttribute(attributeName, attributeValue);
      LDAPModification singleChange = new
LDAPModification(LDAPModification.REPLACE, newAttr);

      try{
        ldc.modify(dn, singleChange);
      }catch (LDAPException e){
        switch(e.getLDAPResultCode()){
          case e.NO_SUCH_OBJECT:System.out.println("The
specified use does not exist.");
            break;
          default:System.out.println("Error number: " +
e.getLDAPResultCode());
            e.printStackTrace();break;
        }
      }
    }
  }
```

## LDAPBean

Since most of the code in LDAP beans adheres to the JavaBeans specification, we won't go into the detail of the *LDAPBean* class. However, let's look at the important code snippets.

```
public class LDAPBean implements Serializable {
```

One of the requirements of a bean is that it should implement the Serializable interface for storing persistent information. So, our *LDAPBean* implements the *Serializable* interface:

```
protected transient String username = "", password =
"";
protected transient String disName = "";
protected transient String commonName = "";

private transient boolean loggedIn;
protected transient String attributeName = "",
attributeValue = "";
```

Variables such as *username, password,* and *disName,* which represent DN; *commonName,* which represents CN; *loggedIn;* and *attributeName* and *attributeValue* are all marked transient, because we do not want to serialize this information since it may vary at runtime. Remember that all runtime information should not be serialized and hence needs to be marked transient.

All beans should have a zero argument constructor in order to allow for serialization.

```
public LDAPBean(){
```

Using design patterns, we defined a number of setter and getter methods for obtaining the design time information

```
public void searchLdapServer(){
  ldap = null;
  ldap = new LDAPUtility(organization, orgUnit,
serverName, portNumber);
  if(ldap != null){
```

```
      result = ldap.search(getSearchCriteria());
    }
    fireEvent();
}
```

Method *searchLdapServer()* is the method that is used for searching the LDAP server. We create an instance of *LDAPUtility* before calling *search()*.

```
public synchronized void updateLdapServer(){
  if(!loggedIn){
    sendMessage("Not logged in");
    return;
  }
  if(ldap != null && loggedIn){
    ldap.update(DN, attributeName, attributeValue);
  }
}
```

Similarly, *updateLdapServer()* is used for updating the LDAP server. We always create an instance of *LDAPUtility*.

```
public void logout(){
  username = "";
  password = "";
  loggedIn = false;
}
```

Method *logout()* makes sure that the log-in ID and the password previously typed are null. This prompts the log-in dialog when update is next called. The log-in ID and password are also nullified when the application exits, because the persistence information for these two values is not stored. It is always a good idea to call *logout()* when done.

```
public boolean login(String uname, String pswd){
  if (ldap == null)
    ldap = new LDAPUtility(organization, orgUnit,
serverName, portNumber);

  if(ldap.authenticate(uname, pswd)){
    loggedIn = true;
```

```
      this.username = username;
      this.password = password;
      sendMessage("Login success");
    }
    else{
      loggedIn = false;
      sendMessage("Login failed");
    }
    return loggedIn;
  }
```

Method *login()* needs to be called before performing any updates. If no log-in has taken place, the update will not work and an error will be reported.

```
public synchronized void addLDAPListener(LDAPListener l){
    listeners.addElement(l);
}

public synchronized void removeLDAPListener(LDAPListener l){
    listeners.removeElement(l);
}

protected void fireEvent(){
    Vector l = (Vector)listeners.clone();
    LDAPEvent e = new LDAPEvent(this, result);
    e.setMessage("Success");
    for(int i = 0; i < l.size(); i++){
        ((LDAPListener)l.elementAt(i)).result(e);
    }
}

protected void sendMessage(String err){
    Vector l = (Vector)listeners.clone();
    LDAPEvent e = new LDAPEvent(this, null);
    e.setMessage(err);
    for(int i = 0; i < l.size(); i++){
        ((LDAPListener)l.elementAt(i)).result(e);
    }
}
```

Methods *addLDAPListener()*, *removeLDAPListener()*, *fireEvent()*, and *sendMessage()* all take care of registering and initiating the registered listeners when an event is fired.

## LDAPBeanListener The Listener Interface

*LDAPBeanListener* is an interface that declares the methods that will be fired as events. In this case, our *LDAPBean* will fire an event called result:

```java
import java.util.*;


public interface LDAPListener extends EventListener{
  public void result(LDAPEvent e);
}
```

## LDAPEvent The Event class

LDAPEvent has two methods that set and get the result obtained from a LDAP search or update.

```java
public String getResult(){
  return this.result;
}


public void setResult(String searchResult){
  this.result = result;
}
```

Here is the text of LDAPEvent.java:

**Listing 8-4**
LDAPEvent

```java
import java.util.*;


public class LDAPEvent extends EventObject{
  protected Vector result;
  protected String message;

  public LDAPEvent(Object o){
    this(o, null);
  }
```

```
public LDAPEvent(Object o, Vector result){
  super(o);
  this.result = result;
}

public Vector getResult(){
  return this.result;
}

public void setResult(Vector result){
  this.result = result;
}

public void setMessage(String message){
  this.message = message;
}

public String getMessage(){
  return message;
}
}
```

Here is the text of LDAPBean.java:

```
import java.beans.*;
import java.io.*;
import java.lang.*;
import java.util.*;

public class LDAPBean implements Serializable{
  protected int portNumber;
  protected String serverName;
  protected String DN = "";
  protected transient String username = "", password = "";
  protected transient String disName = "";

  protected String organization = "",orgUnit = "";

  protected transient String searchCriteria = "";

  protected transient String attributeName =
```

```
       "",attributeValue = "";

   protected LDAPUtility ldap;

   protected Vector result = null;
   private transient boolean loggedIn;

   public LDAPBean(){
     this(389, "127.0.0.1");
   }

   public LDAPBean(int portNumber, String serverName){
     this.portNumber = portNumber;
     this.serverName = serverName;
     ldap = null;
     loggedIn = false;
   }

   public void setDN(String dn){
     this.DN = dn;
   }

   public String getDN(){
     return this.DN;
   }

   public void setOrganization(String organization){
     this.organization = organization;
   }

   public String getOrganization(){
     return organization;
   }

   public void setOrganizationUnit(String orgUnit){
     this.orgUnit = orgUnit;
   }

   public String getOrganizationUnit(){
     return orgUnit;
   }
```

```java
    public void setPortNumber(int portNumber){
      this.portNumber = portNumber;
    }

    public int getPortNumber(){
      return portNumber;
    }

    public void setServerName(String serverName){
      this.serverName = serverName;
    }

    public String getServerName(){
      return serverName;
    }

    public void setSearchCriteria(String sc){
      this.searchCriteria = "(" + sc + ")";
    }

    public String getSearchCriteria(){
      return searchCriteria.substring(1,
searchCriteria.length() - 1);
    }

    public void setAttributeName(String attributeName){
      this.attributeName = attributeName;
    }

    public String getAttributeName(){
      return attributeName;
    }

    public void setAttributeValue(String attributeValue){
      this.attributeValue = attributeValue;
    }

    public String getAttributeValue(){
      return attributeValue;
    }
```

```
public void searchLdapServer(){
   ldap = null;
   ldap = new LDAPUtility(organization, orgUnit,
serverName, portNumber);
   if(ldap != null){
     result = ldap.search(getSearchCriteria());
   }
   fireEvent();
}

public synchronized void updateLdapServer(){
   if(!loggedIn){
     sendMessage("Not logged in");
     return;
   }
   if(ldap != null && loggedIn){
     ldap.update(DN, attributeName, attributeValue);
   }
}

public void logout(){
   username = "";
   password = "";
   loggedIn = false;
}

public boolean login(String uname, String pswd){
   if (ldap == null)
     ldap = new LDAPUtility(organization, orgUnit,
serverName, portNumber);

   if(ldap.authenticate(uname, pswd)){
     loggedIn = true;
     this.username = username;
     this.password = password;
     sendMessage("Login success");
   }
   else{
     loggedIn = false;
     sendMessage("Login failed");
   }
```

```
      return loggedIn;
   }

   public Vector getResult(){
      return result;
   }

   protected Vector listeners = new Vector();

   public synchronized void addLDAPListener(LDAPListener l){
      listeners.addElement(l);
   }

   public synchronized void
removeLDAPListener(LDAPListener l){
      listeners.removeElement(l);
   }

   protected void fireEvent(){
      Vector l = (Vector)listeners.clone();
      LDAPEvent e = new LDAPEvent(this, result);
      e.setMessage("Success");
      for(int i = 0; i < l.size(); i++){
         ((LDAPListener)l.elementAt(i)).result(e);
      }
   }

   protected void sendMessage(String err){
      Vector l = (Vector)listeners.clone();
      LDAPEvent e = new LDAPEvent(this, null);
      e.setMessage(err);
      for(int i = 0; i < l.size(); i++){
         ((LDAPListener)l.elementAt(i)).result(e);
      }
   }
}
```

You can find the complete source code under the *chap8\sample3* subdirectory on the CD-ROM. Compile all the javafiles. Make sure to point to ldap10.jar in your CLASSPATH apart from the core java classes. You'll find ldap10.jar when you install Netscape Communicator under *<netscape installed directory>\communicator\program\java\classes*. Once you have successfully compiled the code, create the LDAPBean.jar file using the jar utility. On the command line, you'll type:

```
jar cvf LDAPBean.jar *.class
```

Of course, the jar file in the Netscape Directory SDK for Java would also work.

# Summary

In this chapter we learned all about LDAP. We also learned how to write Java programs to update and search LDAP servers. At the end of this section we developed an LDAP bean that is a reusable component. In Part 3 of this book, we'll use this LDAP bean to develop an employee tracking system.

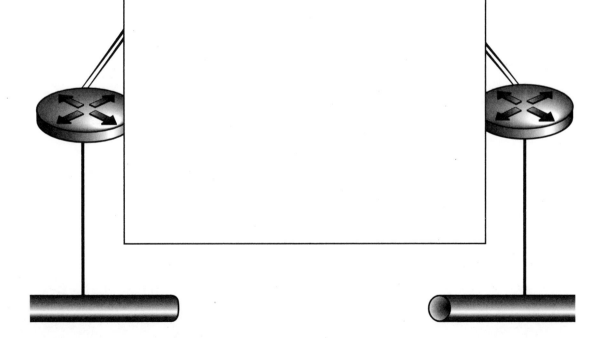

# CHAPTER 9

# Java Naming and Directory Interface

As we discussed in the previous chapter, a scalable directory service is an essential tool for an organization to manage different software applications and deal with personnel changes. Before the advent of LDAP, proprietary protocols have been the main vehicles for providing this service. These protocols include Novell's Netware Directory Service (NDS), Banyan's StreetTalk, and a few application-specific protocols such as Lotus's Enterprise Messaging Exchange (EMX). Novell has since embraced LDAP in NDS and has given it the acronym Novell Directory Service, but strong demand exists for applications to communicate with directory protocols other than LDAP. Java Naming and Directory Interface (JNDI) reflects Sun's desire to meet such a demand in Java.

# Introduction to JNDI

JNDI provides a uniform way of accessing directories regardless of their vendors or protocols. Figure 9-1 shows the simplified view of the architecture.

**Figure 9-1**
JNDI architecture
(simplified)

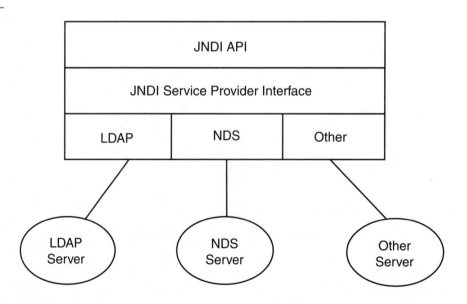

JNDI includes a set of APIs for developers to access directories, including searching and updating. However by itself JNDI doesn't have the code to access any particular directory server. In a way JNDI is analogous to an abstract method in Java. It only states the set of services it provides, but doesn't have the code to do the actual work. The entity that does the work is called a service provider. JNDI has included a set of APIs for directory vendors to plug in their modules that do the actual work of directory access.

The JNDI API doesn't make any assumptions on what kind of directory server it accesses. Therefore once a program is written, the application will run on top of any directory service provider.

With this architecture, developers do not need to know beforehand what directory they need to access. They only need to write the JNDI code, and later, if the targeting directory is found to be an NDS directory, for example, they will only need to plug in the NDS modules into JNDI. The same application code will also work in the case of other directory servers, such as an LDAP server.

## JNDI and Naming Service

Entries in directories often have attributes. Attribute-based access is a hallmark of directory service. There are times when software applications need a lightweight service that performs name lookups—the *naming service*.

A naming service associates a human memorable name with a machine understandable object. For example, when we try to invoke the Netscape Navigator application, we only need to type **netscape** on the command line. The operating system will find the file object that "netscape" represents and start executing it. This process involves translating a name—netscape—to an application file object, and this service is provided by the file system.

Like directory services, currently each application comes with its own routines or programs to perform the naming service. For example, CORBA comes with a COSNaming service, and network systems include Domain Name Service, to translate Internet hostnames like www.foo.com to their corresponding IP addresses (say 192.96.24.116).

In addition to uniting programming interfaces for directory services, which mainly deal with attributes of objects, JNDI also attempts to provide a uniform programming interface for naming services, which deal with the association between objects and their mnemonic names. The JNDI architecture we discussed in the previous section is designed with both naming and directory services in mind. Figure 9-2 shows the complete JNDI architecture, including naming services.

**Figure 9-2**
JNDI architecture
with naming services

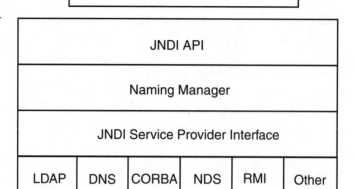

As of today, the naming and directory services available under JNDI include the following:

- LDAP—Lightweight Directory Access Protocol
- NIS—Network Information System, Sun's yellow pages service
- NIS+—NIS, DNS, and other enhancements
- COSNaming—CORBA's naming service
- File system
- RMI registry—Naming service of Java Remote Method Invocation
- Service Location Protocol—A protocol that allows network applications to advertise services
- Novell Directory Service™
- Tengah—The naming service for WebLogic's Java application server

## Advantages and Disadvantages of JNDI

JNDI's biggest advantage is that it furthers Java's promise to "Write Once, Run Anywhere." An application program utilizing JNDI will run under any directory service or any naming service. JNDI also allows developers to concentrate on the main functions of the application rather than learning different naming services. Distributed application frameworks have all brought their own flavors of naming services, and not all of them are easy to learn.

Of course, JNDI pays for simplicity by sacrificing flexibility. In creating a uniform API, JNDI programmers will not be able to take advantages of certain features that a particular directory or naming service may possess.

# JNDI API

There are three packages in JNDI:

- javax.naming
- javax.naming.directory
- javax.naming.spi

The naming package provides classes and interfaces that allow developers to access naming services. The *naming.directory* package enables developers to access directories. The *naming.spi* package provides hooks for vendors to hook their services into JNDI as service providers. The discussion of this package is beyond the scope of our book. (Also, if you were wondering, the "x" in javax stands for extension.)

Central to the JNDI API is the concept of a *context*. Context means the existing binding of objects and names. Before a JNDI application is invoked, it has to create an initial context, which specifies the kind of service provider it wishes to use, among other things. In the case of the LDAP service provider, it will also need to specify where the LDAP server resides and the root DN.

Not surprisingly, JNDI API provides an interface called *Context*. That interface is included in the naming package and provides methods for looking up a name, binding an object to a name, and listing all the bindings for a particular context.

The equivalent interface in naming.directory of *Context* is *DirContext*. This interface includes methods to search a directory, modify objects in a directory, insert objects into a directory, and delete objects from a directory. In fact, the structure of *DirContext* bears a remarkable similarity to *LDAPConnection* in the LDAP API.

The following sections will tell you how to search and update LDAP entries with the JNDI API. Of course, before we start, there is some preparation we need to do. Here are the steps to follow to set up the JNDI environment to access an LDAP server:

1. Download the JNDI (jndi111.zip, LDAP(ldap10.zip), and CosNaming (cosnaming-ea1.zip) service providers from *http://java.sun.com/products/jndi/#download*.

2. Unzip all the zip files mentioned above. Unzip jndi111.zip to, for example, *C:\jndi* and ldap10.zip and cosnaming-ea1.zip to, for example, *C:\jndi\ldap*.

3. Set the CLASSPATH environment variable to include jndi.jar, ldap.jar, cosnaming.jar, and providerutil.jar, as shown: *c:\jndi\lib\jndi.jar;c:\jndi\ldap\lib\ldap.jar;c:\jndi\ldap\lib\providerutil.jar;c:\jndi\ldap\cosnaming.jar*.

Now we are ready to do some programming.

## Initial Context

As we discussed earlier, one of the first things a JNDI program does is to establish an initial context stating that it wants to access an LDAP server. The code piece that accomplishes this looks like this:

```
Hashtable env = new Hashtable();
// specify the need for the LDAP service provider
env.put(Context.INITIAL_CONTEXT_FACTORY,
"com.sun.jndi.ldap.LdapCtxFactory");

// specify the LDAP server and the port number
env.put(Context.PROVIDER_URL, "ldap://localhost:389");

// create the initial context
DirContext ctx = new InitialDirContext(env);
```

The last statement creates the initial context for the program, and we pass initial information through the *env* hashtable.

It is also possible to include initial context information at runtime, using the *−D* option of the java command. For example, if we wanted to provide the PROVIDER_URL at runtime, we could use this option:

```
java −Djava.naming.provider.url=ldap://localhost:389
Search
```

**NOTE**

We are assuming that you have completed Chapter 8 by this point, since we use the LDAP server that we installed there.

# Searching the LDAP Server

The search operation is done by the *search()* method of the *DirContext* interface. The JNDI search should look familiar to an LDAP programmer. A typical form looks like this:

```
NamingEnumeration search(Name name, String filterExpr,
SearchControls cons) throws NamingException
```

Here, name is equivalent to the *searchBase* of an LDAP search, *filterExpr* corresponds to the filter string, and *cons* is translated to *LDAPSearchConstraint.* An example of a search operation looks like this:

```
//specifies the search options
SearchControls searchOptions = new SearchControls();

//the search covers the whole subtree
SearchOptions.setSearchScope
(SearchControls.SUBTREE_SCOPE);

//returns maximum 10 entries.
searchOptions.setCountLimit(10);

//specifies search base and filter, much like the LDAP
API
String searchBase = "o=Airius.com";
String filter = "(uid=tclow)";

//return the first 10 entries of the LDAP database
NamingEnumeration results = ctx.search(searchBase,
filter, searchOptions);
```

If we do not set search options, the default options will be used. The search will then perform in only the first level of its subtree, and it will return all the entries.

The search result is an enumeration of objects of type *SearchResults*, which represents an entry in a directory. For each such object, you can use the *getAttributes()* method to obtain all the attributes. These attributes are stored in an object of type *Attributes,* and you can use the *getAll()* method of interface *Attributes* to retrieve an enumeration of attributes. An attribute is of type *Attribute*. If this all sounds too confusing, Figure 9-3 illustrates the relationships more clearly.

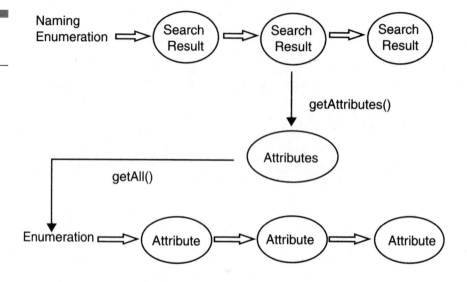

**Figure 9-3**
Extracting search results with JNDI

The code looks like this:

```
// traverse the SearchResult enumeration
while (results != null && results.hasMore()) {
  SearchResult entry = (SearchResult)results.next();

  // getName returns the DN
  System.out.println("DN: " + entry.getName());

  Attributes attrs = entry.getAttributes();
  if (attrs == null) {
    System.out.println("No attributes");
  } else {
    // getAll returns an enumeration of
    // attributes
    for (NamingEnumeration ae = attrs.getAll();
ae.hasMoreElements();) {
      Attribute attr = (Attribute)ae.next();
      String attrName = attr.getID();

      // An attribute may have more than
```

```
                    // one values
                    for (Enumeration vals = attr.getAll();
                       vals.hasMoreElements();
                         System.out.println(attrName + ": " +
vals.nextElement()));
                  }
               }
             System.out.println();
         }
```

## Put it Together for Search

Here is the complete program that performs an LDAP search for entries
whose user ID attribute is "tclow":

■■ ■■ ■■ ■■ ■■ ■■

**Listing 9-1**

Listing for searching
LDAP server using
JNDI

**Search.java:**

```
import java.util.Hashtable;
import java.util.Enumeration;
import javax.naming.*;
import javax.naming.directory.*;

class Search{
  public static void main(String[] args)throws
NamingException{
      Hashtable env = new Hashtable();
      env.put(Context.INITIAL_CONTEXT_FACTORY,
"com.sun.jndi.ldap.LdapCtxFactory");
      env.put(Context.PROVIDER_URL, "ldap://
localhost:389");

      DirContext ctx = new InitialDirContext(env);
      try{
        SearchControls searchOptions = new
SearchControls();

searchOptions.setSearchScope(SearchControls.SUBTREE_SCOPE);
        searchOptions.setCountLimit(10);
        String searchBase = "o=Airius.com";
```

```
        String filter = "(uid=tclow)";

        NamingEnumeration results =
ctx.search(searchBase, filter, searchOptions);

        while (results != null && results.hasMore()){
          SearchResult entry =
(SearchResult)results.next();

        System.out.println("DN: " + entry.getName());

        Attributes attrs = entry.getAttributes();
        if (attrs == null){
          System.out.println("No attributes");
        }else{
          for (NamingEnumeration ae = attrs.getAll();
ae.hasMoreElements();){
            Attribute attr = (Attribute)ae.next();
            String attrName = attr.getID();
            for (Enumeration vals = attr.getAll();
vals.hasMoreElements();System.out.println(attrName + ":
" + vals.nextElement()))
               ;
          }
        }
      }
    }catch(SizeLimitExceededException
se){System.out.println("\nthere are more entries ..");}
  }
}
```

The complete source code for Listing 9-1 can be found under the *chap9\sample1* subdirectory on the CD-ROM. If your CLASSPATH is set as shown at the beginning of this section you should be able to compile the source successfully. After compiling and running this program, you'll get the following:

```
name: uid=tclow, ou=People
givenname: Torrey
telephonenumber: +1 408 555 8825
sn: Clow
```

```
ou: Human Resources
ou: People
l: Santa Clara
roomnumber: 4376
mail: tclow@airius.com
facsimiletelephonenumber: +1 408 555 1992
objectclass: top
objectclass: person
objectclass: organizationalPerson
objectclass: inetOrgPerson
uid: tclow
cn: Torrey Clow
```

# Updating LDAP Server

As in the LDAP API, updating in JNDI requires authentication. Authentication information is passed to the context as an environment variable. Here is the code that specifies the username and password that will be supplied to the directory server:

```
Hashtable env = new Hashtable();
env.put(Context.SECURITY_AUTHENTICATION, "simple");
env.put(Context.SECURITY_PRINCIPAL, "cn=Directory Man-
ager")
env.put(Context.SECURITY_CREDENTIALS, "admintest");
DirContext ctx = new InitialDirContext(env);
```

Here *SECURITY_AUTHENTICATION* specifies the level of the security. The three possible levels are "none", "simple", and "strong". *SECURITY_PRINCIPAL* specifies the identity of the principal that is authenticated for the update operation, and *SECURITY_CREDENTIALS* is passed as the password. See the LDAP chapter, Chapter 8, for a discussion of the management DN and the password.

To update a certain attribute of an entry, we'll need to create an object of *BasicAttribute* type. For example:

```
BasicAttribute attribute1 = new BasicAttribute("ou",
"Product Development");
```

This statement creates an attribute whose name is "ou" and with the value "Product Development."

Once an attribute is created, we want to specify what operation we want to perform on an entry. There are three types of operations: add, replace, and modify. If we wanted to change the organization unit of a person to "Product Development," we would do the following:

```
BasicAttribute attribute1 = new BasicAttribute("ou",
"Product Development");
ModificationItem mod1 = new
ModificationItem(DirContext.REPLACE_ATTRIBUTE, at-
tribute1);
```

Now we need to tell the directory server which entry we want to modify; here is how we do it:

```
ModificationItem[] modItemArray = new
ModificationItem[1];
modItemArray[0] = mod1;
String entryDN = "uid=tclow, ou=People, o=airius.com";
ctx.modifyAttributes(entryDN, modItemArray);
```

Notice that we need to call the *modifyAttributes()* method of *DirContext* to do the actual modification. That method takes an array of *ModificationItem* objects as input. Even though we have only one attribute to modify, we need to create an array with one item.

## Put it Together for Update

Here is the code that will perform the following modifications to the entry whose DN is: "uid=tclow, ou=People, o=airius.com".

- Change the organization unit to Product Development
- Modify the "Description entry" to the last modification date
- Delete the "room number" attribute

**Modification.java:**

```java
import java.util.Hashtable;
import java.util.Date;
import javax.naming.*;
import javax.naming.directory.*;

class Modification{
  public static void main(String[] args){
    Hashtable env = new Hashtable();
    env.put(Context.INITIAL_CONTEXT_FACTORY,
"com.sun.jndi.ldap.LdapCtxFactory");
    env.put(Context.PROVIDER_URL, "ldap://
localhost:389");
    env.put(Context.SECURITY_AUTHENTICATION, "simple")
    env.put(Context.SECURITY_PRINCIPAL, "cn=Directory
Manager");
    env.put(Context.SECURITY_CREDENTIALS, "admintest");

    try{
      DirContext ctx = new InitialDirContext(env);
      BasicAttribute attribute1 = new
BasicAttribute("ou", "Product Development");
      ModificationItem mod1 = new
ModificationItem(DirContext.REPLACE_ATTRIBUTE, at-
tribute1);
      BasicAttribute attribute2 = new
BasicAttribute("Description", "last modified: " + (new
Date()).toString());
      ModificationItem mod2 = new
ModificationItem(DirContext.ADD_ATTRIBUTE, attribute2);
      BasicAttribute attribute3 = new
BasicAttribute("roomnumber");
      ModificationItem mod3 = new
ModificationItem(DirContext.REMOVE_ATTRIBUTE, at-
tribute3);
      ModificationItem[] modItemArray = new
ModificationItem[3];

      modItemArray[0] = mod1;
      modItemArray[1] = mod2;
      modItemArray[2] = mod3;
```

```
    String entryDN = "uid=tclow, ou=People,
o=airius.com";
    ctx.modifyAttributes(entryDN, modItemArray);

    System.out.println("Modification succeeded");
  }catch (NamingException e)
{System.err.println("modification
failed.");e.printStackTrace();}
  }
}
```

The complete source code for Listing 9-2 can be found under the *chap9\sample2* subdirectory on the CD-ROM. If the CLASSPATH is set properly as discussed at the beginning of this section, the code should compile successfully. After the code successfully completes its run, you may want to run Search sample again to make sure the changes are reflected.

If you run the search again, you'll see the following results:

```
name: uid=tclow, ou=People
givenname: Torrey
sn: Clow
telephonenumber: +1 408 555 8825
ou: Product Development
l: Santa Clara
mail: tclow@airius.com
facsimiletelephonenumber: +1 408 555 1992
objectclass: top
objectclass: person
objectclass: organizationalPerson
objectclass: inetOrgPerson
uid: tclow
cn: Torrey Clow
description: last modified: Wed Aug 19 23:48:26 PDT
1998
```

See that ou has changed from Human Resources to Product Development, the description entry holds the last modified date, and the room number no longer shows.

# ▰▰ ▰▰ **JNDI Bean for LDAP**

To show you how we can write JNDI applications in the form of JavaBeans, we have modified the LDAP JavaBean in the previous chapter so that it uses the JNDI API instead. It achieves the same functionality—this bean and the LDAP bean are interchangable in building future applications.

Like the *LDAPUtility* class, *JNDIUtility* has search, update, and authenticate methods. Here is the source for JNDIUtility.java:

▰ ▰ ▰ ▰ ▰ ▰ **JNDIUtility.java**

**Listing 9-3**
JNDI utility class

```java
import java.io.*;
import java.net.*;
import java.util.*;
import javax.naming.*;
import javax.naming.directory.*;

public class JNDIUtility{
    String organization = null;
    String organizationUnit = null;
    String commonName = null;
    String searchBase = null;
    String host;
    int port;
    DirContext ctx;
    static DirContext modCtx;
    SearchControls searchOptions;

    JNDIUtility(){}

    JNDIUtility(String organization, String
organizationUnit, String host, int port){
        this.organization = organization;
        this.organizationUnit = organizationUnit;
        searchBase = organization;
        this.host = host;
        this.port = port;

        Hashtable env = new Hashtable();
        env.put(Context.INITIAL_CONTEXT_FACTORY,
"com.sun.jndi.ldap.LdapCtxFactory");
        env.put(Context.PROVIDER_URL, "ldap://" + host +
":" + port);
```

```
    try{
      ctx = new InitialDirContext(env);
    }catch(NamingException e){e.printStackTrace();}

    searchOptions = new SearchControls();

searchOptions.setSearchScope(SearchControls.SUBTREE_SCOPE);
    }

  private String getSearchBase(){
    String searchBase;
    searchBase = "o=" + organization;

    if (!organizationUnit.equals("")){
      searchBase = "ou=" + organizationUnit + ", " +
searchBase;
    }

    return searchBase;
  }

  private String getDN(String cn){
    commonName = cn;
    return ("cn=" + cn + ", ou=" + organizationUnit +
", o=" + organization);
  }

  private String getNetscapeDN(String cn){
    commonName = cn;
    return ("uid=" + cn + ", ou=" + organizationUnit +
", o=" + organization);
  }

  public Vector search(String filterString){
    String searchBase = getSearchBase();
    String filter = filterString;
    String[] attrs = null;
    boolean attrsOnly = false;

    NamingEnumeration results = null;

    try{
```

```
        results = ctx.search(searchBase, filter,
searchOptions);
    }catch(Exception e){System.err.println("Search
failed");
        e.printStackTrace();
    }


    if (results != null){
      return (extractResults(results));
    }else{
      return (null);
    }
  }

  private Vector extractResults(NamingEnumeration res){
    Vector resultVec = new Vector();

    try{
      while ((res != null) & (res.hasMore())){
        SearchResult entry = (SearchResult)res.next();
        String nextDN = entry.getName();

        String stringValue = "DN="+nextDN;
        resultVec.addElement (stringValue);

        Attributes attrs = entry.getAttributes();
        NamingEnumeration attrsInSet = attrs.getAll();

        while (attrsInSet.hasMoreElements()){
          Attribute nextAttr =
(Attribute)attrsInSet.next();
          String attrName = nextAttr.getID();

          for (Enumeration valsInAttr =
nextAttr.getAll(); valsInAttr.hasMoreElements();){
            try{
              String nextValue =
(String)valsInAttr.nextElement();
              resultVec.addElement (attrName + "=" +
nextValue);
            }catch(NullPointerException e){}
          }
```

```
        }
      }
    }catch(NamingException
e){e.printStackTrace();return (null);}
      return (resultVec);
    }


  public boolean authenticate(String cn, String
passwd){
    Hashtable env = new Hashtable();
    env.put(Context.INITIAL_CONTEXT_FACTORY,
"com.sun.jndi.ldap.LdapCtxFactory");
    env.put(Context.PROVIDER_URL, "ldap://" + host +
":" + port);
    env.put(Context.SECURITY_AUTHENTICATION, "simple");
    env.put(Context.SECURITY_PRINCIPAL, cn);
    env.put(Context.SECURITY_CREDENTIALS, passwd);

    try{
      modCtx = new InitialDirContext(env);
    }catch(NamingException e){return false;}
    return true;
  }


  void update(String dn, String attributeName, String
attributeValue){
    BasicAttribute attribute1 = new
BasicAttribute(attributeName, attributeValue);

    ModificationItem mod1 = new
ModificationItem(DirContext.REPLACE_ATTRIBUTE, at-
tribute1);
    ModificationItem[] modItemArray = new
ModificationItem[1];

    modItemArray[0] = mod1;
    try{
      modCtx.modifyAttributes(dn, modItemArray);
    }catch(NamingException
e){System.out.println("Modification failed");
e.printStackTrace();}
  }
}
```

Like the *LDAPBean*, *JNDIBean* is a bean wrapper over the *JNDIUtility* class. Here is the source code for JNDIBean.java:

**Listing 9-4**
JNDI bean class

**JNDIBean.java**

```java
import java.beans.*;
import java.io.*;
import java.lang.*;
import java.util.*;

public class JNDIBean implements Serializable{
  protected int portNumber;
  protected String serverName;
  protected String DN = "";
  protected transient String username = "", password =
"";
  protected transient String disName = "";
  protected String  organization = "", orgUnit = "";
  protected transient String searchCriteria = "";
  protected transient String attributeName = "",
attributeValue = "";
  protected JNDIUtility ldap;
  protected Vector result = null;
  private transient boolean loggedIn;

  public JNDIBean(){
    this(389, "127.0.0.1");
  }

  public JNDIBean(int portNumber, String serverName){
    this.portNumber = portNumber;
    this.serverName = serverName;
    ldap = null;
    listeners = new Vector();
    loggedIn = false;
  }

  public void setDN(String dn){
    this.DN = dn;
  }

  public String getDN(){
    return this.DN;
  }
```

```java
    public void setOrganization(String organization){
      this.organization = organization;
    }

    public String getOrganization(){
      return organization;
    }

    public void setOrganizationUnit(String orgUnit){
      this.orgUnit = orgUnit;
    }

    public String getOrganizationUnit(){
      return orgUnit;
    }

    public void setPortNumber(int portNumber){
      this.portNumber = portNumber;
    }

    public int getPortNumber(){
      return portNumber;
    }

    public void setServerName(String serverName){
      this.serverName = serverName;
    }

    public String getServerName(){
      return serverName;
    }

    public void setSearchCriteria(String sc){
      this.searchCriteria = "(" + sc + ")";
    }

    public String getSearchCriteria(){
      return searchCriteria.substring(1,
searchCriteria.length() - 1);
    }
```

```java
public void setAttributeName(String attributeName){
  this.attributeName = attributeName;
}

public String getAttributeName(){
  return attributeName;
}

public void setAttributeValue(String attributeValue){
  this.attributeValue = attributeValue;
}

public String getAttributeValue(){
  return attributeValue;
}

public void searchLdapServer(){
  ldap = null;
  ldap = new JNDIUtility(organization, orgUnit,
serverName, portNumber);
  if(ldap != null){
    result = ldap.search(searchCriteria);
  }
  fireEvent();
}

public synchronized void updateLdapServer(){
  if(!loggedIn){
    sendMessage("Not logged in");
    return;
  }

  ldap = null;
  ldap = new JNDIUtility(organization, orgUnit,
serverName, portNumber);

  if(ldap != null && loggedIn){
    ldap.update(this.getDN(), attributeName,
attributeValue);
    ldap.search(searchCriteria);
  }
}
```

```
public void logout(){
  username = "";
  password = "";
  loggedIn = false;
}


public void login(String username, String password){
  if (ldap == null){
    ldap = new JNDIUtility(organization, orgUnit,
serverName, portNumber);
  }

  if(ldap.authenticate(username, password)){
    loggedIn = true;
    this.username = username;
    this.password = password;
    sendMessage("Login success");
  }
  else{
    loggedIn = false;
    sendMessage("Login failed");
  }
}

public Vector getResult(){
  return result;
}

protected Vector listeners = new Vector();

public synchronized void addJNDIListener(JNDIListener l){
  listeners.addElement(l);
}

public synchronized void removeJNDIListener(JNDIListener
l){
  listeners.removeElement(l);
}

protected void fireEvent(){
  Vector l = (Vector)listeners.clone();
```

```
      JNDIEvent e = new JNDIEvent(this, result);
      e.setMessage("Success");
      for(int i = 0; i < l.size(); i++){
        ((JNDIListener)l.elementAt(i)).result(e);
      }
    }

    protected void sendMessage(String err){
      Vector l = (Vector)listeners.clone();
      JNDIEvent e = new JNDIEvent(this, null);
      e.setMessage(err);
      for(int i = 0; i < l.size(); i++){
        ((JNDIListener)l.elementAt(i)).result(e);
      }
    }
  }
```

In addition, we have the class for events—JNDIEvent.java:

**Listing 9-5**
JNDIEvent class

**JNDIEvent.java**

```
import java.util.*;

public class JNDIEvent extends EventObject{
  protected Vector result;
  protected String message;

  public JNDIEvent(Object o){
    this(o, null);
  }

  public JNDIEvent(Object o, Vector result){
    super(o);
    this.result = result;
  }

  public Vector getResult(){
    return this.result;
  }

  public void setResult(Vector result){
    this.result = result;
  }
```

```
public void setMessage(String message){
  this.message = message;
}

public String getMessage(){
  return message;
}
}
```

And finally, JNDIListener.java:

■ ■ ■ ■ ■ ■
**Listing 9-6**
JNDIListener class

**JNDIListener.java**

```
import java.util.*;

public interface JNDIListener extends EventListener{
  public void result(JNDIEvent e);
}
```

Complete source code for this bean can be found in the *chap9/sample3* subdirectory on the CD-ROM. Compile all the source code. Then create JNDIBean.jar archive using the jar utility. For now we'll assume that the bean works as expected. In Chapter 19 we will use this bean to develop an Employee Tracking System.

# JNDI & COSNaming

Distributed application environments have all built their own naming systems. RMI has its naming registry and CORBA has its COSNaming specfication. JNDI has united the object naming service APIs so that developers don't have to learn a new specific naming scheme whenever they write for a different environment. The unified naming API also makes distributed applications more portable.

Like the directory services, a naming application needs to obtain an initial context first. That initial context implements interface *Context,* within which many of the naming related methods are defined. Some of the more frequently used methods include the following:

■ *lookup()*—Given a name, return the object associated with it.

■ *bind()*—Binds an object to a name.

■ *rebind()*—Like bind, although it overwrites the existing binding.

## JNDI API for COSNaming

In Chapter 12 we cover CORBA's COSNaming feature in detail, so we will briefly review the way COSNaming provides the naming service here. For details on CORBA's COSNaming feature, please refer to Chapter 12.

In CORBA's COSNaming, on the server-side, you need to first find the object reference for the name service, then create a *NameComponent* object, and finally bind the servant object reference with the name as shown below.

```
org.omg.CORBA.Object obj =
orb.resolve_initial_references("NameService");
NamingContext ncObj = NamingContextHelper.narrow(obj);
NameComponent nc = new NameComponent("PCConfig", "");
NameComponent path[] = {nc};
ncObj.rebind(path, configObj);
```

On the client-side, you need to find the object reference of the name service and then look up the name:

```
org.omg.CORBA.Object obj =
orb.resolve_initial_references("NameService");
NamingContext ncObj = NamingContextHelper.narrow(obj);
NameComponent nc = new NameComponent("PCConfig", "");
NameComponent path[] = {nc};
Config config =
ConfigHelper.narrow(ncObj.resolve(path));
```

Let's see how we can provide the same services with JNDI. On the server side, we create a naming context with an environment variable that specifies which ORB to use. We then bind the object reference to a name.

```
Hashtable env = new Hashtable();
env.put("java.naming.corba.orb", orb);
Context ic = new InitialContext(env);
ic.rebind("DBAccess", DBObj);
```

That's a bit simpler, isn't it?

Similarly, here is the code for the client-side:

```
Hashtable env = new Hashtable();
env.put("java.naming.corba.orb", orb);
Context ic = new InitialContext(env);
DBAccess dbObject =
DBAccessHelper.narrow((org.omg.CORBA.Object)ic.lookup("DBAccess"));
```

# Put it Together for JNDI & COSNaming

Here's the sample IDL file:

**Listing 9-7**

Sample IDL file for demonstrating JNDI and COSNaming

**DBAccessApp.idl:**

```
module DBAccessApp
{
  interface DBAccess
  {
    string inquire();
    void update();
  };
};
```

You need to compile this IDL file using idltojava. For more information about IDL files and compiling, refer to the CORBA programming tutorial in Chapter 12. A subdirectory called *DBAccessApp* will be created with all necessary classes for binding.

Here is the server implementation code, which uses JNDI naming:

**Listing 9-8**

Server implementation

**DBAccessServer.java**

```
import DBAccessApp.*;
import org.omg.CORBA.ORB;
import javax.naming.InitialContext;
import javax.naming.Context;
import java.util.Hashtable;

class DBServant extends _DBAccessImplBase{
  public String inquire(){
```

```
        return "some database inquiry routines are called
here \n";
    }

  public void update(){
     System.out.println ("Some database updating rou-
tines are called here.");
    }
}

public class DBAccessServer{
  public static void main(String args[]){
    try{
      ORB orb = ORB.init(args, null);
      DBServant DBObj = new DBServant();
      orb.connect(DBObj);

      Hashtable env = new Hashtable();
      env.put("java.naming.corba.orb", orb);

      Context ic = new InitialContext(env);
      ic.rebind("DBAccess", DBObj);

      java.lang.Object sync = new java.lang.Object();
      synchronized (sync){
        sync.wait();
      }

    }catch (Exception e){System.err.println("ERROR: " +
e); e.printStackTrace(System.out);}
    }
}
```

And for the client:

**DBAccessClient.java**

```
import DBAccessApp.*;
import org.omg.CORBA.ORB;
import org.omg.CORBA.Object;
import javax.naming.InitialContext;
```

```
import javax.naming.Context;
import java.util.Hashtable;

public class DBAccessClient{
  public static void main(String args[]){
    try{
      ORB orb = ORB.init(args, null);
      Hashtable env = new Hashtable();
      env.put("java.naming.corba.orb", orb);

      Context ic = new InitialContext(env);
      DBAccess dbObject =
DBAccessHelper.narrow((org.omg.CORBA.Object)ic.lookup("DBAccess"));

      String result = dbObject.inquire();
      System.out.println(result);

    }catch(Exception e){System.out.println("ERROR : " +
e) ; e.printStackTrace(System.out);}
  }
}
```

The complete source code can be found under the *chap9\sample4* subdirectory on the CD-ROM. Compile the Java files along with the DBAccessApp subdirectory. Make sure CLASSPATH is also pointing to ldap.jar and cosnaming.jar that you installed at the beginning of this chapter. You'll need to use JDK1.2 for compilation and testing.

Type the following commands on separate command prompts to test the sample:

```
tnameserv -ORBInitialPort 1050
java -
Djava.naming.factory.initial=com.sun.jndi.CosNaming.CNCtxFactory
myServer -ORBInitialPort 1050
java -
Djava.naming.factory.initial=com.sun.jndi.CosNaming.CNCtxFactory
DBClient -ORBInitialPort 1050
```

And you get the following :

```
some database inquiry routines are called here
```

The above string is passed from the CORBA server to the client, and is printed by the client.

You can also use the batch files provided with the source. Instead of executing the java commands indicated above, you can call *runserver* and then *runclient* after starting the name server.

## Summary

JNDI API provides a uniform way of accessing directory and naming services. It relieves programmers of the tedious task of learning a new API every time they encounter a new directory or naming service. It is a step forward in realizing Java's "write once, run anywhere" promise. In the third part of this book, we will build an electronic commerce application with CORBA, we will use JNDI to look up CORBA services, and we will also show that the JNDI bean discussed in this chapter is interchangeable with the LDAP bean discussed in the previous chapter.

CHAPTER **10**

# Servlet

With increased usage of the Web, the need for improving the processing of user inputs has become a major focus. Initially, Common Gateway Interface (CGI)—binary executables that would reside on the server—would take care of processing the user input. CGI can be written in any native language pertaining to the platform on which it runs. In the initial stages of the Web, error detection and data processing would take place on the server by CGI programs. Later, with the invention of scripting languages for the client, like JavaScript and others, the error detection would be taken care of on the client-side. CGI programs would need to take care of the data processing only. This resulted in eliminating a lot of overhead, which resulted in faster data processing. A major bottleneck with CGI is performance, because every request that comes from the client for a CGI program execution creates a new process. So CGI requires heavyweight startup and initialization code on each request. This results in slow performance and more usage of system resources. Another disadvantage of the CGI programs is that they are not cross-platform in nature, since they are binary executables. So, let's see what servlet technology has to offer.

Java, a cross-platform language, is used mostly for client-side applications/applets. It isn't meant for just the client anymore. Servlet technology brings Java to the server too. Also, since multi-threading is built into Java, developing server-side applications is even easier.

## Servlet Architecture

Servlets are protocol- and platform-independent components that extend the capabilities of java-enabled servers like Java Web Server from Javasoft, Enterprise Server from Netscape, and so on. Servlets are Java code modules that get invoked when any request is made on them from the client and send a response back to the client. Since servlets run inside the servers, they do not have a graphical user interface. Servlets can be thought of as a counterpart to client-side applets. They can be downloaded and used on demand.

**NOTE**

To develop servlets you'll need a specialized server that supports Java. Later in the chapter, we will show you how to obtain and install the Java Web Server from Sun Microsystems. However you can use any server that supports servlets, specifically JSDK 2.0.

Servlets can do the following:

1. Process data submitted by client over HTTP/HTTPS from an HTML form.
2. Handle multiple requests concurrently because of the multi-threading capabilities built into Java.
3. Use other servlets or forward request to other servlets.
4. Maintain states between different requests from the same users using the Session tracking mechanism.

All servlets implement the *Servlet* interface directly or indirectly. Since we'll be dealing with the HTML form processing over the Internet, we'll deal with the *HttpServlet,* which implements the servlet interface indirectly. *HttpServlet* is an abstract class that has a number of methods that are useful in form processing, that will be discussed in detail.

**NOTE**

More information about the servlet package can be obtained from the Java Servlet Development Kit (JSDK).

When a servlet accepts a client request, it receives two objects. They are:

1. *ServletRequest*—An interface used for getting client information into the servlet. Some data provided by this interface includes parameter names, their values, and so on. It also provides access to the input stream, from which the servlet can get the data sent by the client. *HttpServletRequest* is an interface that extends *ServletRequest* to provide HTTP-related data.
2. *ServletResponse*—An interface used for sending data to the client from a servlet's method. Any MIME bodies can be returned by the servlet to the client. *HttpServletResponse* is a special interface that allows the servlet's methods to set HTTP headers and send data to the client. Again, this class also provides an output stream for the servlet to write data back to the client.

Classes and interfaces described in this section make up a basic servlet. Advanced features such as session tracking capabilities are also available and are discussed in Chapter 17.

## Which Servers Support Servlets?

As mentioned earlier, servlets are supported by all the major competent servers. Javasoft's Java Web Server fully supports servlets, because the technology is integrated into the server architecture. However, as of this writing, Netscape's Enterprise and Fast Track server, Microsoft's IIS, and Apache only support servlets to a certain extent. Servlet support by these servers is vendor-dependent. Jigsaw from W3 consortium supports JSDK 2.0 fully. For our purposes, we'll use the Java Web Server.

## The Servlet Lifecycle

A servlet can be loaded during the server start-up or when a client request comes in. Servlet execution depends entirely on how the servlet is configured. Regardless of when or how it is loaded, the following events take place:

1. The server runs servlet's *init()* method. This method is called once every servlet's lifetime. The method *init()* is not called again until the servlet is removed by calling the destroy method. Initialization is completed before processing any client request.

2. After initialization is complete, the servlet is now ready to process any client request. The request is processed in the *service()* method. Each client request executes the *service()* method of the servlet in a separate servlet thread. This thread will receive the client's request and send the client its response. Servlets can execute multiple service requests at a time. It is therefore important to make your code threadsafe. In case the servlet should not handle multiple concurrent requests, then it should implement *SingleThreadModel*. Servlets that are developed specially for processing HTTP requests, such as servlets that extend *HttpServlet*, might execute *doPut()*, *doGet()*, *doDelete()*, or *doPost()*.

3. When a servlet is removed, its *destroy()* method is called. This method performs cleanup, as its name indicates.

**NOTE**

Servlets do not usually override the service() method.

# Advantages of Servlets

There are a number of advantages in using servlets over the conventional CGI programs. All of these advantages are covered directly or indirectly in the previous sections. Here is an overview of all the advantages:

1. Since servlets are written using Java, they are cross-platform in nature.
2. Servlets are loaded only once, unlike CGI, which is loaded each time a request for the program comes from the client. The *init()* method initializes the servlet, which is a one-time affair, therefore intensive initialization code can be placed in this method.
3. Since Java supports multithreading, servlets can handle concurrent requests as threads. This has advantages over CGI since CGI programs are executed as a separate process for every request consuming system resources.
4. Servlets can maintain persistent data between sessions for a single user using Session Tracking features

# Java Web Server

Java Web Server is an HTTP server from Javasoft. This server is officially supported on Windows NT and Solaris Sparc. This Web server is written in Java. Apart from other advanced built-in features, it also supports servlets directly. In this section we will see how to download, install, and use Java Web Server.

## Downloading and Installing Java Web Server

If you have Internet access, you can visit *http://jserv.java.sun.com* and download the latest version of the Java Web Server product. Here we'll explain how to install and configure the Java Web Server.

Here are the steps to follow to install Java Web Server 1.1 on Windows NT:

1. Copy the self-extracting executable "jws11-try-win32-gl-ssl.exe" into a temporary directory, for example, `C:\temp`.
2. Double-click to execute the application.
3. An installer wizard should start. Follow the instructions to install the server in the drive you want; for example, the C: drive.

4. Retain all the setup information as default. The Web server will be installed in *C:\Java WebServer1.1,* also known as the server root directory.

5. At the end of the installation, you will be asked if you want to install NT Service application. You can either click Yes or No.

## Running the Java Web Server

Here are the steps you'll follow to set up the environment and run the Web server:

1. Open the Control Panel and double-click the System icon.
2. In the Environment folder, add a user variable called CLASSPATH, as shown: .;c:\javawebserver1.1\lib\javac.jar;c:\javawebserver1.1\lib\ x509v1.jar;c:\javawebserver1.1\lib\jws.jar.
3. On Windows Explorer, change the directory to *C:\Java Web Server1.1\bin.*
4. Double-click the httpd application.
5. This will start your Web server. Minimize the DOS™ window.
6. Open your browser and type: **http://local_host_name:8080**.
7. This will display the default page of the Java Web Server.

**NOTE**

All pages that are accessible via the browser are under the *public_html* subdirectory under the server root directory. We will retain all the default values, since we are using them for testing purposes only.

# Developing and Testing a Simple Servlet

Before we get into the development of servlet beans, let's first get a feel for how to write and test a servlet. This section will show how to develop and test a simple servlet.

This servlet will take input from the user, and output the same. It will use an HTML form for obtaining the input in both POST and GET methods.

# Coding the Simple Servlet

Below is the listing of a Simple Servlet.

**Listing 10-1**
A simple Servlet

**SimpleServlet.java**

```java
import javax.servlet.http.*;
import java.io.*;
import javax.servlet.*;

public class SimpleServlet extends HttpServlet{

  public void doGet (HttpServletRequest req,
HttpServletResponse res) throws ServletException,
IOException{
    PrintWriter out;

    res.setContentType("text/html");

    out = res.getWriter();

    sendDataToClient(out,
req.getParameterValues("text1")[0]);

    out.close();
  }

  public void doPost(HttpServletRequest req,
HttpServletResponse res)  throws ServletException,
IOException{
    PrintWriter out;

    res.setContentType("text/html");

    out = res.getWriter();

    sendDataToClient(out,
req.getParameterValues("text1")[0]);

    out.close();
  }
```

```
    private void sendDataToClient(PrintWriter out, String
dataToSend) throws IOException{
        out.println("<html><head><title>");
        out.println("Test result of SimpleServlet</title></
head>");
        out.println("<body> You entered <p>");
        out.println(dataToSend);
        out.println("</body></html>");
    }
}
```

Let's look into some of the important code snippets.

```
import javax.servlet.http.*;
import javax.servlet.*;
```

These import statements (above) are necessary for importing the *HttpSevlet* and *Servlet* related classes.

```
protected void doGet(HttpServletRequest req,
HttpServletResponse res) throws IOException
```

This method is called when the HTML form accesses the servlet using the GET method.

We set the content type of the servlet's output data by calling the *setContentType()* of *HttpServletResponse* as shown below:

```
res.setContentType("text/html");
```

We set the content type to "text/html" because we are outputting HTML content. Next we have to get an output stream to write data back to the client.

```
out = res.getWriter();
```

We get the PrintWriter by calling *getWriter()* as shown above.

**NOTE**

When writing ascii data we recommend that you use *PrintWriter* instead of *ServletOutputStream*. You can obtain this using *getOutputStream()*.

It is also necessary that the content type is set before calling *getWriter()*. If *getWriter()* is called before the content type is set then the error shown in Figure 10-1 will be displayed. For more information on *getWriter()* and *getOutputStream()* please refer to the servlet API documentation.

**Figure 10-1**
Error displayed when the PrintWriter is obtained before setting the content type

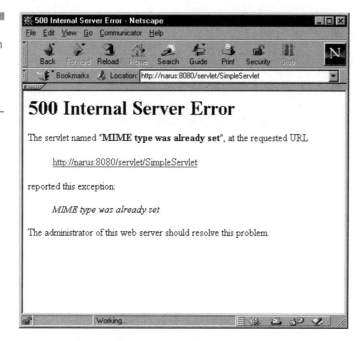

After these are done we extract the form values as shown below.

```
req.getParameterValues("text1")[0]
```

This call will return the value typed in by the user in the "text1" field, which is a textfield in the HTMLfile. Since *getParameterValues("text1")* returns an array of string values, we extract the required values by indexing. Since there is only one "text1" element in the HTML form, we extract the zeroeth element to get the value.

**NOTE**

In this case, if you try to access the values beyond the zeroeth element, JVM will throw an *ArrayIndexOutOfBoundsException* exception. If you have a number of "text1" elements, then the array will have as many elements as "text1" form elements.

Method *sendDataToClient()* returns the data back to the client.

Source code for the Simple Servlet can be found under the chap10/ sample1 directory on the CD-ROM. Copy the source file to a directory convenient to you. Make sure you have set your CLASSPATH as explained in the previous section on installing the Java Web Server. Compile SimpleServlet.java and copy SimpleServlet.class to the *servlets* subdirectory under the server root directory.

## Testing a Simple Servlet

To test the servlet, two things need to be done:

1. Load the servlet. Here are the steps to follow:

   - Make sure your server is running.
   - Open the default home page of the server by typing **http://host_name:8080**.
   - Click on the Administer the Web Server link.
   - Click on Start the Administration Tool. This will load the log-in screen. The default user name is "admin" and the password is also "admin." Click the Login button.
   - This will log you in successfully and load the administration applet. Select "Web Service" and click the Manage button at the bottom.
   - This will load the Web Service application. In the toolbar, select servlets. This is where you configure your servlets. Select Add.
   - Type *SimpleServlet* as the servlet name and *SimpleServlet* as the servlet class.
   - This will load the configuration screen. Click "Yes" in the Loaded Now radio button. This will load the servlet. Our servlet is ready for use.

2. On the CD-ROM under the *chap10/sample1* subdirectory, you will find the HTML files to test the *SimpleServlet* class. Copy these three HTML files, for example, frame.html, SimpleServlet.html, and blank.html, into

the *public_html/* subdirectory under the server root directory. Open frame.html by typing **http://host_name:8080/frame.html**. When you click the Submit Query buttons, the servlet response can be seen in the other frame as shown in Figure 10-2. You can also change text and test it.

**Figure 10-2**
Output of
SimpleServlet
displayed in the
bottom frame

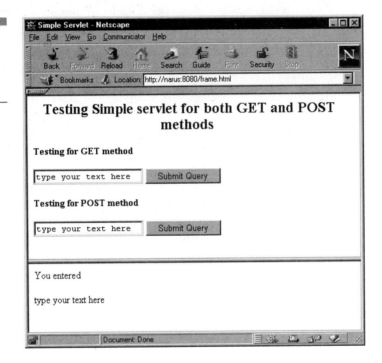

**NOTE**

All the samples in this chapter carry "localhost:8080" as the default hostname. Make sure to change the hostname "localhost" to the hostname that you have. Otherwise these samples will not work properly.

# Servlet Beans

Servlets can be used as JavaBeans, and all JavaBeans can be used in servlets. In the next two sections, let's see how the bean technology can be used in servlets.

If servlets themselves are written as JavaBean components, they offer two major advantages:

- Servlet persistence information can be stored automatically as a serialized file.
- If the servlet configuration is changed, it takes effect immediately.

All servlet beans follow the JavaBeans design patterns to expose the properties, which means they have a pair of get/set methods to read/write the property value. This helps the Java Web Server to set all the properties of the servlet beans using Introspection mechanism. Also, the Java Web Server assumes all the servlets are beans. Servlet beans are usually distributed in JAR files. However they can also be distributed as the .class files or serialized files.

It is recommended that all servlet beans reside either in the servlet or in the *servletbeans* subdirectory under the server root directory. They can reside in any directory under the CLASSPATH, though. In this case the only disadvantage is that automatic reloading of the servlets is not performed by the classloader in the event of any changes.

Properties are initial arguments passed to the servlet for initialization purposes. You can pass the properties in the *init()* method of the servlet or explicitly call the SET methods to set the properties.

## Servlet Bean: an Example

In this section let's see how to develop a servlet bean.

This servlet bean will send a "Hello World" string back to the client. We'll manipulate the bean property using the Java Web Server administration tool and see how the changes are propagated to the client.

Here's the code for the HelloWorldBean:

**Listing 10-2**
Servlet bean sample

**HelloWorldBean.Java**

```java
import javax.servlet.http.*;
import javax.servlet.*;
import java.io.*;

public class HelloWorldBean extends HttpServlet{
  private String message = "HelloWorld";

  public String getMessageString(){
    return message;
  }
```

```
   public void setMessageString(String newMessage){
     message = newMessage;
   }

   public void service(HttpServletRequest req,
HttpServletResponse res) throws IOException{
      res.setContentType("text/html");
      PrintWriter out = res.getWriter();
      out.println("<html><head><title>HelloWorld Sample
Servlet Bean</title></head>");
      out.println("<body>Servlet contains the following
message stored for you<p><strong>");
      out.println(this.message);
      out.println("</body></html>");
      out.close();
   }
}
```

Our bean has a property called *message,* which can be changed, and its persistence information can be saved in a serialized file. Also note that our *HelloWorldBean* does not explicitly implement *Serializable* because *HttpServlet* implements *Serializable.*

```
public String getMessageString(){
   return message;
}

public void setMessageString(String newMessage){
   message = newMessage;
}
```

Methods *getMessageString()* and *setMessageString()* are responsible for manipulating the *message* variable. Whenever message property is changed via the Java Server Administration tool, *setMessageString()* gets called. Also, in this example, we are overriding the service method. This method just writes back the HTML file with the message string.

Source code for the HelloWorldBean can be found under the *chap10/ sample2* directory on the CD-ROM. Make sure you have the CLASSPATH set to jws.jar in the subdirectory named *lib* under the Java server installed directory, also known as the server root directory. Compile this program, create HelloWorldBean.jar using the jar utility that is bundled with the JDK, and copy the HelloWorldBean.jar to the *servletbeans* subdirectory under the server root directory.

## Testing HelloWorldBean Servlet

To test the HelloWorldBean servlet, two things need to be done:

1. Load the servlet. Here are the steps to follow:

   ▪ Bring up the Web Service application. In the toolbar, select servlets. This is where you configure your servlets. Select Add. (Steps to bring up the Web Service Application are explained in detail when testing sample1.)

   ▪ Type **HelloWorldBean** as the servlet name and **HelloWorldBean** as the servlet class.

   ▪ Select Bean Servlet as "Yes" and type **HelloWorldBean.jar**.

   ▪ Click Add.

   ▪ This will load the configuration screen. Click "Yes" on the Loaded Now radio button. This will load the servlet. Our *HelloWorldBean* servlet bean is ready for use. When you view the *Properties* sheet, you'll find that the *messageString* property is set to its initial value, which is "Hello World."

2. To test the servlet, open your browser and type **http://host_name:8080/ servlet/HelloWorldBean**. You'll see that the "HelloWorld" message is displayed. Go back to the Web Service Application and change the property to Hello. To change the property, double-click the item and type. Click the Modify button and then Save. Reload the page in your browser. It should display "Hello" now as shown in Figure 10-3.

**NOTE**

A serialized file named *HelloWorldBean.ser* will be created in your *servletbeans* subdirectory automatically. Every time the servlet is loaded from now on, the persistence information in the serialized file is used. So the next time you load HelloWorldBean, it will print the message "Hello" and not "Hello World." If the serialized file is absent, then the *Servlet* class will be used for creating the new instance.

■■ ■■ ■■ ■■ ■■ ■■

**Figure 10-3**
Output of
HelloWorldBean after
changing the
property to Hello

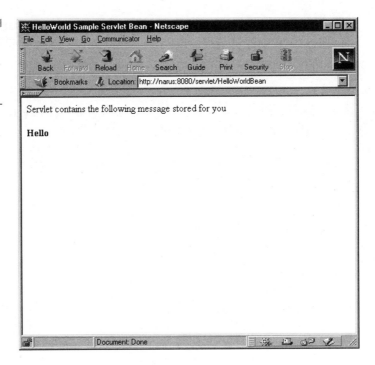

# Beans in Servlet

In the last section we saw how servlets can be designed as beans. In this section we'll see how existing beans can be used in servlets. This is one of the important concepts of the servlet architecture, in the sense that it allows us to use existing beans. Javabeans developed for purposes like parsing, computing, and so on, that do not have any GUI components, can be reused on the server too. Servlets use the JavaBeans API to access existing JavaBeans and reuse them.

We'll develop a sample that will demonstrate the use of beans with servlets. We'll also develop an HTML bean that will generate an HTML file. Later in Part 3 we'll reuse these beans to develop enterprise applications.

JavaBeans are reusable components packaged with other dependent classes in a JAR file. JavaBeans used on a server are non-GUI-based components. They all reside in the server directory. Using JavaBeans in servlets is very similar to using JavaBeans within JavaBeans. We use the *Beans.instantiate()* method to use a bean. Similarly, servlets also use the same *instantiate()* method call to use a JavaBean component on a server.

Since all JavaBeans components are packaged in JAR files, one needs to copy these JAR files into the *lib* subdirectory under the server root directory.

The server needs to be restarted after the JAR files are copied. JavaBeans are ready to be used in servlets. No other special installation or coding is required.

**NOTE**

You shouldn't forget to restart the server after copying the JAR files containing JavaBeans under the *lib* subdirectory. Otherwise the server won't be aware of the existence of the JavaBeans and will throw a *ClassNotFoundException* when any servlet attempts to instantiate a JavaBean.

# Beans and Servlet: an Example

In this section we'll develop a simple non-GUI-based JavaBean and then try to use it in a servlet. We'll develop an AccumulatorBean that will just accumulate all the data given to it. We'll display the accumulated data using a servlet.

The code given here is the complete listing for AccumulatorBean:

**Listing 10-3**
Accumulator bean

**AccumulatorBean.java**

```java
import java.lang.*;
import java.util.*;
import java.io.*;

public class AccumulatorBean implements Serializable{
  private Vector accumulator;

  public AccumulatorBean(){
    accumulator = new Vector();
  }

  public Vector getAccumulatorData(){
    return accumulator;
  }

  public synchronized void setAccumulatorData(Object
dataObject){
```

```
      if(dataObject instanceof Vector){
        accumulator = (Vector)dataObject;
      }
      else if(dataObject instanceof String){
        accumulator.addElement(dataObject);
      }
    }
  }
```

The code above is self-explanatory and is written like any other JavaBean component. Source code for the AccumulatorBean can be found under the *chap10/sample3* subdirectory on the CD-ROM. Compile AccumulatorBean.java and create a JAR file called AccumulatorBean.jar with AccumulatorBean.class in it. Copy the JAR file into the *lib* subdirectory under the server root directory. Start the Java Web Server, if it's not running. Otherwise restart the Web server after the JAR file is copied.

The code given below is the complete listing for the AccumulatorServlet:

■ ■ ■ ■ ■ ■ ■  **AccumulatorServlet.java**

**Listing 10-4**
Servlet using
Accumulator bean

```
import javax.servlet.http.*;
import javax.servlet.*;
import java.beans.*;
import java.util.*;
import java.io.*;

public class AccumulatorServlet extends HttpServlet{
  public void service(HttpServletRequest req,
HttpServletResponse res) throws IOException{
    AccumulatorBean ab = null;

    res.setContentType("text/html");
    PrintWriter out = res.getWriter();

    try{
      ab = (AccumulatorBean)Beans.instantiate(null,
"AccumulatorBean");
    }catch(ClassNotFoundException
e){e.printStackTrace();}
```

```
        out.println("<html><head><title>Bean Result</
title></head>");

    if(ab != null){
       ab.setAccumulatorData("Test String 1");
       ab.setAccumulatorData("Test String 2");

       Vector data = ab.getAccumulatorData();
       out.println("<body><p>Bean returns");

       for(Enumeration e = data.elements();
e.hasMoreElements();){

out.println(((String)e.nextElement()).toString());
       }
    }

    else{
       out.println("<b>Bean class not found");
    }
    out.println("</body></html>");
    out.close();
  }
}
```

Again, this piece of code is pretty straightforward. Source code for the *AccumulatorServlet* can be found under the *chap10/sample3* subdirectory on the CD-ROM. Compile the servlet and copy AccumulatorServlet.class into the *servlets* subdirectory under the Java web server root directory. Load the servlet (follow the steps given in the previous examples) and test it by typing **http://host_name:8080/servlet/AccumulatorServlet**. You should see the output as shown in Figure 10-4.

**Figure 10-4**
Output of
AccumulatorServlet

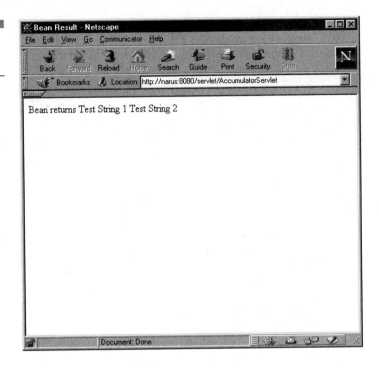

**Figure 10-4**
Output of
AccumulatorServlet

# Beans for Enterprise Applications

In this section we'll develop a non-GUI bean component that will generate HTML files. Later, in Part 3 of the book, we'll see how this bean will be
reused to develop enterprise applications.

## Bean for Generating HTML Files

Our objective: To develop a bean component that will generate an HTML
file based on the input data.

Assumption: This bean may get data as a vector or a string. If the data is
a vector, each vector element is assumed to have a name value pair. Under
this circumstance, the bean would generate an HTML file with each name
and its corresponding value populated into a table. If the bean gets data as
a string, it would just write the data into the body of the HTML file.

Design: The execution is as follows:

1. You can add a default header and footer, set/unset cache if the file
   should/should not be cached in the client, set the file name to output
   HTML strings to, set refresh URL and refresh time if you need to
   continuously refresh the HTML file.

2. A routine to add custom headers should also be provided.

3. The data may come as a vector or a string.

4. All vector-based data—which come in name-value pair formats like name1=value1—will be extracted and stored as strings.

5. Have a vector member in the bean that will store all the data as strings.

6. When data arrives, update the vector.

7. All data is inserted as the last-but-one element in the vector, because the last element is always the footer.

## Code for the Sample HtmlGenerator Bean

Let us take a look at the complete bean code, which is simple and self-explanatory.

**Listing 10-5**
Bean for generating
HTML file

**HtmlGeneratorBean.java**

```
import java.io.*;
import java.util.*;

public class HtmlGeneratorBean implements Serializable{

    protected String fileName;
    protected String refreshURL;
    protected boolean cache;
    protected int refreshTime;
    protected transient Vector vectorData;
    protected transient String title;
    protected transient String defaultBodyMessage;


    public HtmlGeneratorBean(){
       this("");
    }

    public HtmlGeneratorBean(String fileName){
       this.fileName = fileName;
       this.refreshURL = "";
       this.refreshTime = 10;
       this.cache = true;
       vectorData = new Vector();
```

```
      title = "";
      defaultBodyMessage = "";
   }

  public void writeHeaderFooter(String title, String
defaultBodyMessage){
     this.title = title;
     this.defaultBodyMessage = defaultBodyMessage;
     vectorData.removeAllElements();

     vectorData.addElement("<html><head>");

     if(!refreshURL.equals("")){
       vectorData.addElement("<META HTTP-EQUIV='Refresh'
CONTENT=" + refreshTime + " URL=" + refreshURL + ">");
     }

     if (!cache){
       vectorData.addElement("<META HTTP-EQUIV='Pragma'
CONTENT=no-cache>");
     }

     vectorData.addElement("<title>" + title + "</
title></head><body>");

     if(defaultBodyMessage != null){
       vectorData.addElement(defaultBodyMessage);
     }
     vectorData.addElement("<hr align=left
width='100%'></body></html>");
   }

  public void writeBody(Object data){
     if(data instanceof Vector){

       vectorData.insertElementAt("<table border cols=2
width='100%'>", vectorData.size() - 1);

       for(Enumeration e = ((Vector)data).elements();
e.hasMoreElements();){
         String s = (String) e.nextElement();
         vectorData.insertElementAt("<tr><td>" +
```

```
s.substring(0, s.indexOf('=')) + "</td><td>" +
s.substring(s.indexOf('=') + 1) + "</td></tr>",
vectorData.size() - 1);
        }


        vectorData.insertElementAt("</table>",
vectorData.size() - 1);
    }

    else if(data instanceof String){
        vectorData.insertElementAt("<p>" + data,
vectorData.size() - 1);
    }

    synchronized(this){
        try{
            FileOutputStream file = new
FileOutputStream(getFileName());
            Vector newdata = getData();

            for (int index = 0; index < newdata.size();
index++){

file.write(((String)newdata.elementAt(index)).getBytes());
            }

            file.close();
            newdata = null;

        }catch(IOException e){System.out.println("Cannot
create file");}
    }

  }

  public Vector getData(){
    return (Vector) vectorData.clone();
  }

  public void removeData(){
    vectorData.removeAllElements();
    writeHeaderFooter(title, defaultBodyMessage);
  }
```

```
      public void setFileName(String fileName){
        this.fileName = fileName;
      }

      public String getFileName(){
        return fileName;
      }

      public void setRefreshURL(String refreshURL){
        this.refreshURL = refreshURL;
      }

      public String getRefreshURL(){
        return refreshURL;
      }

      public void setRefreshTime(int refreshTime){
        this.refreshTime = refreshTime;
      }

      public int getRefreshTime(){
        return refreshTime;
      }

      public void setCache(boolean cache){
        this.cache = cache;
      }

      public boolean getCache(){
        return cache;
      }

      public void deleteFile(){
        if((fileName != null) && !(fileName.equals(""))){
          new File(fileName).delete();
        }
      }
    }
```

Source code for the HtmlGeneratorBean can be found under the *chap10/ sample4* subdirectory on the CD-ROM. Compile the code and run the jar utility to create HtmlGeneratorBean.jar archive.

# Summary

In this chapter we read about the advantages of servlets over CGI. We also did some exercises to write a simple servlet, a servlet bean, and using an existing bean in a servlet. In Part 3 of this book, we'll use the *HtmlGeneratorBean* to create enterprise applications.

CHAPTER **11**

# Internet
# Security

# Security Technology Overview

## The Need for Security

Internet commerce is growing at an astounding speed and many market research firms predict that hundreds of billions of dollars of revenue consumer and business transactions will occur on the Internet by early next century. The number one concern of companies or consumers who buy and sell online is security. People don't want their credit card numbers to fall into the hands of malicious hackers, and companies don't want their business transactions known to the outside world. Worse yet, without adequate network security, criminals can even alter messages and create false transactions, causing bigger financial losses.

In addition to Internet commerce, many other areas of the Web require tight security implementation. For example, more and more companies are using extranets to share important proprietary information online with their business partners, but they want to exclude access to that information by outsiders.

Even within a company, it's a good practice to implement network security in important applications. Studies have shown that disgruntled employees are often the biggest threat to the integrity and confidentiality of proprietary company information.

## What is Security?

The way in which the Internet delivers messages is similar to a relay service. The process is analogous to a situation in which you want to pass a package to your friend at the other end of a hallway, and you pass the package to the person who is standing next to you. That person will pass the package to the next person who's closer to your friend, and the relay ends when your friend finally gets the package. During the process, everybody who touches your package has the ability to open it, take a look at what's inside, and do whatever they want with the contents.

Because of the open nature of the Internet's infrastructure, Internet security technologies are needed to ensure the four characteristics of network security. These characteristics are confidentiality, integrity, authenticity, and non-repudiation.

## Confidentiality

Maintaining the confidentiality of a message means eavesdroppers are not able to learn the content of messages. The most effective way of maintaining confidentiality is through encryption.

## Integrity

Since the Internet is an open medium, an intruder may intercept your message and change the content without your knowledge. For example, you may instruct your bank to send $200 to your friend. An intruder may change the message and instruct the bank to send the money to himself. Maintaining the integrity of a message means ensuring that the message has not been changed. The most commonly used tool to ensure message integrity is called message digest. We will have a more detailed discussion on message digest in the next section of this chapter

## Authenticity

Authenticity concerns making sure the person sending the message is really the person that they claim to be. When we go to a bank to withdraw some cash, we are asked to present identification (such as driver's license). If we want to pay our bills on the Internet, how can the bank make sure we are who we claim to be without seeing identification? A unique ID and a password have been the traditional methods of authentication. Modern cryptography has allowed us to use an even safer way of authentication—the certificate. We'll discuss certificate technology in more detail later in this chapter.

## Non-repudiation

Since there is no signature on a check when we make an electronic payment, banks need to make sure that customers will not be able to deny that they have made a request for payment. The tool that banks may use is called a digital signature.

Recently, a lot of progress has been made in the field of cryptography, and computer scientists are now able to utilize cryptographic algorithms to provide all four characteristics of network security to the Internet.

# Introduction to Cryptographic Algorithms

There are three classes of cryptographic algorithms that are in use today: symmetric key, public key, and message digest. Together these algorithms form an infrastructure that provides the Internet with the four characteristics of network security.

## Symmetric Key Algorithms

Symmetric key algorithms use keys that are shared between senders and receivers. The keys are used both to encrypt messages and to decrypt messages. This type of algorithm is the workhorse of today's secure network. They are fast and relatively easy to implement. Many of them are designed to be implemented in hardware.

The Data Encryption Standard (DES) algorithm is the most widely used symmetric key algorithm in use today. It was first developed by IBM in the late 1960's and early 1970's, and later adopted (in 1977) as Federal Information Processing Standard 46. For the past two decades, DES has enjoyed wide deployment in financial institutions around the world. However, its short key size (56 bit) has gradually become a potential weakness as microprocessors have become more powerful. It has been shown that a well-equipped opponent can break DES within a few hours.

In cryptographic terminology, the message text is called plain text before it is encrypted, while the encrypted message text is called cipher text. Brute force attack is a method that an opponent can use to find the secret to a symmetric key algorithm. With this method, an opponent enumerates all possible keys and uses them to decrypt the cipher text and guess the original plain text. Figure 11-1 shows the flow of text in symmetric key algorithms:

Many good symmetric key algorithms have been proposed to replace DES. Here are a few of them:

### Triple DES

One way to improve on DES is to design an algorithm with a larger key size, while another alternative is to reuse DES with multiple keys. The second alternative has the advantage of preserving the hardware and software investment already made in DES. Triple DES uses either two or three DES keys and applies the DES algorithm three times as an encryption algorithm. Many researchers agree that triple DES is much stronger than DES and more capable of withstanding a brute force attack.

**Symmetric Key Algorithm**

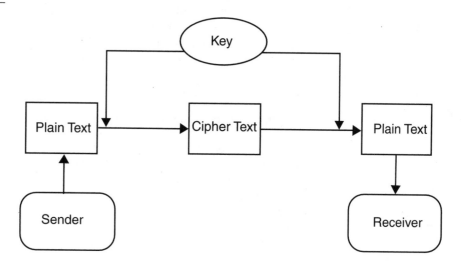

## IDEA

The International Data Encryption Algorithm (IDEA) was developed by Xuejia Lai and James Massey of the Swiss Federal Institute of Technology. It has a key length of 128 bits and was designed very carefully so that it is easy to implement on hardware. IDEA is included in a popular email encryption program called PGP (Pretty Good Privacy). With its larger key size, IDEA is believed to be much stronger than DES.

## RC-5

RC-5 is an algorithm developed by Ron Rivest, who is best known as one of the inventors of the RSA public key algorithm. RC-5 is a fast, easy-to-implement algorithm with variable key length. It's also designed to have low memory requirements.

**NOTE**

A stream cipher algorithm encrypts one bit or one byte at a time, and a block cipher algorithm encrypts one block of data at once. All of the previously mentioned algorithms are block ciphers. DES, triple-DES, and IDEA use 64-bit blocks; RC-5 uses variable size blocks depending on users' needs.

# The Drawback of Symmetric Key Algorithms

The most glaring drawback of symmetric key algorithms is that the sender and the receiver have to agree on a shared key before the message exchange starts. On the wide-open Internet, there is no simple and safe way of distributing these keys. Another type of encryption—the public key algorithm—has risen up and taken an important role in managing key distributions.

## Public Key Algorithm

The public key algorithm was first discovered by Whitfield Diffie and Martin Hellman in 1976. Diffie and Hellman were then researchers at Stanford University. In 1978, Ron Rivest, Adi Shamir, and Len Adelman developed the RSA public key algorithm, which has since become the most widely used public key algorithm in the world. The threesome later founded RSA Data Security, Inc.

A public key algorithm is asymmetric in the sense that each user has two keys, say key one and key two. Messages encrypted by key one may only be decrypted by key two, but not by key one itself, and vice versa. Furthermore, it's impossible to deduce the value of one key from the value of another key, even with the cipher text and knowledge of the algorithm present.

So how does this help us in solving the key distribution problem associated with the symmetric key algorithms? The answer lies in the asymmetric nature of the public keys. We divide the two keys into a public key and a private key and we advertise our public keys to the outside world. We keep the private key only to ourselves.

Now suppose you want to send a secret message to your friend Nick. You first obtain Nick's public key (which is advertised openly), and then encrypt your message with the public key. Since Nick has the private key, he will be able to read your message. On the other hand, no one else has the private key and the public key doesn't decrypt the message, so your message is safe from other people, even if they eavesdrop and listen to every exchange between you and Nick. Figure 11-2 shows the process.

The mathematical foundation of the public key algorithm is number theory. To date, there is no easy way of factoring large numbers, and the designers of public key algorithms take advantage of this fact by making it impossible for eavesdroppers to determine the private key with knowledge of the public key. Most key-generating algorithms give users the key size choices of 512, 1024, and 2048 bits. The last two are generally considered uncrackable for the next few years.

Public key algorithms are often hundreds of times slower than symmetric key algorithms, and are not suited to do the bulk of message encryption. However, they are very useful in key distribution. For example, your first secret message to your friend can be a key that will later be used in a symmetric key algorithm. The type of encryption that uses the public key algorithm to negotiate a session key and then uses a symmetry key algorithm to encrypt the bulk of the transmission is called a hybrid scheme. Popular encryption algorithms such as Pretty Good Privacy (PGP), Secure Socket Layer (SSL), and IP level security (IPSec) all fall into this category. We will discuss SSL, the algorithm suited for Internet commerce, in more detail in a later section of this chapter.

**Figure 11-2**

Public key algorithm

**Public Key Encryption**

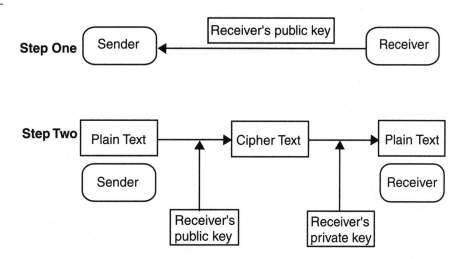

## Message Digest

We have an arsenal of encryption algorithms to protect us from eavesdroppers. What if some of the eavesdroppers decide to intercept your message, alter it, and then send it to your friend? The class of algorithms that ensures message integrity is called message digest, or one-way hash.

The one-way hash function takes any document as an input and produces a long integer as a result. The integer is called a message digest and is of fixed length, often 128 bits or 256 bits in length. Figure 11-3 shows the process.

**Message Digest**

The hash function is designed to catch any tampering of your message and makes it very difficult to forge another message that results in the same message digest. The idea is that you send the message digest along with your message to your friend, so that any tampering of your message will be detected by the accompanying message digest.

Here are some characteristics of the hash function:

■ It applies to documents of any size, and produces message digests of the same length

■ For a given message digest, it is computationally unfeasible to concoct a different document from the original one.

■ The function is simple enough for practical software and hardware implementation.

Popular message digest algorithms include Message Digest #2 (MD2), Message Digest #4 (MD4), and Message Digest #5 (MD5), all developed by RCA; and Secure Hash Algorithm (SHA) and SHA-1, developed by the National Security Agency.

# Digital Signature

Message digest does not address a serious attack in which your potential adversaries intercept your message and the message digest, and then supply the intended recipient with altered documentation and the message digest of this new, altered documentation. The solution to preventing this kind of attack is called digital signature.

A digital signature is a message digest encrypted with the sender's private key. Figure 11-4 shows the process.

You first create a message digest for the document you want to send. Then you use your private key to encrypt the message digest. The resulting cipher text is called a digital signature, and the process of creating the digital signature is called digital signing. Notice that the document itself may not be encrypted.

**Figure 11-4**
Digital signature

**Digital Signature**

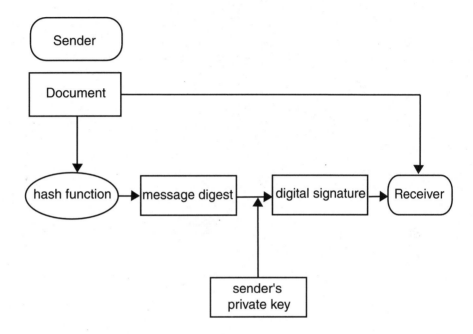

Once your friend receives the document and the digital signature, they use your public key to decrypt the digital signature into the original message digest form. They then create a message digest from the document. If the two message digests match, then the document has truly been sent by you. That is because if your message was intercepted by someone who then created an altered message digest and encrypted it with a forged private key, your friend will still use your public key to decrypt the message, and the resulting message digest from the decryption will be different from the message digest created directly from the original document. Figure 11-5 shows the process.

**Figure 11-5**
Digital signature
verification

**Digital Signature Verification**

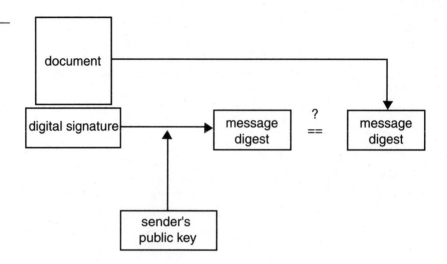

Coupled with digital time-stamping, digital signature is the key to maintaining non-repudiation. People will not be able to deny sending messages that they have sent.

## Digital Certificates

We have skipped an important issue during our discussion of public key algorithms and digital signatures—the issue of public key distribution. Namely, how do you pass your public key to your friend? You could email it to them but the email could be forged. You could publish them on the Web, but how can your friend be sure the Web site hasn't been forged? The current solution to this problem is the digital certificate, or a "stamp" issued by some trusted third party.

In a non-digital world, you can be authenticated by some independent and universally recognized authority such as the Department of Motor Vehicles (DMV). In the digital world, you can be authenticated by a well-established Internet security firm, such as Verisign, or by the U.S. Postal Service.

The process of obtaining a digital certificate goes as follows:

1. You generate a pair of keys on your local machine and store the private key securely.

2. You then present the public key to a certificate authority, along with some additional personal information about you such as your name and email address.

3. The certificate authority creates a document containing the public key and your personal information and digitally signs it with its private key.

4. The documentation, along with the digital signature, forms a digital certificate. The format of the certificate often conforms to the X.509 standard, and therefore they are often called X.509 certificates.

Verisign, Inc., a spin-off of RCA, is a popular choice for digital certificate requests. The company issues two kinds of personal certificates with two levels of authentication. A class one certificate only verifies the sender's email address. A class two certificate is verified with a credit reporting agency. As of this writing, the class one certificate costs $9.95 (and you can obtain a 60-day free trial period), and the class two certificate costs $19.95. Different types of certificates are issued for Web servers, corporations, and software developers who want to digitally sign their software. Verisign's Web site, *http://www.verisign.com,* has more details about each of these types of certificate.

## Certificate Chaining

Corporations and schools often want to issue certificates by themselves so that they don't have to go to a certificate authority every time they add a new employee. They can do this by installing a certificate server in their enterprise and using the certificate server to issue certificates. However, many software applications, such as Netscape Navigator and the Java Web server, only accept a few of the certificate authorities.

The remedy to this problem is called certificate chaining. In this case, the root certificate of the issuer is signed by a known certificate authority. In other words, the end user certificate is signed by a certificate server whose public key is signed by a certificate authority. The net effect is that a certificate often contains a chain of certificates, with the last one belonging to a certificate authority.

# Secure Socket Layer

Secure Socket Layer (SSL) was developed by Netscape Communications in 1994 and has since become the *de facto* standard for secure consumer electronic commerce on the Web.

SSL is a hybrid scheme in the sense that it has two phases. The first phase includes a handshake protocol, which specifies how the client and the server may exchange certificates, chooses the right algorithms for one-way hash, and determines a session key, which is used in the second phase. The type of symmetric key algorithm to use is also determined in the first phase. The second phase encompasses the bulk of the transmission, which is encrypted by a symmetric key algorithm.

SSL supports all the cryptographic algorithms mentioned so far in this chapter. For example, symmetric key algorithms that are supported include RC2, RC4, DES, IDEA, and triple DES. Public key algorithms that are supported include RSA and Diffie-Hellman.

SSL has the ability to ensure all four components of Internet security, namely confidentiality, integrity, authenticity, and non-repudiation.

## Acquiring a Certificate for the Java Web Server

In an SSL handshake, the client will always ask for a server certificate, although it is optional for the server to ask for a certificate from the client. To enable SSL on a Web server, we need to obtain a server certificate. Let's review the process of getting a certificate:

1. Generate a private/public key pair.
2. Submit your information along with the public key to a certificate authority.
3. The certificate authority digitally signs the information you provide and sends you the resulting certificate.

The Java Web server contains a tool that assists you in performing these steps. This tool is a command called *authstore*, which is located in the bin directory of the Web server installation directory. Once you type **authstore** on the command line, the AuthStore GUI comes up. Click "Passphrase" and enter Passphrase. To protect the server keys, enter **admin** and **admin**. Click on OK. Now you can use *authstore* to perform the three steps previously outlined.

## Generate a Key Pair

Click on the "Create" button, and *authstore* shows you a screen containing default choices for your key pair. We'll use the default choices, so click on Continue. Next, you are shown a form that asks for some information about you. Fill it out and make sure that you enter the complete state name in the State or Region field and not the abbreviation. (For example, enter California instead of CA.) Click on Save.

Now a small window pops up asking for a pass phrase, which is the password that protects your key database. Enter the password of your choice and click on OK, and you're done!

The panel now shows an available certificate with a key called "ssl-RSA-default." This is a certificate that has not yet been signed by a certificate authority. You now have a certificate for your Java Web server that you can use for testing purposes.

## Submit the Public Key to a Certificate Authority

Click on the "ssl-RSA-default" key and click on Request. The next screen asks you to provide some information about yourself. This information, combined with the public key, forms a Certificate Signing Request (CSR) and should be saved in a file. The file is signed with the private key. You should specify the full path of the file (for example, in Windows you may specify the path as *C:\temp\mycsr.txt*) and click on Save.

A typical CSR file looks like this:

```
Webmaster Name:          Nick
Webmaster Email:         nick@foo.com
Webmaster Telephone:     408 222 2222

Server Software:         Java Web Server
Server Version:          1.0

Common Name:             localhost
Organizational Unit:     Marketing
Organization:            My Company Name
Locality:                San Jose
State:                   California
Country:                 US

—BEGIN NEW CERTIFICATE REQUEST—-
MIIBszCCARwCAQAwczELMAkGA1UEBhMCVVMxCzAJBgNVBAgTAkNBMR
EwDwYDVQQHEwhTYW4gSm9zZTEWMBQGA1UEChMNQ21zY28gU3lzdGVt
```

```
czEYMBYGA1UECxMPR2xvYmFsIEFsbGlhbmNlMRIwEAYDVQQDEwlsb2
NhbGhvc3QwgZ8wDQYJKoZIhvcNAQEBBQADgY0AMIGJAoGBAKx3yTiq
cNxHlbz01wiB5w8Rq3knejp74WJZqwmNhFY55PuIx2EYaWUksg1EX6
Dul6MrKWyexVXqQAE1FzkM9P7y51ixuBwVVuz5X4svGt4FSf2ifCq7
SCytewYPYDus0hqHJnlJqEvxpsXXPQphQ1IB4nucqdKEUcjoKrCvXE
LAgMBAAGgADANBgkqhkiG9w0BAQQFAAOBgQBsnfGlaGzQv265PtiT6
p93wZIZhOSKYTTOmP3/F5aQPgHwTzQb1lv15iXhj4kmo07sYpw5wxu
Y8gg2uJOtwyXg13uY32Sb1D0QmCetLt27pAv8+jdqcDljyUBd8KIO8
JLCJ68wTmDPsLk0137N71S0xQ0Z/NCdnqu30gWFv51A==
```
—END NEW CERTIFICATE REQUEST—-

Now you can send the CSR to a certificate authority, which is normally done via email.

### Certificate Signed by a Certificate Authority

The certificate authority that receives your CSR will ask you to submit some information about yourself, including your email address. Depending on the level of security you need, the certificate authority will complete some form of authentication and then sign your CSR with its own private key. A free certificate often only involves verifying your email address, and the certificate is sent back to you via email.

Certificates are first encoded into ASCII characters using a standard called Base64. ASCII is used because different computers have different ways of representing data, but they all agree on how to represent ASCII characters. The certificate is decoded back to binary form before it is used.

## Example: Acquiring a Server Certificate from Verisign

As an example, we will show you how you can acquire a server certificate from Verisign.

Start up your browser, and connect to the URL: *http://www.verisign.com/*. As of this writing the site has a button called "Web Site Security" on the left frame of the home page. Click this button. On the next screen, click on "Get your Secure Server ID now" or "Test drive a trial server ID for Free" link, which is in the right frame. On the next screen, click on the "Enroll Now" button, which is located in the right bottom corner. Follow the instructions on the following screen. Verisign will show you the five steps to getting a server certificate:

**NOTE**

The steps that you'll follow for either a paid or a trial certificate are the same. However, with the trial certificate you won't be able to import the certificate into the current version of the Java Web server (1.1).

## Step One: Generate CSR

We have already completed this step, so we click on Continue.

## Step Two: Submit CSR

If you have saved the contents in *C:\temp\mycsr.txt*, you'll have to open this file in a notepad and copy the entire contents of the CSR file, including the lines that contain the begin and end statements, and paste it into the text area provided on the screen. Click on Continue to submit the CSR.

## Step Three: Complete Application

Again, fill in some information about yourself. Read the terms and conditions of the agreement on the page. If it is acceptable to you, click on Accept.

## Step Four: Wait for Processing

If you agree to be bound by all the terms and conditions that appear on the next screen, then click on Accept. Verisign will sign the public key and email you the certificate. Depending on your browser, you will then be shown a series of screens that contain questions such as "do you trust the particular host?" You may click on the buttons that reaffirm that you agree to these provisions. Also, you'll be asked to type in a nickname. You can use anything you want here.

## Step Five: Receive the Verisign Certificate From Email

Verisign will email you the certificate. It will look something like this:

```
—BEGIN CERTIFICATE—-
QZZCYjCCAgwCEDI2u9uhIFdqK5DEF2sxrB0wDQYJKoZIhvcNAQEE
BQAwgakxFjAUBgNVBAoTDVZlcmlTaWduLCBJbmMxRzBFBgNVBAsT
Pnd3dy52ZXJpc2lnbi5jb20vcmVwb3NpdG9yeS9UZXN0Q1BTIElu
```

```
Y29ycC4gQnkgUmVmLiBMaWFiLiBMVEQuMUYwRAYDVQQLEz1Gb3Ig
VmVyaVNpZ24gYXV0aG9yaXplCB0ZXN0aW5nIG9ubHkuIE5vIGFz
c3VyYW5jZXMgKEMpVlMxOTk3MB4XDTk4MDkxOTAwMDAwMFoXDTk4
MTAwMzIzTk1OVowezELMAkGA1UEBhMCVVMxEzARBgNVBAgTCkNh
bGlmb3JuaWExETAPBgNVBAcUCFNhbiBKb3NlMRYeFAYDVQQKFA1D
aXNjbyBTeXN0ZW1zMRgwFgYDVQQLFA9HbG9iYWwgQWxsaWFuY2Ux
EjAQBgNVBAMUCWxvY2FsaG9zdDCBnzANBgkqhkiG9w0BAQE123AO
BjQAwgYkCgYEA2pSb6FncFSEcQ6jx2al4VbtUWQ6bNk8oO3U2XVN
2r3mUIaDdn5hEAMTrzfT/ubnwbqP4Re9ZlQXQncGXuiqRtKgI7IT
pZRvsI/CIacQI/Meu0iBocwCqHH5DXHO5lZMLwh/JK1FWhju/z8f
YUbpvW+nzOwJRkcTJibTA+pJPsCAwEAATANBgkqhkiG9w0BAQQFA
ANBACR6r15R1DuQYfev3+Zgs1auITkItYUIyR7Ntlf0Nt6yh1zuE
RN3tvHpLpA5FWjXDg0A7uCier4sKbJlQinA61E=
```
—END CERTIFICATE—-

Copy the email contents from Begin Certificate to End Certificate, including the Begin and End statements, and save it in a file. In Windows, you may save it under C:\temp\mycert.txt.

## Enabling SSL on the Java Web Server

Once you have acquired a server certificate, you are ready to enable SSL on the Java Web server. Here are the steps to import the certificate to the server key database (if you have a trial certificate, you can skip ahead to step 5 right away):

1. Invoke the *authstore* command. Type in the pass phrase when prompted. Remember that you have to type **admin**, and click on OK.
2. Highlight the key for which you sent a CSR (the "ssl-RSA-default" key if you have followed the steps of this book) and click on Import.
3. On the next screen, input the path of the file where you saved the certificate and click on Save.
4. Start the Java Web server. You will be prompted for the pass phrase that you typed in for the key database.
5. Start the administration server.
6. Highlight "Secure Web Server" in the administration page, and click on Start.

Now you should be able to access the Java Web server through SSL with the following URL: *https://hostname:7070.* For example, if you want to invoke the date Servlet through SSL, you use the URL: *https://hostname:7070/servlet/Date.*

# Internet Security Bean

## The X.509 Certificate

JDK 1.2 contains a package called java.security.cert, which includes many classes that you'll need to manipulate certificates, including the X.509 format certificates. Within the package, three classes are of particular importance to us: *Certificate, X509Certificate,* and *CertificateFactory.*

The class *Certificate* represents a general certificate and includes methods that most types of certificates support, such as *toString()* and *getPublicKey().* Particular certificate types, such as PGPs, are subclasses of the class *Certificate.*

The class *X509Certificate* represents the X.509 format certificate, which has become the *de facto* standard for certificates. This class includes methods that obtain information contained in an X.509 format certificate. These methods include:

- *getSubjectDN()* returns the distinguished name of the person whom the certificate represents
- *getIssuerDN()* returns the distinguished name of the certificate authority who issues the certificate
- *getNotBefore()* returns the date when the certificate starts being valid
- *getNotAfter()* returns the date when the certificate expires
- *getSigAlgName()* returns the signing algorithm

Both *Certificate* and *X509Certificate* come with a default constructor. The preferred way of creating an instance of a certificate is by using the *CertificateFactory* class. For example, if you want to create an X509Certificate, you should call the *getInstance()* method in *CertificateFactory.* Currently only the X.509 format is supported by *CertificateFactory.*

The following program reads a file that contains a certificate and prints some of the information. It uses the classes and methods previously described. It also uses the *BASE64Encoder* class in the sun.misc package. That is not a supported package, but the encoder comes in handy.

We first read the whole file into a *ByteArrayInputStream* object:

```
FileInputStream in = new FileInputStream(args[0]);
DataInputStream dis = new DataInputStream(in);

byte[] bytes = new byte[dis.available()];
dis.readFully(bytes);
ByteArrayInputStream bais = new
ByteArrayInputStream(bytes);
```

Then we create a *CertificateFactory* object that produces X.509 certificates:

```
CertificateFactory cf =
CertificateFactory.getInstance("X.509");
```

Now we are ready to create an X.509 certificate that holds the information read from the file:

```
X509Certificate cert =
(X509Certificate)cf.generateCertificate(bais);
```

Once the certificate is created, we are able to use the methods in the *X509Certificate* class to read information within the certificate. If we want to print the public key of the certificate, we need to convert the key into an ASCII string first, using base 64 encoding, like this:

```
BASE64Encoder encoder = new BASE64Encoder();
System.out.println("Public key: " +
encoder.encode(cert.getPublicKey().getEncoded()));
```

Here is the complete program:

■■ ■■ ■■ ■■ ■■ ■■   **CertReader.java**

**Listing 11-1**
A program that prints
an X.509 certificate

```
import java.io.*;
import java.security.cert.*;
import sun.misc.*;

public class CertReader {
```

```
public static void main (String [] args){
  String inputString = "";
  String str;

  try {
    FileInputStream in = new
FileInputStream(args[0]);
    DataInputStream dis = new DataInputStream(in);

    byte[] bytes = new byte[dis.available()];
    dis.readFully(bytes);
    ByteArrayInputStream bais = new
ByteArrayInputStream(bytes);

    CertificateFactory cf =
CertificateFactory.getInstance("X.509");

    X509Certificate cert =
(X509Certificate)cf.generateCertificate(bais);

    System.out.println("The certificate is for: " +
cert.getSubjectDN() + "\n");
    System.out.println("Issuer: " +
cert.getIssuerDN() + "\n");
    System.out.println("Valid from: " +
cert.getNotBefore().toString() + "\n");
    System.out.println("Valid until: " +
cert.getNotAfter().toString() + "\n");
    System.out.println("Signing Algorithm: " +
cert.getSigAlgName() + "\n");

    BASE64Encoder encoder = new BASE64Encoder();
    System.out.println("Public key: " +
encoder.encode(cert.getPublicKey().getEncoded()));
    }catch (FileNotFoundException e){
      e.printStackTrace();
    }catch (IOException e){
      e.printStackTrace();
    }catch (CertificateException e){
      e.printStackTrace();
    }
  }
}
```

The complete source for this sample can be found under the *chap11\sample1* subdirectory on the CD-ROM. When you compile this sample code, make sure that your CLASSPATH points to rt.jar, which is packaged with JDK1.2. It is present under the *jre\lib* subdirectory under the JDK 1.2 installed directory.

Run the program with the server certificate (or the trial certificate) obtained from Verisign. If you have the trial certificate, make sure to copy the contents between Begin Certificate and End Certificate, including the Begin and End statements, into a file called server-cert.txt using Notepad (if you are using Windows) and save it as something like C:\temp\server-cert.txt. You can run the program from the command line as shown below:

```
java CertReader C:\temp\server-cert.txt
```

All the details of the certificate should be printed on the console.

# Obtaining the Client Certificate from a Servlet

On today's Internet, password authentication is no longer a sufficient means of security. That's because users often use obvious passwords (such as their birthday or their name), or they write down the password on a piece of paper, thus making the password easily compromised. Certificate authentication, along with password authentication, is a much stronger security system because a potential attacker would have to obtain something that is on the user's computer—the certificate. In this section we will introduce a Servlet that will print out the certificate chain of a browser.

The request for a client certificate is done during the SSL negotiation period. In order for the Servlet to obtain the certificate chain, we need to configure the server so that it makes the request during the SSL connection. The configuration file for such a request is:

```
<Webserver-root>\properties\server\javawebserver
\secureservice\endpoint
```

The last line of this file looks like this by default:

```
endpoint.main.ssl.need-clnt-auth=false
```

Turning the "false" into "true" causes the Web server to ask for the certificate from the browser during an SSL connection. This is a very important step that you will have to perform in order to obtain the client certificate.

The current version of the Java Web server does not recognize the free trial version of the Verisign certificate. Therefore in order for the following servlet example to work, the reader will need to obtain a class 2 personal certificate from Verisign (the one that costs $19.95). In addition, the current version of the Java Web server (1.1) only supports certificates issued by Verisign, by default, although the *authstore* tool has some options that allow other certificate authorities to be trusted.

## The PrintClientCertChain Servlet

JDK1.2 includes an SSL package called *java.net.ssl*. Within the package there is an interface called *SSLSession*. *SSLSession* includes methods that describe the characteristics of the particular SSL connection. Those methods include:

- *getCipherSuite()* returns the cryptographic algorithm used in the SSL connection
- *getPeerHost()* returns the hostname of the client machine
- *getPeerCertificateChain()* returns the certificate chain stored on the client

The way to obtain the *SSLSession* object is by calling a method of the *ServletRequest* interface: *getAttribute()*. This method takes a string as a parameter. Possible choices of the string are: "javax.net.ssl.cipher_suite," "javax.net.ssl.peer_certificates," and "javax.net.ssl.session." They return the cryptographic algorithm used, the client certificate chain, and the *SSLSession* object, respectively. Of course, once we obtain the *SSLSession* object, the other two also become available.

```
SSLSession sslSession =
(SSLSession)req.getAttribute("javax.net.ssl.session");
```

Then we call the *getAttribute()* method of *HttpServletRequest* to obtain the *SSLSession* object:

```
X509Certificate[] certChain =
sslSession.getPeerCertificateChain();
out.println("<b>Number of certificates in the
certificate chain: " + certChain.length + "</
b><br><br>");

for (int i=0; i<certChain.length; ++i)
{
  out.println("<b>Certificate " + i + "</b><br><br>");
  printCert(out, certChain[i]);
}
```

Once we receive a good certificate chain, we want to traverse it and print the content of each certificate:

```
private void printCert(PrintWriter out, X509Certificate
cert){
  out.println("<b>DN: </b>" + cert.getSubjectDN() +
"<br>");
  out.println("<b>Issuer: </b>" + cert.getIssuerDN() +
"<br>");
  out.println("<b>Valid from: </b>" +
cert.getNotBefore().toString() + "<br>");
  out.println("<b>Valid until: </b>" +
cert.getNotAfter().toString() + "<br><br>");
}
```

In this Servlet, we print the subject DN, the issuer DN, the effective date, and the expiration date.

Putting it all together, we have:

**Listing 11-2**

A Servlet that prints the client certificate

**PrintClientCertChain.java**

```
import javax.servlet.http.*;
import javax.servlet.*;
import java.io.*;
import javax.net.ssl.*;
import javax.security.cert.*;
import sun.security.x509.*;
import sun.security.util.*;
```

```java
import java.security.*;

public class PrintClientCertChain extends HttpServlet {

  private void printCert(PrintWriter out,
X509Certificate cert){
    out.println("<b>DN: </b>" + cert.getSubjectDN() +
"<br>");
    out.println("<b>Issuer: </b>" + cert.getIssuerDN()
+ "<br>");
    out.println("<b>Valid from: </b>" +
cert.getNotBefore().toString() + "<br>");
    out.println("<b>Valid until: </b>" +
cert.getNotAfter().toString() + "<br><br>");
  }

  public void doGet (HttpServletRequest req,
HttpServletResponse res)throws ServletException,
IOException{
    PrintWriter out;
    String temp;

    res.setContentType("text/html");
    out = res.getWriter();

    SSLSession sslSession =
(SSLSession)req.getAttribute("javax.net.ssl.session");

    out.println("<html>");
    out.println("<head><title>Client Certificate Chain
</title></head>");
    out.println("<body>");

    if (sslSession == null){
      out.println ("Not an SSL session<br>");
    }
    else{
    try{
      X509Certificate[] certChain =
sslSession.getPeerCertificateChain();
      out.println("<b>Number of certificates in the
certificate chain: " + certChain.length + "</
```

```
b><br><br>");

     for (int i=0; i<certChain.length; ++i){
        out.println("<b>Certificate " + i + "</
b><br><br>");
        printCert(out, certChain[i]);
     }
  }catch(SSLPeerUnverifiedException e){

out.println("<br>SSLPeerUnverifiedException<br>");
     }
  }
  out.println("</body></html>");
  out.close();
  }
}
```

The complete source code for this sample can be found under the *chap11\sample2* subdirectory on the CD-ROM. To compile this code make sure that jws.jar (of Java Web Server) and rt.jar (packaged with JDK1.2) are in your CLASSPATH. Once you compile the servlet successfully, copy the class file into the *servlets* subdirectory under the Java Web server installed root directory.

## Test the Servlet

To test the Servlet, we need to obtain a class 2 Verisign certificate. Go to the URL *http://www.verisign.com/client/enrollment/index.html* and click on the "Class 2 Digital ID" option. Follow the instructions and install the certificate on your browser. The process is not nearly as complicated as the server certificate installation.

If this is the first time you have installed a certificate, the browser will prompt you for a password to protect your certificate database. When the Web server asks for a certificate during an SSL connection setup, you will be prompted for the password again. This is to protect you from someone who is trying to access your computer illegally.

Once the class 2 certificate is installed on your browser, you should verify that the certificate is indeed the one sent to the Web server at the time of a request. The way to verify this on Netscape Navigator 4.x is to click on the "security" button. A new screen will pop up displaying all the security-related information. Click on "Yours" under "Certificates" on the left bar, and you should see something similar to this line:

```
Nick's    VeriSign, Inc. ID #2
```

Click on Navigator on the left bar, and you should see the same certificate name under "Certificate to identify you to a Web site:".

Now you are ready to test the servlet by going to the URL *https://hostname:7070/servlet/PrintClientCertChain.* You will see something like the following on your browser:

```
Number of certificates in the certificate chain: 3

Certificate 0

DN: OID.1.2.840.113549.1.9.8="111 E. El Camino Real 000
Sunnyvale, CA 94087 US",
OID.1.2.840.113549.1.9.1=nick@foo.com, CN=Nick,
OU=Digital ID Class 2 - Netscape, OU="www.verisign.com/
repository/RPA Incorp. by Ref.,LIAB.LTD(c)98",
OU=VeriSign Trust Network, O="VeriSign, Inc."
Issuer: CN=VeriSign Class 2 CA - Individual Subscriber,
OU="www.verisign.com/repository/RPA Incorp. By
Ref.,LIAB.LTD(c)98", OU=VeriSign Trust
Network, O="VeriSign, Inc."
Valid from: Tue Sep 22 17:00:00 PDT 1998
Valid until: Thu Sep 23 16:59:59 PDT 1999


Certificate 1

DN: CN=VeriSign Class 2 CA - Individual Subscriber,
OU="www.verisign.com/repository/RPA Incorp. By
Ref.,LIAB.LTD(c)98", OU=VeriSign Trust Network,
O="VeriSign, Inc."
Issuer: OU=Class 2 Public Primary Certification
Authority, O="VeriSign, Inc.", C=US
Valid from: Mon May 11 17:00:00 PDT 1998
Valid until: Tue Jan 06 15:59:59 PST 2004


Certificate 2

DN: OU=Class 2 Public Primary Certification Authority,
O="VeriSign, Inc.", C=US
Issuer: OU=Class 2 Public Primary Certification
```

```
Authority, O="VeriSign, Inc.", C=US
Valid from: Sun Jan 28 16:00:00 PST 1996
Valid until: Fri Dec 31 15:59:59 PST 1999
```

In case you invoke this Servlet in a normal HTTP connection by accessing the URL *http://hostname:8080/servlet/PrintClientCertChain,* you will see the following message in your browser:

```
Not an SSL session
```

**NOTE**

Make sure to set endpoint.main.ssl.need-clnt-auth=false after the test. Otherwise, the server will ask for the client certificate every time you access applications over SSL.

# Internet Security Bean

In this section, we will introduce the Internet Security Bean. This bean is pretty simple. It will read the client certificate and give the owner's common name (CN). This bean will later be reused in Chapter 18 as part of the project tracking system.

## Extract the CN From the Certificate

If the *getPeerCertificateChain()* call returns a valid certificate chain, then the integrity of the Web server ensures that the certificate has been signed by a proper certificate authority that the Web server trusts. Otherwise, the *SSLPeerUnverifiedExeption* will be thrown.

Because the distinguished name returned by *getSubjectDN()* is a long string that contains a lot of other information, we need a small routine to extract the common name out of the DN string. (Please refer to Chapter 8 for a detailed discussion on the terms DN [Distinguished Name] and CN [Common Name].) Notice that the DN looks like this:

```
OID.1.2.840.113549.1.9.8="111E. El Camino Real 000
Sunnyvale, CA 94087 US",
OID.1.2.840.113549.1.9.1=nick@foo.com, CN=Nick,
OU=Digital ID Class 2 - Netscape, OU="www.verisign.com/
repository/RPA Incorp. by Ref.,LIAB.LTD(c)98",
OU=VeriSign Trust Network, O="VeriSign, Inc."

private String getCN(String dn){
  StringTokenizer st = new StringTokenizer(dn, ",");
  while (st.hasMoreTokens()){
    String tmp = st.nextToken().trim();
    if (tmp.startsWith("CN=")){
      return (tmp.substring(tmp.indexOf('=')+1));
    }
  }
  return null;
}
```

We use the *StringTokenizer* class to extract substrings delimited by a comma, and then search for strings starting with "CN=".

Of course, we need a routine to obtain the client certificate. In a certificate chain, the first certificate is always the one belonging to the identity the certificate represents. The code snippet is shown below:

```
public String getCertCN(HttpServletRequest req){
  SSLSession sslSession =
SSLSession)req.getAttribute("javax.net.ssl.session");
  if (sslSession == null){
    return null;
  }
  else{
    try{
      X509Certificate[] certChain =
sslSession.getPeerCertificateChain();
      String subjectDN =
certChain[0].getSubjectDN().getName();
      return(getCN(subjectDN));
    }catch(SSLPeerUnverifiedException e){
      return null;
    }
  }
}
```

This routine returns null if it turns out that the connection is not SSL based, if the client doesn't supply a certificate, or if the certificate supplied is not trusted by the Web server.

Here's the complete code for the Security Bean:

**Listing 11-3**

A bean that returns the CN of a client certificate

**SecurityBean.java**

```java
import javax.servlet.http.*;
import javax.servlet.*;
import java.io.*;
import java.util.StringTokenizer;
import javax.net.ssl.*;
import javax.security.cert.*;
import java.security.*;
import sun.security.x509.*;
import sun.security.util.*;


public class SecurityBean implements Serializable{
  public transient SSLSession sslSession = null;

  public void setSSLSession(SSLSession sslSession){
    this.sslSession = sslSession;
  }

  public SSLSession getSSLSession(){
    return (this.sslSession);
  }

  private String getCN(String dn){
    StringTokenizer st = new StringTokenizer(dn, ",");
    while (st.hasMoreTokens()){
      String tmp = st.nextToken().trim();
      if (tmp.startsWith("CN="))
        return (tmp.substring(tmp.indexOf('=') + 1));
    }
    return null;
  }

  public String getCertCN(){
    if (sslSession == null){
      return null;
    }
```

```
    else{
       try{
          X509Certificate[] certChain =
sslSession.getPeerCertificateChain();
          String subjectDN =
certChain[0].getSubjectDN().getName();
          return(getCN(subjectDN));
       }catch(SSLPeerUnverifiedException e){
          return null;
       }
    }
  }
}
```

The complete source code for this sample can be found under the *chap11\sample3* subdirectory on the CD-ROM. To compile the source code make sure your CLASSPATH is also pointing to rt.jar (packaged with JDK1.2).

# Summary

In this chapter we learned about security on the Internet, including the various algorithms that are used to provide security. We also learned how to set up a secure Web site using the Java Web server. In addition, we developed some samples to verify the digital certificate. A practical example for using security will be provided in Chapter 18 of this book.

# Common Object Request Broker Architecture

# Problems Solved by CORBA

The history of enterprise computing is composed of roughly three stages. The first one is mainframe computing, where enterprises run their important applications on a mainframe, with dumb terminals as the user interfaces. The second one is client/server computing, where major applications are run on server class machines and users access the application services via a network through a PC. Now we are entering a third stage where multi-tier distributed applications will gradually dominate enterprise computing.

Common Object Request Broker Architecture (CORBA) is the ideal programming environment for the third phase of enterprise computing. It is also a great facilitator of the gradual shift of mainframe/host computing to distributed computing.

Many large organizations invested millions of dollars in applications that run on mainframes. In order to move into distributed computing, they have to provide the mainframe application service on the network. One way of doing this is to rewrite the application on an open environment such as UNIX, but that is often prohibitively expensive. Another way of doing this is through CORBA. We will explain in later sections how CORBA can enable the re-use of applications in a networked environment.

CORBA is also very effective when integration of diverse applications is needed. For example, when two banks merge, their branch offices need to be able to access a different kind of application. CORBA provides much more cost-effective and timely solutions for integrating two computer systems than traditional client/server solutions.

# Traditional Client/Server Programming

The two traditional ways of solving the problems of reusing existing applications and integrating diverse software applications are:

- using network APIs (i.e., Socket)
- using Remote Procedural Call (RPC)

Programmers of network APIs often need to know the intricacies of network-specific issues, including dealing with lower level network connections, data representations, and packing and unpacking network requests.

These networking modules are often similar in different applications and are tedious to write.

Enter the Remote Procedure Call (RPC). RPC allows a developer to signal a remote machine to execute some procedure. The syntax of calling a remote function resembles a local procedure call.

Figure 12-1 shows how it works.

**Figure 12-1**

How RPC works

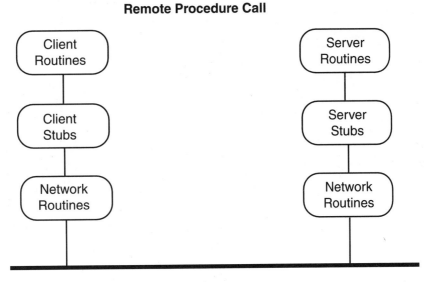

**Remote Procedure Call**

**Network**

In the client routines, a programmer simply makes a function call. The client *stub* routines will pack the call parameters and send them to the server. The server stub unpacks the parameters and calls a server routine on the client's behalf, and then passes the result back to the client.

Traditional RPC has a clear advantage over network API programming, since it hides the complexity of low-level network programming and takes care of data representation and parameter passing.

On the other hand, RPC still leaves something to be desired. For example, RPC is synchronous in nature. The client is blocked after making the remote procedure call and only gets started executing again after the result comes back. Many users prefer applications that have the option of calling remote procedures asynchronously.

Some other drawbacks of RPC include the following: the caller has to know the hostname of the server machine, the server process has to be active at the time of the RPC call, and RPC is procedural in nature (compared to the more advanced object model).

# CORBA

CORBA is RPC in the distributed computing age. It is designed to fix some of the shortcomings of traditional RPC. The Object Request Broker (ORB) is a layer between the network and stubs, as shown in Figure 12-2:

**Figure 12-2**
Simple CORBA
architecture

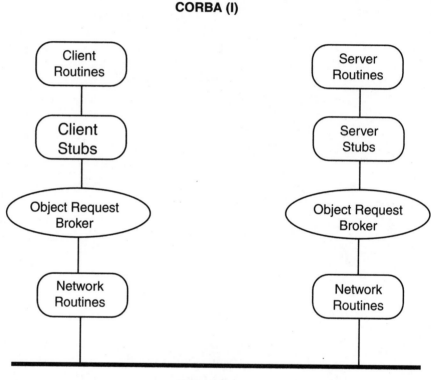

CORBA (I)

Network

The additional ORB layer allows the remote request to be made either synchronously or asynchronously. It also allows the server to be activated only when a client has made some requests. Furthermore, it has become an object environment where methods of an object, rather than procedure calls, are invoked.

CORBA has also defined a number of services on top of the ORB. Those services are essential for distributed applications. For example, with the CORBA naming service, a client may request services from a server without knowing its physical location.

Figure 12-3 shows where CORBA fits into all the services:

**Figure 12-3**

CORBA architecture
with services

**CORBA (II)**

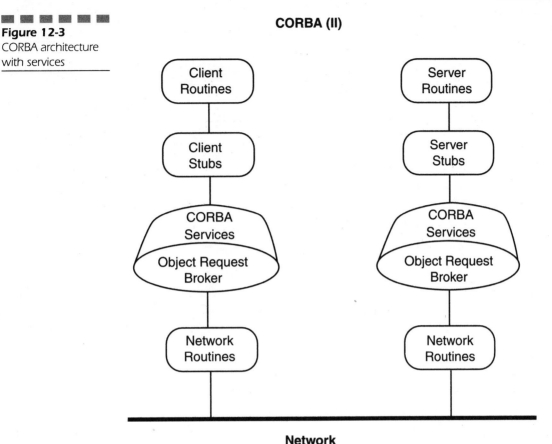

**Figure 12-3**

CORBA architecture
with services

CORBA is a middleware because it sits between application-specific code and network routines. It allows developers to concentrate on the problem they are trying to solve rather than spending time doing tedious network code.

## CORBA Architecture

CORBA has five components: the ORB core, object services, common facilities, domain objects, and application objects.

Figure 12-4 shows the relationship among the components. The ORB does the basic plumbing of invoking remote methods and passing parameters. All other parts use the services provided by ORB.

Application objects are created by developers of specification applications. They are only used in those applications. All other components are specified because they are often commonly needed objects for applications.

**Figure 12-4**
Complete CORBA
architecture

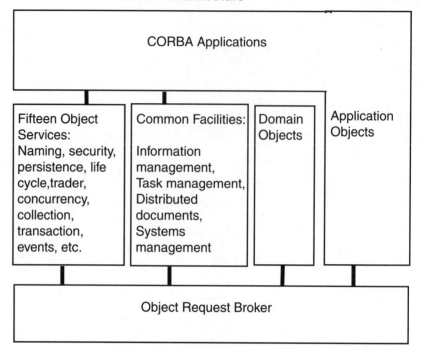

Domain objects are used in domain-specific applications. Here domain means industry type; examples of domain include the telecommunication industry, medical industry, financial industry, and so on.

Object services are domain-independent services. These services are used in applications of all domains. Examples of object services include the naming service, trader services, event services, and so on. There are fifteen object services in CORBA.

Common facilities are user-interface–related objects. An example of this is a compound document.

## ORB Architecture

So how does the ORB deliver all the wonderful features we described? The answer lies in some crucial components of the ORB that Figure 12-5 shows:

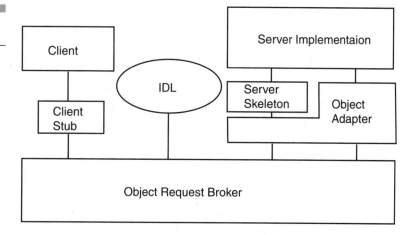

**Figure 12-5**
ORB architecture

The Interface Definition Language (IDL) is the glue that connects the client and the server, and it is often the first piece that needs to be developed in a CORBA application. IDL lets the client know what methods are available on the server and their parameters. It also allows the client and server to be written in different programming languages. IDL is a declarative language, which means you use IDL to define the interface between the client and the server, but you don't include the actual implementation. Some IDL examples will be presented in later sections of this chapter.

Once the IDL is available, a developer uses an IDL compiler to create client *stubs* and server *skeletons* (see Figure 12-6). Stubs and skeletons take care of passing parameters between the two sides. Once a request is passed from a client to a server, a component called *object adapter* is responsible for the actual invocation of the server object (which is called the server implementation in CORBA).

**Figure 12-6**
IDL compiler
generates client stubs
and server skeletons

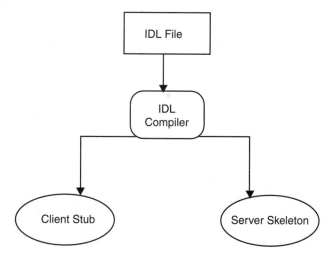

## Object Adapter

CORBA supports a variety of server implementations, including both legacy applications written way before CORBA was conceived in a language such as COBOL, and ones written in newer languages such as Java. Once the server implementation is registered with the ORB, it has to provide a way to let ORB invoke its methods. For a language such as C, a pointer to the function would be enough for method invocation. On the other hand, COBOL or Java programs would need to provide something different.

In order to deal with different types of distributed server implementations, CORBA provides the object adapter that takes care of the nitty-gritty of distributed server programming. An object adapter allows CORBA to provide flexible services and, at the same time, unburdens developers from dealing with some of the common problems associated with server programming.

Some of the duties of an object adapter include the following:

- Object registration—registers the server implementation with the ORB
- Request demultiplexing—demultiplexes client requests and sends them to the right server implementations
- Server implementation upcall—invokes the requested methods on behalf of the client
- Object reference generation—generates an object reference for each server object

Figure 12-7 shows some of the duties of an object adapter.

An object reference is a string that uniquely identifies an object on the ORB. The latest CORBA specification includes the interoperable object reference (IOR), which allows objects to be uniquely identified across different CORBA platforms.

To support object persistence, IOR can be converted to a string and stored in a file. Here is an example of IOR:

```
IOR:00000000000001349444c3a48656
c6c6f576f726c643a312e30000000000
0100000000000000044000100000000000
d3230372e312e3134372e343900009da2
0000002800504d4300000000010000000134
9444c3a48656c6c6f576f726c643a312e
3000000000000019bc0aab9
```

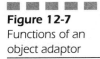

**Figure 12-7**

Functions of an
object adaptor

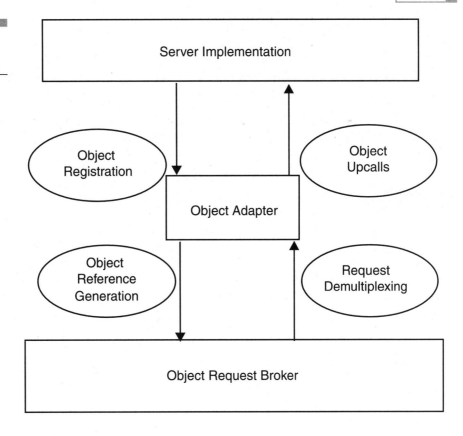

It is a long string since it has to be unique among all ORBs. Some of the information included in an IOR are the ORB version, hostname, port number, and object ID.

## Object Service Example: Naming Service

The naming service is the yellow pages of the distributed system. It allows the client to invoke services without knowing the physical location of the CORBA server implementation.

The way it works is also similar to the yellow pages system. When we start a CORBA service, we register it with the name server. The name server contains a database that stores all the mapping of service names and the object reference. The physical location of the server implementation is encoded in the object reference.

When the client wants to invoke certain CORBA services, it queries the name server with the service name. The name server returns the object reference of the service, which allows the client to contact the server. Figure 12-8 shows the process.

The naming service—specification in CORBA is called COSNaming (Common Object Services Naming). It stores names and object references in a tree structure.

**Figure 12-8**
CORBA name service

**CORBA Name Service**

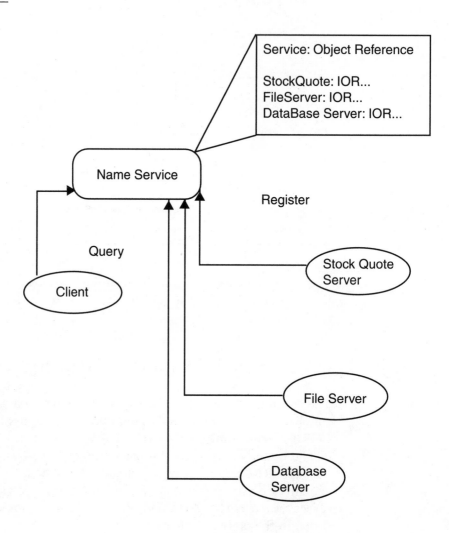

# CORBA Programming Tutorial

A visible benefit of CORBA is that it allows you to reuse existing software applications. In this section we will show you how to add CORBA abilities to some server applications so that any CORBA client may receive the services.

The application we want to build will allow users to calculate the price of PCs configured to their specifications that they want to buy. The client will first be presented with a default PC configuration and price. They will also be shown options for each device—the processor type, memory size, hard drive size, and so on. Users may substitute default options with their own choices. When they're finished, they will have the option of calculating the prices of the personally designed PC they have specified.

## Step 1: Preparation

JDK 1.2 has included a CORBA called *java idl*. However, you will also need to download a tool called *idltojava* from the JavaSoft Web site. The URL is:

```
http://developer.java.sun.com/developer/earlyAccess/
jdk12/idltojava.html
```

Please make sure you are a member of Java Developer Connection Program. The registration is free.

The **idltojava** tool utilizes the native C/C++ compilers as preprocessors, so if you are running our examples on Windows NT, you'll want to make sure you have Visual C++ installed. Otherwise, if you have access to a Solaris machine, you can compile the *idl* program on a Solaris and ftp the results back to the Windows NT machine.

## Step 2: IDL

IDL is the contract between the server and the client. It is the first piece of a CORBA application. Some features of IDL include the following:

- Syntax is similar to C
- Supports *long* (32bit), *long long* (64 bit), and *short* (16bit)
- Supports *float, double,* and *long double*
- Supports *char* and *wchar* (wide-character type)
- Supports *string*
- Supports *boolean, octet* (8 bit), *enum,* and *any* (any IDL type)

- Has "in," "out," and "inout" types of parameter passing
- No pointers, constructors, or destructors

CORBA's parameter passing is directional. A parameter is either an input to the method, an output from the method, or both. So if the parameter passing is of type "in," it means the parameter is an input. If it is of type "out" that means the parameter is an output, and type "inout" means the parameter is both an input and an output.

For our purposes, we only need three methods:

- *getDefaultConfig()*—this method will return to the default configuration
- *getDeviceChoice()*—this method will return the choices available for a device type
- *getPrice()*—this method will return the price of a certain type of a device

Here is the idl:

**Listing 12-1**

Simple IDL file for the tutorial sample

**PCSelect.idl:**

```
module PCSelect
{
  interface Config
  {
    string getDefaultConfig();
    string getDeviceChoice(in string deviceName);
    long getPrice(in string deviceSelection);
  };
};
```

Use *idltojava* to compile the previous program:

**idltojava PCSelect.idl**

Running this command will create a directory called "PCSelect" with the following files:

- Config.java: Contains the Java version of the IDL interface.
- ConfigHolder.java: Deals with the directional nature of CORBA in Java, which can only pass by value.

■ ConfigStub.java: Stub file is the client stub, which acts as a proxy for the server implementation object.

■ ConfigHelper.java: Contains some utility methods, including the *narrow()* method, which assigns the appropriate object type to the object reference passed to the CORBA client.

■ ConfigImplBase.java: This is the server skeleton, which allows the server implementation to connect with the ORB and register itself.

These are the client stub and the server skeleton files, which do all the lower level plumbing.

## Step 3: Write the Server Implementation

This step includes two phases—the server implementation and its registration. In the CORBA release of Java, an implementation is called a servant. In this section, we will use dummy functions so we can concentrate on CORBA programming. In the next section of this chapter, we will explain how we can combine CORBA and JDBC. The following piece of code performs the actual implementation of the interfaces that are exposed to the CORBA client. The server implementation class needs to extend the skeleton class, which does the actual work of connecting to the ORB.

```
class ConfigServant extends _ConfigImplBase{
  public String getDefaultConfig(){
    return ("Default Config");
  }

  public String getDeviceChoice(String deviceName){
    return ("Device Choice for: " + deviceName);
  }

  public int getPrice(String deviceSelection){
    return (100);
  }
}
```

In registering the servant, we mean to register it both to the ORB and to the name service. First we need to get hold of an object that represents the ORB. The following statement will do the trick:

```
ORB orb = ORB.init(args, null);
```

The port number of the name server is passed from the command line with the *-ORBInitialPort* parameter.

Then we want to create an instance of the servant object and register it with the ORB:

```
ConfigServant configObj = new ConfigServant();
orb.connect(configObj);
```

The *connect()* method of ORB utilizes the object adapter and takes care of all the low-level details of the ORB, including registering the servant object with the ORB and object reference generation.

Now we want to find the name service:

```
org.omg.CORBA.Object obj =
orb.resolve_initial_references("NameService");
NamingContext ncObj = NamingContextHelper.narrow(obj);
```

The first statement retrieves the object reference of the naming service, which is often passed in as a command line argument. The second statement specifies that the object retrieved is of the *NamingContext* interface. This interface contains methods for binding objects to a name, query objects with names, and so on. Chapter 9 discusses naming concepts in more detail.

Once we have the name service, we want to register our service with it:

```
NameComponent nc = new NameComponent("PCConfig", "");
NameComponent path[] = {nc};
ncRef.rebind(path, configObj);
```

The first two statements create the actual name we want to register, and the last statement registers it.

*NameComponent* is the building block of a name. The constructor takes two arguments: the name and its description. The association of an object and a name is called binding. Rebind will simply overwrite any existing binding. The reason binding or rebinding takes an array of *NameComponent* objects is that an object may have more than one name.

The last thing we do is wait for the client requests:

```
java.lang.Object sync = new java.lang.Object();
synchronized (sync) {
  sync.wait();
}
```

Figure 12-9 shows the flow of CORBA server programming.

**Figure 12-9**
Steps for CORBA
server programming

**CORBA server programming**

get ORB object

create the servant object

register with the ORB

locate the naming service

register with the naming service

wait for client requests

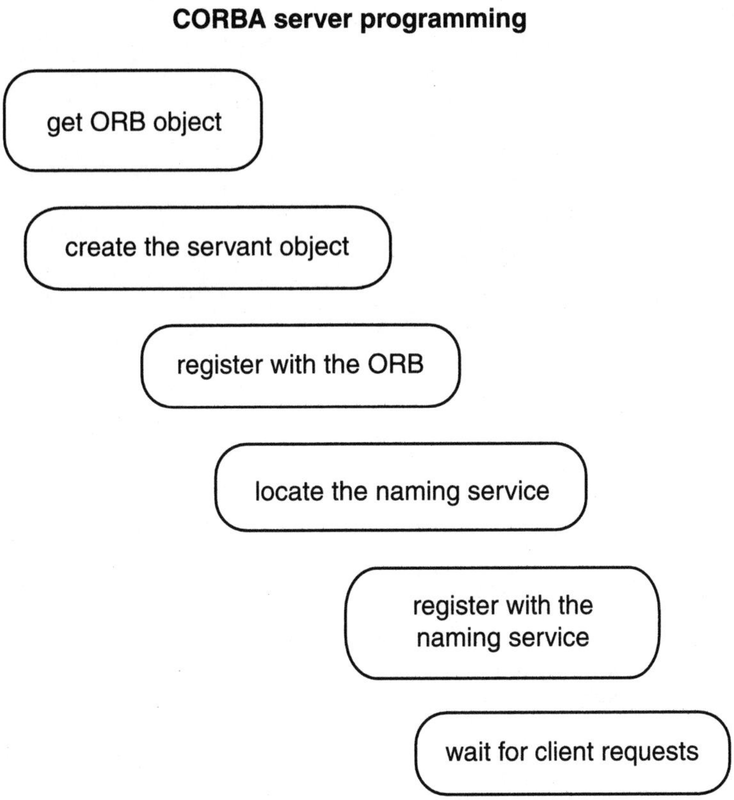

Now use Listing 12-2 to put it all together for the server side of the application.

**Listing 12-2**
Complete server
implementation

**ConfigServer.java**

```
import PCSelect.*;
import org.omg.CosNaming.*;
import org.omg.CosNaming.NamingContextPackage.*;
import org.omg.CORBA.*;
```

```java
class ConfigServant extends _ConfigImplBase{
  public String getDefaultConfig(){
    return ("Default Config");
  }

  public String getDeviceChoice(String deviceName){
    return ("Device Choice for: " + deviceName);
  }

  public int getPrice(String deviceSelection){
    return (100);
  }
}
public class ConfigServer{
  public static void main(String args[]){
    try{
      ORB orb = ORB.init(args, null);

      ConfigServant configObj = new ConfigServant();
      orb.connect(configObj);

      org.omg.CORBA.Object obj =
orb.resolve_initial_references("NameService");

      NamingContext ncObj = NamingContextHelper.narrow(obj);
      NameComponent nc = new NameComponent("PCConfig", "");
      NameComponent path[] = {nc};
      ncObj.rebind(path, configObj);

      System.out.println ("\nServer object
registered\n");

      java.lang.Object sync = new java.lang.Object();
      synchronized (sync){
        sync.wait();
      }
    }catch (Exception e){System.err.println("ERROR: " +
e);e.printStackTrace(System.out);}
  }
}
```

## Step 4: Write the Client

The client program is somewhat simpler than the server, since there is no servant and registration to take care of.
    We still need to get the ORB object:

```
ORB orb = ORB.init(args, null);
```

Now we need to locate the name server, just like we needed to do for the server:

```
org.omg.CORBA.Object obj =
orb.resolve_initial_references("NameService");
NamingContext ncObj = NamingContextHelper.narrow(obj);
```

The port number of the name server is passed from the command line with the *-ORBInitialPort* parameter. The exact syntax is shown in the "Run the Programs" section.
    Then we query for the server object:

```
NameComponent nc = new NameComponent("PCConfig", "");
NameComponent path[] = {nc};
Config config =
HelloHelper.narrow(ncRef.resolve(path));
```

Notice that the object name is the same as the interface name in the *idl* file.
    With the service object in hand, we may invoke those services:

```
String defaultConfig = config.getDefaultConfig();
String  deviceChoice =
config.getDeviceChoice("Memory");
int price = config.getPrice("Memory32");
```

Figure 12-10 shows the client programming diagram.

■ ■ ■ ■ ■ ■
**Figure 12-10**
Steps for CORBA
client programming

**CORBA Client Programming**

get the ORB object

locate the name server

query the name server

invoke remote services

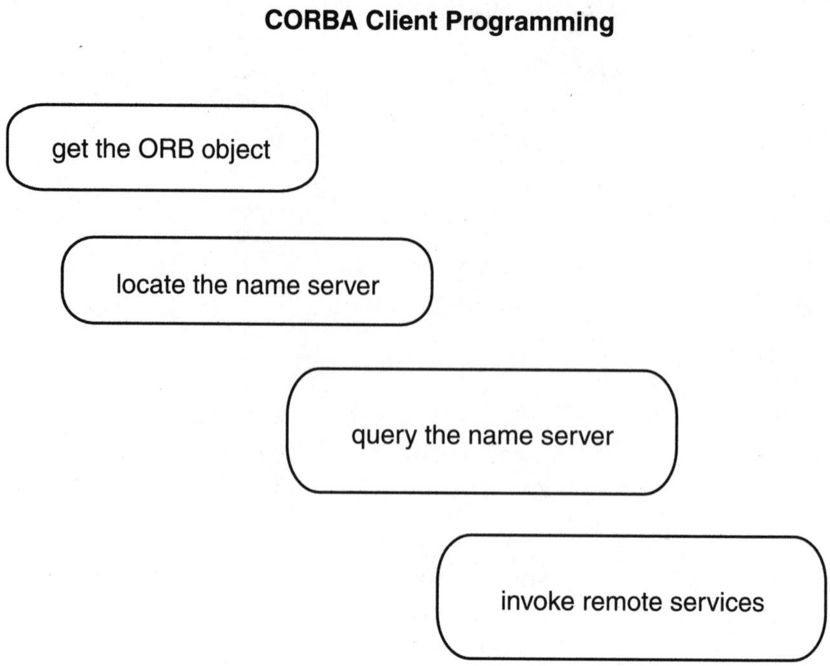

Now use Listing 12-3 to put it all together for the client.

■ ■ ■ ■ ■ ■
**Listing 12-3**
Complete client
implementation

**ConfigClient.java**

```java
import PCSelect.*;
import org.omg.CosNaming.*;
import org.omg.CosNaming.NamingContextPackage.*;
import org.omg.CORBA.*;
public class ConfigClient
{
  public static void main(String args[]){
    try{
      ORB orb = ORB.init(args, null);
      org.omg.CORBA.Object obj =
      orb.resolve_initial_references("NameService");

      NamingContext ncObj = NamingContextHelper.narrow(obj);
```

```
        NameComponent nc = new NameComponent("PCConfig", "");
        NameComponent path[] = {nc};
        Config config = ConfigHelper.narrow(ncObj.resolve(path));

        String defaultConfig = config.getDefaultConfig();
        String deviceChoice =
config.getDeviceChoice("Memory");
        int price = config.getPrice("Memory32");

        System.out.println("return value:");
        System.out.println(defaultConfig + ", " +
deviceChoice + ",
            and " + price);
    }catch(Exception e){System.err.println("ERROR: " +
e); e.printStackTrace(System.out);}
    }
}
```

# Run the Programs

Follow these steps to test our example:

## Step 1: Start the name service:

```
tnameserv -ORBInitialPort 1050
```

## Step 2: Start the server:

```
java ConfigServer -ORBInitialPort 1050
```

Once the server is started, you will see the message "Server Object Registered."

### Step 3: Run the client:

```
java ConfigClient -ORBInitialPort 1050
```

The client should produce the following output:

```
return value:
Default Config, Device Choice for: Memory, and 100
```

# CORBA Bean Utilizing JDBC

In this section we will design a CORBA bean that will interact with the JDBC Bean we developed in Chapter 7.

We want to design a CORBA bean that is not exactly a JavaBean but just a service that will return all of the specified table entries from a specified database. The CORBA service will return all the table information as a single string for the table. The table name will be passed by the user. The return value will have the following format:

```
<number of columns>, [<column name1>, <column
name2>...], [<column value1>, <column value2>...],
[<column value1>, <column value2>...], [<column
value1>,<column value2>...]
```

Let's assume that we have a table in a database as shown below:

**Table 12-1**

Sample Table

| ID | Employee Name |
|----|---------------|
| 1  | name1         |
| 2  | name2         |
| 3  | name3         |

The CORBA bean will return the following string:

```
2, Id, EmployeeName, 1, name1, 2, name2, 3, name3
```

Now let's write a CORBA service that will give us the table information shown above.

The first step is to write the IDL file that will define all the methods that can be accessed using the CORBA service. In our case, we will just have a single service responsible for getting all the table entries. Our IDL file, PCSelect.idl, is shown below:

**Listing 12-4**
IDL file for providing *getTableEntries()* CORBA service

**PCSelect.idl**

```
module PCSelect
{
    interface Config
    {
        string getTableEntries(in string tableName);
    };
};
```

When you run *idltojava* on PCSelect.idl, a directory called PCSelect will be created that contains all the necessary binding files. Our next step is to write a server that will contact the database when *getTableEntries()* is invoked by the client.

The code is very simple. Most of it is initialization that utilizes the JDBCBean and string manipulation to return the result in a format discussed at the beginning of this section.

**Listing 12-5**
Complete implementation of *getTableEntries()*

**ConfigServer.java**

```
import PCSelect.*;
import org.omg.CosNaming.*;
import org.omg.CosNaming.NamingContextPackage.*;
import org.omg.CORBA.*;
import java.io.*;
import java.beans.*;
import java.util.*;

class ConfigServant extends _ConfigImplBase implements
Serializable{

    public String getTableEntries(String deviceName)
    {
```

```
    JDBCBean jb = null;
    boolean resultAvailable = false;
    Vector columnNames, columnValues;
    JDBCListenerImpl jdbcListener = new
JDBCListenerImpl();

    columnNames = new Vector();
    columnNames.addElement("*");
    resultAvailable = false;

    try{
       jb = (JDBCBean)Beans.instantiate(null,
"JDBCBean");
       jb.setUserid("admin");
       jb.setPassword("admin");

jb.setURL("jdbc:oracle:thin:@127.0.0.1:1521:ORCL");
       jb.addJDBCListener(jdbcListener);
    }catch(ClassNotFoundException
cnf){cnf.printStackTrace();}
    catch(IOException ioe){ioe.printStackTrace();}

    jb.setTableName(deviceName);
    jb.setColumnNames(columnNames);
    jb.readTable(null);

    int i = 0;

    while(!(jdbcListener.resultAvailable()) && i < 10){
      try{
        Thread.sleep(1000);
        i++;
      }catch(InterruptedException ie){}
    }

    if(!jdbcListener.resultAvailable()){
      return null;
    }

    columnNames = jdbcListener.getColumnNames();
    columnValues = jdbcListener.getColumnValues();
```

```
        String result = "";

        result += columnNames.size() + ",";

        for(i = 0; i < columnNames.size(); i++){
          result += columnNames.elementAt(i) + ",";
        }

        for(i = 0; i < columnValues.size() - 1; i++){
          result += columnValues.elementAt(i) + ",";
        }

        result += columnValues.elementAt(i);

        return result;
      }
    }

public class ConfigServer{
  public static void main(String args[]){
    try{
      ORB orb = ORB.init(args, null);
      ConfigServant configObj = new ConfigServant();
      orb.connect(configObj);

      org.omg.CORBA.Object obj =
orb.resolve_initial_references("NameService");

      NamingContext ncObj = NamingContextHelper.narrow(obj);

      NameComponent nc = new NameComponent("PCConfig", "");
      NameComponent path[] = {nc};
      ncObj.rebind(path, configObj);

      System.out.println ("\nServer object registered\n");

      java.lang.Object sync = new java.lang.Object();
      synchronized(sync){
        sync.wait();
      }
    }catch(Exception e){
```

```
            System.err.println("ERROR: " + e);
            e.printStackTrace(System.out);
        }
    }
}
```

**Listing 12-6**
JDBCListener
implementation

**JDBCListenerImpl.java**

```
import java.util.*;

public class JDBCListenerImpl implements JDBCListener{
    private Vector columnNames, columnValues;
    private String error;
    private boolean result;

    public JDBCListenerImpl(){
        columnNames = columnValues = null;
        error = "";
    }

    public void result(JDBCEvent e){
        columnValues = e.getColumnValues();
        columnNames = e.getColumnNames();
        result = true;
    }

    public void error(JDBCEvent e){
        error = e.getErrorMessage();
        result = false;
    }

    public Vector getColumnNames(){
        return columnNames;
    }

    public Vector getColumnValues(){
        return columnValues;
    }

    public String getError(){
```

```
      result = false;
      return error;
  }

  public boolean resultAvailable(){
    return result;
  }
}
```

The complete source code for Listings 12-5 and 12-6 can be found under the *chap12\sample2* subdirectory on the CD-ROM. To compile this code, make sure you copy JDBCBean.jar from the *chap7\sample5* subdirectory to the directory where the source files are present, or ensure that the CLASSPATH points to the JDBCBean.jar. We'll use this CORBA service in Chapter 17 to develop an electronic commerce application.

# Summary

CORBA is very effective in helping developers create truly scalable distributed applications. However, its complexity has kept many developers away. The marriage of CORBA and JavaBean brings together the best of both worlds—the distributed programming nature of CORBA, and the ease of development in Java. In Chapter 17 we will show you how you can use the CORBA bean to create useful applications quite easily.

CHAPTER **13**

# Developing
# Enterprise
# JavaBean

# Introduction

This chapter assumes that the developer has already read Chapter 3 or has previous knowledge of Enterprise JavaBeans (EJB). In this chapter we'll concentrate on developing Enterprise JavaBeans. To keep things simple we'll develop Entity beans with container managed persistence. Entity beans usually represent persistent storage of data, commonly in a database or another form of persistent storage.

The Entity beans that we'll develop in this chapter will use the Oracle database that we already installed in Chapter 7. We'll also use a server that supports Enterprise JavaBeans called EJBHome server. This chapter is written around the .4 release of EJBHome. If you need to get the server, the new .5 release—called HomeBase—is freely available at *http://www.ejbhome.com*. If you use HomeBase, refer to Appendix D for code changes needed for deployment.

In this chapter we'll go through the development process as we develop the code. Where necessary, we will give detailed explanations. We'll develop two EJBs in this chapter whose functionality is the same. One EJB will access the Privilege table in a database and create some entries. The other EJB will access the ProjectTracker table in the same database and obtain entries, depending on the user's privileges.

# Downloading and Installing EJBHome Server

You can download the latest EJBHome server from *http://www.ejbhome.com*. Unzip the contents and extract them into the drive root directory, say *C:\*. Once you have unzipped the contents make sure to modify your CLASSPATH to include ejbhome.jar. This file is present under the *lib* subdirectory of the EJB Server root directory, which may be *C:\EJBHome-0.4.0*. So your CLASSPATH may have another entry that looks like *C:\EJBHome-0.4.0\lib\ejbhome.jar*. That's pretty much it. The installation is complete. In later sections of this chapter we'll learn how to start the server and how to use the built-in tools to generate the Container classes.

**NOTE**

As of this writing, EJBHome Server does not support JDK 1.2. Make sure, whenever you use Java or the Javac command with EJBHome server, that you use JDK 1.1.x and have CLASSPATH pointing to core java classes that belong to JDK 1.1.x.

# Developing the Privilege EJB

The Privilege bean will access the Privilege table in the database to create some entries. It will also find the privilege level of the specified user. The Privilege table in our database will have the properties shown in Table 13-1. This particular bean can be used in your applications wherever you need to create a table with a first column of type Varchar(32) and second column of type number. We'll use this bean to store names and privilege levels. But you can reuse it to store book names and prices or component names and stock availability, and so on.

**Table 13-1**

Privilege Table

| Name | PrivilegeLevel |
|---|---|
| Varchar(32) | Number |

**NOTE**

Name should be a primary key.

## The Remote Interface

Every EJB should have a remote interface that extends *EJBObject*. The Remote interface defines all the business methods (businesss methods are high level methods containing business logic) that the client can call. The client will see this remote interface only. Any method in the remote interface called by the client will execute the actual implementation on the server.

Our remote interface will have just one public method, called *getPrivilegeLevel()*, which will return the privilege level of the specified user. The complete code for the remote interface is shown in Listing 13-1.

**Listing 13-1**

Remote interface for Privilege bean

```
Privilege.java
package sample1;

import javax.ejb.*;
import java.rmi.*;
```

```
public interface Privilege extends EJBObject{
   int getPrivilegeLevel() throws RemoteException;
}
```

**NOTE**

All remote interfaces must follow the rules of RMI (Remote Method Invocation). This means that all the methods must throw *RemoteException* and the arguments to the method or the method's return type must be *Serializable,* so that they can be passed over the wire.

## The Home Interface

Every EJB Component has a home interface, which is a contract between the EJB Component class and the container. The home interface describes the life-cycle of a bean such as construction, destruction, and lookup of EJB instances. Every home interface should extend *EJBHome.* A home interface may define create and finder. Since currently there are no specifications for the interface between the EJB Server and the container, vendor tools are responsible for providing the container that implements the home interface and for returning the home object (that implements the interface) to the client. Our home interface for the Privilege bean is shown in Listing 13-2.

**Listing 13-2**
Home interface for Privilege bean

**PrivilegeHome.java**

```
package sample1;

import javax.ejb.*;
import java.rmi.*;

public interface PrivilegeHome extends EJBHome{
   Privilege create(String name, int privilegeLevel)
throws CreateException, RemoteException;
   Privilege findByPrimaryKey(PrivilegePKey name) throws
FinderException, RemoteException;
}
```

Our home interface has a *create()* method that takes a string and an integer as parameters. Method *findByPrimaryKey()* will extract a particular row from the database that matches the input parameter that has the primary key. It returns this row to the client.

**NOTE**

Apart from throwing *RemoteException*, every *create* method should throw *CreateException* and every *finder* method should throw *FinderException*.

## Developing the Enterprise Bean Component

An Enterprise Bean Component, which is also known as a bean component, provides the implementation for the business methods that the client can call. Let's look at some of the code snippets that comprise an Entity bean.

```
public class PrivilegeBean implements EntityBean{
```

Every bean component must either implement *EntityBean* or *SessionBean*, depending on the type of the bean. Since we are creating Entity bean components, our component implements *EntityBean*.

Every *create()* method in the home interface must have a corresponding *ejbCreate()* method with matching arguments defined in the bean component.

```
public void ejbCreate(String name, int privilegeLevel){
  this.privilegeLevel = privilegeLevel;
  this.name = name;
}
```

Our home interface just had one create method, and its corresponding *ejbCreate()* is shown above.

```
public int getPrivilegeLevel(){
  return privilegeLevel;
}
```

A bean component is also responsible for providing business implementations. Our remote interface had just one business method (*getPrivilegeLevel()*). This method's implementation is shown above.

Any other methods that are needed to satisfy the interface must be defined in the component. Most of these methods are dummies for our purposes.

Complete code for the bean component is shown in Listing 13-3.

**Listing 13-3**
Privilege bean component

**PrivilegeBean.java**

```
package sample1;

import javax.ejb.*;
import java.rmi.*;

public class PrivilegeBean implements EntityBean{
   public int privilegeLevel;
   public String name;
   protected EntityContext ectx;

   public void ejbCreate(String name, int
privilegeLevel){
      this.privilegeLevel = privilegeLevel;
      this.name = name;
   }

   public int getPrivilegeLevel(){
      return privilegeLevel;
   }

   public void setEntityContext(EntityContext ectx)
throws RemoteException{
      this.ectx = ectx;
   }

   public void unsetEntityContext() throws
RemoteException{
      this.ectx = null;
   }

   public void ejbRemove() throws RemoteException,
```

```
RemoteException{
    }

    public void ejbActivate() throws RemoteException{
    }

    public void ejbPassivate() throws RemoteException{
    }

    public void ejbLoad() throws RemoteException{
    }

    public void ejbStore() throws RemoteException{
    }
}
```

## The Primary Key Class

The primary key is a unique identifier that represents a row in a table. All container-managed EJB components must have a primary key class that is serializable, so all primary key classes must implement serializable. The primary key class includes public fields from the set of container-managed fields. In our example, a primary key in the table is Name. So we create a class that implements serializable and wraps the name field. The complete code for our primary key class is shown in Listing 13-4.

**Listing 13-4**
Primary key class for
Privilege bean

**PrivilegePKey.java**

```
package sample1;

import java.io.*;

public class PrivilegePKey implements Serializable{
    public String name;

    public PrivilegePKey(){
    }

    public PrivilegePKey(String name){
```

```
    this.name = name;
  }
}
```

The complete source code for this example can be found under the *chap13\sample1* subdirectory on the CD-ROM. You'll have to copy all the source code, except PrivilegeTest.java, onto your local drive to a subdirectory. You must copy the source code to a subdirectory called *sample1*. Here we'll assume that you copied it to *C:\chap13\sample1*. Include *C:\chap13\* in your CLASSPATH and compile the source files. You should not get any errors if your CLASSPATH is properly configured. Finally, create two files named privilege.properties and environment, as shown in Listings 13-5 and 13-6.

**Listing 13-5**
Properties file for Privilege bean

**privilege.properties**

```
name=sample1.Privilege
type=entity
primaryKeyClass=sample1.PrivilegePKey
containerManagedFields=name,privilegeLevel
environment=environment
transactionAttribute=TX_SUPPORTS
```

**Listing 13-6**
Environment settings file for Privilege bean

**environment**

```
dataSourceName=jdbc/PrivilegeDB
databaseUser=admin
databasePassword=admin
```

These two files can also be found under the *chap13\sample1* subdirectory in the CD-ROM. If you haven't already done so, copy these files to *C:\chap13\sample1*. Now change your directory to *C:\chap13\sample1*, and enter the following command:

**java com.ejbhome.Generator -f**
**sample1\privilege.properties**

A number of files will be generated under *C:\chap13\sample1.* These are the container classes, which comprise the contracts between the container and the server. We won't go into the details of these files. Remember that these files are proprietary to the EJBHome server. These file may vary depending on the type of server you use.

Before running the server to test the EJB we just developed, we need to write a client program. This is covered in the following section.

## Developing a Client to Test Privilege EJB

In this section we'll develop a client to test our Privilege EJB. The client will create a few entries in the database. It will also query the database based on the primary key and extract the result. This code is very simple. Some of the important snippets are discussed below.

```
Properties env = new Properties();
env.put("java.naming.factory.initial",
"com.ejbhome.naming.spi.rmi.RMIInitCtxFactory");
Context ctx = new InitialContext(env);

PrivilegeHome home =
(PrivilegeHome)ctx.lookup("Privilege");
```

The client will have to access the home object using JNDI placed in the naming service.

```
home.create("user1", 0);
```

Every create statement executed by the client will create an entry in the database. The create called by the client should match what was already declared in the home interface, which in our case is *PrivilegeHome.* Our create takes a string parameter and an integer parameter.

```
Privilege p = home.findByPrimaryKey(new
PrivilegePKey(args[0]));
```

Method *findByPrimaryKey()* will return a remote interface object, on which business methods can be called.

```
System.out.println("Privilege level for " + args[0] + "
: " + p.getPrivilegeLevel());
```

Method *getPrivilegeLevel()* will return the privilege level for the specified primary key.

Listing 13-7 shows the complete source listing for the client.

**Listing 13-7**

Client for testing
Privilege bean

**PrivilegeTest.java**

```
import sample1.*;
import java.util.Properties;
import javax.naming.*;

public class PrivilegeTest{

  public static void main(String[] args) throws
Exception{

      Properties env = new Properties();
      env.put("java.naming.factory.initial",
"com.ejbhome.naming.spi.rmi.RMIInitCtxFactory");
      Context ctx = new InitialContext(env);

      PrivilegeHome home =
(PrivilegeHome)ctx.lookup("Privilege");

      home.create("user1", 0);
      home.create("user2", 1);
      home.create("user3", 2);
      home.create("user4", 0);

      Privilege p = home.findByPrimaryKey(new
PrivilegePKey(args[0]));

      System.out.println("Privilege level for " + args[0]
+ " : " + p.getPrivilegeLevel());
  }
}
```

The source code can be found under the chap13\sample1 subdirectory on the CD-ROM. Copy this file onto your local hard drive and make sure your CLASSPATH is pointing to C:\chap13. Any pointers related to C:\chap13 should be removed. Also, you'll need to change your current directory to C:\chap13 in order to compile the source code.

## Testing the Privilege EJB

Here are the steps to follow to test the Privilege EJB. Make sure the table named Privilege has been created in the database. Also, make sure that your JDBC Drivers and C:\chap13\sample1 are in the CLASSPATH.

1. Copy the subdirectory named conf and logs, along with all the files under it, to C:\chap13.
2. Open the datasource.properties file. Make changes if necessary to the JDBC URL. We assume that the Oracle database is on the local machine.
3. Change your directory to C:\chap13.
4. Make sure your CLASSPATH includes C:\chap13\sample1. Anything else related to chap13 in CLASSPATH should be removed.
5. On the command line type start java com.ejbhome.EJBServer.
6. Your server should begin listening on port 9999.

Make changes to your CLASSPATH so that it points to C:\chap13. Anything else related to chap13 in CLASSPATH should be removed. You can now run your client by typing:

```
java PrivilegeTest user1
```

Your output should be

```
Privilege level for user1: 0
```

**NOTE**

If you open your database and explore the Privilege table, you should see three entries created there.

You can also use the browser and type 127.0.0.1:9999 to administer EJBHome server.

# Developing ProjectTracker EJB

The Project Tracker bean will access the ProjectTracker table in the database to obtain table entries depending on the Privilege level. Our database will have the ProjectTracker table with the properties shown in Table 13-2.

**Table 13-2**

ProjectTracker
Table

| PrivilegeLevel | ProjectInfo |
| --- | --- |
| Number | Varchar(32) |

**NOTE**

PrivilegeLevel should be a primary key.

ProjectTracker EJB is similar to Privilege EJB except that there are no create methods in ProjectTracker EJB, which means that the entries in the database must exist already. For this reason, let's create some table entries as shown in Table 13-3.

**Table 13-3**

ProjectTracker
Table populated
with entries

| PrivilegeLevel | ProjectInfo |
| --- | --- |
| 0 | This is level 0 string |
| 1 | This is level 1 string |
| 2 | This is level 2 string |

Most of the code for this sample is in the Privilege EJB, so we won't bother to explain the code in detail here.

## The Remote Interface

Listing 13-8 contains the complete source code for the remote interface for the ProjectTracker bean.

**Listing 13-8**
Remote interface for
ProjectTracker bean

**ProjectTracker.java**

```
package sample2;

import javax.ejb.*;
import java.rmi.*;
```

```
public interface ProjectTracker extends EJBObject{
   String getProjectInfo() throws RemoteException;
}
```

## The Home Interface

The complete code for the home interface is shown in Listing 13-9.

**Listing 13-9**
Home interface for
ProjectTracker bean

**ProjectTracker.java**

```
package sample2;

import javax.ejb.*;
import java.rmi.*;

public interface ProjectTrackerHome extends EJBHome{
   ProjectTracker findByPrimaryKey(ProjectTrackerPKey
privilegeLevel) throws FinderException, RemoteException;
}
```

## The Enterprise Bean Component

The complete code for the bean component is shown in Listing 13-10.

**Listing 13-10**
ProjectTracker bean
component

**ProjectTrackerBean.java**

```
package sample2;

import javax.ejb.*;
import java.rmi.*;

public class ProjectTrackerBean implements EntityBean{
   public String projectInfo;
   public int privilegeLevel;
   EntityContext ectx;
```

```
   public String getProjectInfo(){
     return projectInfo;
   }

   public void setEntityContext(EntityContext ectx)
throws RemoteException{
      this.ectx = ectx;
   }

   public void unsetEntityContext() throws
RemoteException{
      this.ectx = null;
   }

   public void ejbRemove() throws RemoteException,
RemoveException{
   }

   public void ejbActivate() throws RemoteException{
   }

   public void ejbPassivate() throws RemoteException{
   }

   public void ejbLoad() throws RemoteException{
   }

   public void ejbStore() throws RemoteException{
   }
}
```

## The Primary Key Class

The complete source code for the primary key class is shown in Listing 13-11.

**Listing 13-11**
Primary sey class for
ProjectTracker bean

**ProjectTrackerPKey.java**

```
package sample2;

import java.io.*;
```

```
public class ProjectTrackerPKey implements Serializable{
  public int privilegeLevel;

  public ProjectTrackerPKey(){
  }

  public ProjectTrackerPKey(int privilegeLevel){
    this.privilegeLevel = privilegeLevel;
  }
}
```

Complete source code for the ProjectTracker EJB can be found under the *chap13\sample2* subdirectory on the CD-ROM. Copy the complete code, except ProjectTrackerTest.java, into your local hard drive. Change the CLASSPATH to include *C:\chap13*. Once all the sources compile, copy the *ptracker.properties* and environment files to *C:\chap13\sample2*, change the CLASSPATH to include *C:\chap13\sample2*, and execute the command shown here:

**java com.ejbhome.Generator -f ptracker.properties**

## Creating a Client to Test the Privilege EJB

Copy ProjectTrackerTest.java from the *chap13\sample2* subdirectory to your local drive and compile the file. Your CLASSPATH should point to *C:\chap13* and anything else related to *C:\chap13* should be removed. Change the current directory to *C:\chap13* to compile the source code. A complete listing for the ProjectTrackerTest is shown in Listing 13-12.

■ ■ ■ ■ ■ ■
**Listing 13-12**
Client for testing
ProjectTracker bean

**ProjectTrackerTest.java**

```
import java.util.Properties;
import javax.naming.*;
import sample2.*;

public class ProjectTrackerTest {
```

```
    public static void main(String[] args) throws
Exception {

    Properties env = new Properties();
    env.put("java.naming.factory.initial",
"com.ejbhome.naming.spi.rmi.RMIInitCtxFactory");
    Context ctx = new InitialContext(env);

    ProjectTrackerHome home =
(ProjectTrackerHome)ctx.lookup("ProjectTracker");

    ProjectTracker p = home.findByPrimaryKey(new
ProjectTrackerPKey(0));
    System.out.println(p.getProjectInfo());
  }
}
```

To run the server, follow the steps described in the section "Testing Privilege EJB," earlier in the chapter. Make sure your CLASSPATH contains JDBC drivers and C:\chap13\sample2. Anything else related to chap13 in the CLASSPATH should be removed. Once the server is up and running, change CLASSPATH to reflect C:\chap13. Again, anything else related to chap13 in the CLASSPATH should be removed. You should get the following output:

```
This is level 0 string
```

# Summary

In this chapter we learned about simple Enterprise JavaBeans in general, and about Entity Beans in particular. We suggest you go through the EJB specifications for a more thorough understanding of EJB. In Chapter 18, we will reuse these EJB components to build a project tracking system.

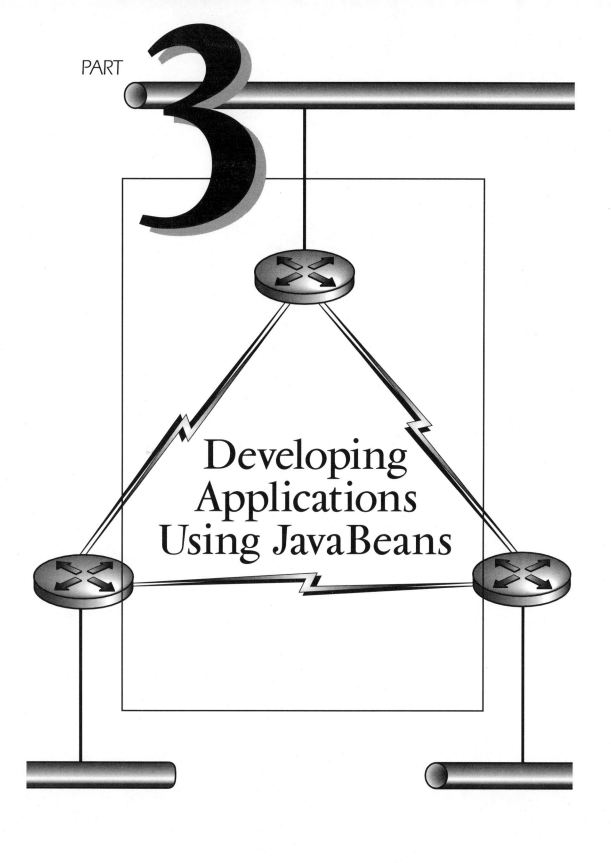

PART

3

Developing
Applications
Using JavaBeans

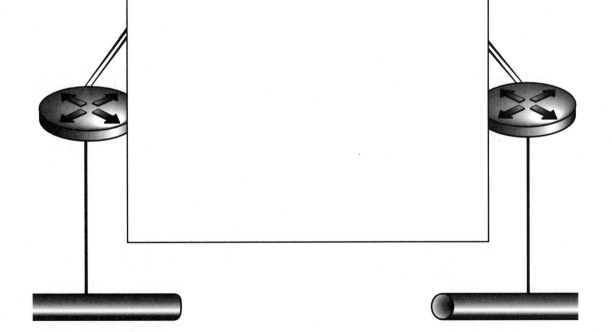

# CHAPTER 14

# Enterprise
# Internet
# Applications

# Introduction

Enterprise Internet applications can generally be categorized as intranet, extranet, or electronic commerce. An intranet is a mini-Internet within a corporation that is protected from the rest of the Internet by a firewall. Originally, intranets were conceived of as a tool for sharing information among departments, but they have since evolved into much more powerful applications and provide groupware applications that foster communication, collaboration, and coordination within a company. An extranet, in its simplest form, is a natural extension of an intranet to a company's customers, partners, and suppliers.

Electronic commerce consists of two types of applications: consumer Internet commerce applications and business-to-business electronic commerce applications. The two types of electronic commerce applications have much in common. They both need to provide an easy-to-navigate interface, personalized service, and security. However, there are still some fundamental differences between them. The biggest difference is probably the payment method. Consumers usually pay by a credit card number, so consumer electronic commerce applications usually need to deal with credit card processing, while the payment method between two companies is usually arranged by those two particular parties, and credit card–style payment is uncommon. In addition, business-to-business electronic commerce systems are usually associated with the companies' extranet. While extranet or business-to-business electronic commerce does not individually provide all the services that are needed for business-to-business communication, together they do.

In this chapter, we will provide some background on these types of Internet applications and also discuss some of the reasons why Java is the right choice for many of these applications.

# Intranet

Intranets were probably one of the first enterprise Internet applications. They were originally viewed as a tool to share documents within a corporation. With an intranet, engineering teams are able to publish their design documents and collaborate on large projects. Salespeople are able to tap into the corporate database and find out pricing information in real-time.

Intranets have gradually evolved into full service groupware applications that provide directory, email, and collaborative functions to a corporation. One of the distinctions between traditional document sharing and a groupware application is that in a groupware application, a user has many ways to instantly inform others what he or she has done about the information. For example, the user may reply to an email message, post a response to a newsgroup, or fill out a form online and submit it.

An intranet is an example of how technology changes business processes. Before the advent of intranets, only large corporations with the wherewithal to implement proprietary groupware applications were able to share some degree of information among different departments. For most corporations, employees are separated by virtual walls between departments, with very little horizontal communication. Intranets have provided an inexpensive means for cross-functional teams to collaborate and collectively bring about solutions. They have torn down the walls that obstruct information flow between departments and have become a must-have for corporations to maintain their competitiveness.

Figure 14-1 shows some of the functions within an intranet.

**Figure 14-1**

Some of the functionality of an intranet

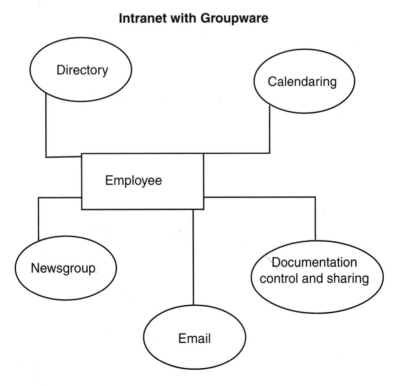

**Intranet with Groupware**

Most intranet applications are fairly simple compared to their Internet commerce peers. They usually involve a Web server and perhaps some CGI applications to take in user input. The CGI applications often interact with existing corporate databases.

Of course, for larger organizations, some of the emerging intranet applications may require a significant amount of effort in their preparation and implementation. For example, single-sign-on applications are becoming popular in large corporations. These applications allow an employee to have one single password for multiple databases. However, implementation of a single-sign-on application often involves building a public-key infrastructure.

# Consumer Electronic Commerce

Consumer electronic commerce applications need to provide personalized service. For example, they need to remember what customers bought the last time, their addresses, and so on, so that customers don't have to input this information repeatedly. The applications also need to be able to handle hundreds of thousands of users simultaneously. The most intriguing issue that a consumer electronic commerce application has to deal with, however, is the issue of credit card numbers.

Credit cards are the choice of payment on the Internet, although consumers are generally very nervous about protecting their credit card numbers from potential fraud. That is why Internet commerce sites use secure connections such as Secure Socket Layer (SSL) to transmit credit card numbers. However, the secure transfer of credit card numbers from consumers' computers to merchants is only a part of the story. What happens after the merchant receives the credit card number is actually quite complex.

## Credit Card Transactions

If a merchant wants to accept a credit card as a form of payment, it is usually associated with a bank that deals with credit card–related issues on the merchant's behalf. This bank is called the merchant's acquiring bank. On the other hand, credit cards such as Visa or MasterCard are issued by the consumer's issuing bank.

When the merchant receives a credit card number from a consumer, it needs to find out if the card has enough credit for the current purchase. Such an operation is called authorization. Once the card is authorized and the products or services are delivered, the money is transferred to the merchant's account. The transfer operation is called settlement.

The merchant passes an authorization request to its acquiring bank, which in turn passes it to the issuing bank through an interchange network operated by credit card operators such as Visa or MasterCard. If the issuing bank approves the transaction, the response is passed back to the merchant and the service or products will be delivered to the consumer. The credit card transaction is settled at a later time (for example, at the time of the shipment). Figure 14-2 shows the process.

**Figure 14-2**

Typical processing of a credit card payment

**Credit Card Transaction**

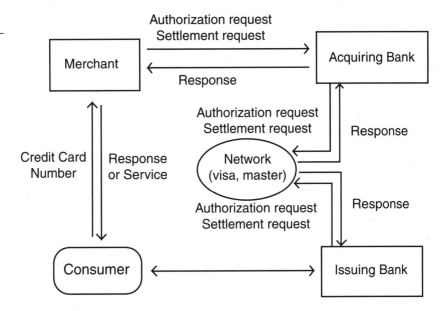

## Secure Consumer Electronic Commerce Systems

The current Internet credit card payment system has a serious security weakness, namely the database that stores all these credit card numbers. For one thing, if the database were accessed illegally by an intruder or a disgruntled employee, major credit card fraud could occur. In addition, a database with this type of sensitive information opens the door for unscrupulous merchants to make illegal charges on them.

There are several protocols and commercial systems available today that address these security problems. Their architectures are quite similar, as Figure 14-3 shows.

**Figure 14-3**
Secure ECommerce

**Electronic Commerce**

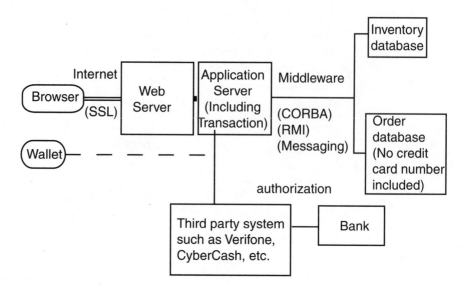

A *wallet*, which is installed on the customer's computer, encrypts credit card numbers. The encrypted credit card number is then passed from the vendor to a third-party system, such as CyberCash or Verifone. The third-party system decrypts the credit card number and passes it to the bank for authorization, and the result is passed back to the vendor. The vendor still has the order database, and perhaps the encrypted credit card number. However the vendor is not able to obtain the real credit card number.

One of the major protocols for Internet electronic commerce is SET, or Secure Electronic Transaction. SET is a group of protocols developed by Visa and MasterCard that has gained wide industry support from corporations such as HP, IBM, and Microsoft. SET installs the wallet as a helper application to a browser, and uses a gateway to process and decrypt the credit card submissions performed by the wallet.

JavaSoft has released its own wallet under the Java Commerce initiative, which also includes support for smart card. The Java solution has the advantage of multiple protocol support and easy downloading and installation. The wallet is made of Java beans that are downloadable. This represents an advantage of the Java wallet over other types of systems since no special software installation is needed.

Despite their advantages, secure consumer electronic commerce systems have attracted little following among consumers. Even SET, the protocol that has strong backing from both the financial industry and the computer industry, seems to have lost its momentum in the marketplace. The reason may lie in the fact that financial institutions such as Visa or MasterCard and online merchants would benefit the most from these systems, not consumers.

## Other Chores

Credit card processing is only one area of doing business online. A consumer electronic commerce application needs to deal with other chores of being an online Internet store. These chores include the following.

### Transaction

The system should maintain the transaction's ACID (Atomicity, Consistency, Isolation, and Durability) property for each customer's order. Even in the case of a system or network crash, the customer should not be billed for a product that is not shipped, and the merchant should not ship a product without billing it to a customer.

### Logging

Orders and invoices must be logged, along with customer's information such as addresses and advertisement information. The application also needs to deal with shipping, calculating shipping charges, generating a receipt, and similar record-keeping tasks.

## Extranet and Business-to-Business Electronic Commerce

Believe it or not, both extranet and business-to-business electronic commerce existed before the Internet became popular. The companies that pioneered those systems are the stalwarts of American industry today, including Wal-Mart and General Electric.

## The Wal-Mart Story

Wal-Mart started out building retail stores in rural areas that were poorly serviced by retail chains at the time. It has since surpassed Sears as the largest retail chain in America. There is a long list of factors in Wal-Mart's success. Its information technology should rank quite high on that list.

To ensure quality services to its customers, Wal-Mart opened up its internal databases to its key suppliers so that the suppliers knew firsthand how their products fared on the market, and thus could plan to ramp up production accordingly, without even seeing orders from Wal-Mart first.

Such an act was revolutionary at the time, because for a long time corporations saw their suppliers as quasi-enemies that they should constantly squeeze prices from, rather than as trusted business partners. But Wal-Mart's success has demonstrated the value of sharing and working together with partners, and it has facilitated the cultural shift to extranets in the last two years.

The network connection between Wal-Mart and its partners was through a private network linked by satellite, and the business-to-business transactions were placed under the Electronic Data Interchange protocol.

## Electronic Data Interchange

Electronic Data Interchange, or EDI, is the electronic exchange of business information in a standard format. It has been in existence for about twenty years and has produced considerable savings in the cost of doing business for large corporations.

Business transactions between two companies usually involve a few phases, including sending catalogs, placing orders, checking order status, invoicing, and generating receipts. These transactions involve a large number of phone calls, faxes, and printed paper. In addition, mistakes can often occur because of human error or confusion between different form formats between companies.

EDI was designed to use computers to perform these transactions, thus eliminating the costs associated with phone calls and printed paper, as well as the human errors and time associated with redundant data entry. General Electric Information Service, for example, has developed an EDI system for its vendors and suppliers to better manage the procurement process, and has achieved substantial savings in time and cost.

EDI does have one drawback—namely, its cost. That is because it runs on private networks, called Value Added Networks, that are usually leased lines. The high cost associated with EDI represents a high barrier of entry into EDI systems, and smaller vendors who cannot afford EDI are automatically excluded from becoming suppliers of companies who do business using EDI.

## Doing Business on the Internet

Because of the high costs associated with Wal-Mart–style private networks and EDI, businesses are gradually moving these networks toward the Internet. The result is the rapid development of extranet and Internet business-to-business electronic commerce.

Secure transmission, the biggest advantage of private networks, has been matched by the Internet because of recent advancements in a technology called Virtual Private Network (VPN). VPN systems carve out a chunk of Internet bandwidth for a corporation and securely transmit those messages as if they were on a private leased line. These messages are encrypted to ensure privacy.

GE Information Systems, for example, expanded their EDI system to the Internet and can now reach all 25,000 of their suppliers. In addition to business transactions, the system also takes bids for commodities that GE purchases. GE recently announced that it has reached $1 billion worth of annual trading transactions on its Internet EDI system.

Business-to-business Internet commerce and extranet systems are probably the most complex Internet applications. Not only do they deal with many of the issues associated with intranet and consumer Internet commerce applications, they also need to deal with security issues such as VPN, firewalls, secure segregation of partner data, and legacy systems (such as EDI).

## Why Java?

Most of today's Internet applications are written in languages other than Java. The platforms range from Microsoft Transaction Server to Netscape Application Server. The languages used are mostly C and C++. The existing platforms and languages do the job well, so why use Java?

Java is the best choice because Java represents the next generation in technology. Java will replace C and C++, just like C replaced COBOL in many areas. In this section, we will present some reasons for using Java to develop Internet applications. They are by no means scientific studies, but rather passionate arguments from our own experiences.

# Arguments Against Java

Let's first examine some of the biggest arguments against Java.

## Write Once, Debug Everywhere

Java comes with the promise of being able to "Write Once, Run Anywhere." That promise has not been realized in many places—mostly on the client-side, where graphic displays vary from platform to platform. The situation is better on the server-side since there is no graphical user display involved. However, because JavaSoft only lists specifications for most technologies, vendors' different implementations may create compatibility problems. For example, different JDBC drivers may behave differently on certain method invocations. Thus Java obtained another label along the way—"write once, debug everywhere."

But Java still represents a giant step toward a uniform platform when it is compared to C. There are many thousand-line Java programs that run flawlessly on both NT and UNIX. Even when some tweaking is needed, the effort is often trivial when compared to the effort required to make C programs run on different platforms. Many of the incompatibilities arise because of Java's immaturity. As SUN and other Java platform vendors learn more about those incompatibilities, we expect less and less debugging to be necessary, especially in basic functionality.

## Java Is Slow

Yes and no. Our experiences show that Java is noticeably slower than C or C++ programs at this time. But C was noticeably slower than assembly languages when it was first introduced. Distributed applications were noticeably slower than monolithic ones for a long time. Even relational databases were deemed slow at one time. However, these initially "slower" technologies eventually have become dominant in the industry because they represent a significant value for customers and developers. Java, by all accounts, is just such a next-generation technology.

# Arguments for Java

A strong reason to use Java is that it is a good language. It forces programmers to make object-oriented designs. Its many features prevent programmers from making mundane mistakes. Our experiences show that writing large applications in Java takes significantly less time than in C, and Java's pure object-orientedness often prevents applications from breaking in future extensions.

Java is also ideally suited for component-style programming. Its security features make it easier for enterprises to deploy third-party modules, and the language design makes it much easier to achieve fault isolation. Coupled with Java's promise of "Write Once, Run Anywhere," Java is on the verge of creating a true, robust, third-party component market.

We believe that Java, despite its immaturity, represents the future of computing. It will leave the C/C++/Client-server paradigm that we are familiar with behind, and create a new paradigm that we are just beginning to envision. SUN's Jini may be an indication of what lies ahead. (See Chapter 3 for a more detailed description of Jini.)

# Summary

The rest of this book presents a few examples of Internet Java applications. They are by no means complete. Our intention is to demonstrate how cross-platform enterprise applications can be built in Java.

# CHAPTER 15

# Email
# Application

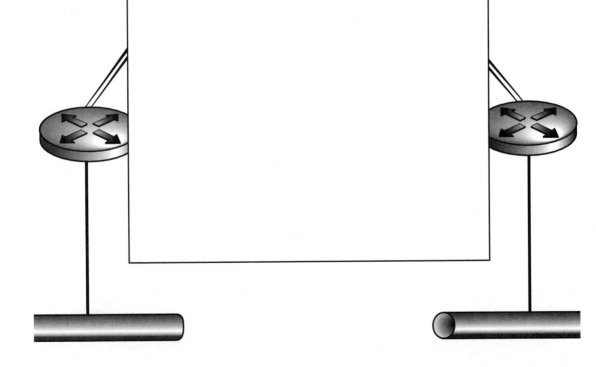

In this chapter we'll develop an email application using JavaStudio 1.0 and the JavaBeans we developed in Chapter 6. We'll learn how to develop two email client applications; one sends an email message, and the other receives and displays it. We'll also see how to use a third-party bean. We'll use a printer JavaBean developed by WildCrest to add printing capability to our application.

# Developing an Email Client to Send Email Messages

To develop this application, let's use the *SendMailBean* we developed in Chapter 6. Since we'll be using Java Studio to wire the components to develop the application, we must first wrap *SendMailBean* into a Java Studio component class. We learned in Chapter 5 how to wrap a JavaBean into a Java Studio component, so we won't be dealing with that in detail here. For more information you may want to refer to Chapter 5.

## Converting SendEmailBean to VJSendEmail

The *VJSendEmail* component will have the input connectors to accept the following information:

- To: address
- From: address
- Cc: address
- Bcc: address
- Subject title
- Body of the message
- Connector that will send email

The only output connector VJSendEmail component we'll have is the one that displays status messages. Here's the complete listing of *VJEmailBean* component:

**VJSendEmail.java**

```java
import com.sun.jpropub.vj.vjcomp.*;
import com.sun.jpropub.vj.vjcomp.util.*;
import java.lang.reflect.*;

public class VJSendEmail extends VJComponent implements
EmailListener{
  VJBoundPort messagePort, toPort, fromPort, ccPort,
bccPort, subjectPort, bodyPort, sendPort;

  public VJSendEmail(){
    super();
  }

  public void VJComponentInit(String nm){
    SendEmailBean eb = new SendEmailBean();
    StringToBasicOutputTransfer stringOut = new
StringToBasicOutputTransfer();
    BasicToStringInputTransfer stringIn = new
BasicToStringInputTransfer();
    ObjectInputTransfer objectIn = new
ObjectInputTransfer();

    Class emailClass = eb.getClass();
    Class myClass = this.getClass();

    try{
      Class outargs[] = {Class.forName("EmailEvent")};
      Class inargs[] =
{Class.forName("java.lang.String")};
      Method outMethod1 =
myClass.getMethod("emailBeanMessage", outargs);

      Method inMethod1 =
emailClass.getMethod("setFromAddress", inargs);
      Method inMethod2 =
emailClass.getMethod("setToAddress", inargs);
      Method inMethod3 =
emailClass.getMethod("setCcAddress", inargs);
      Method inMethod4 =
emailClass.getMethod("setBccAddress", inargs);
      Method inMethod5 =
```

```
emailClass.getMethod("setSubject", inargs);
     Method inMethod6 =
emailClass.getMethod("setMessage", inargs);
     Method inMethod7 = emailClass.getMethod("send",
inargs);

     messagePort = new VJBoundPort(this, outMethod1,
stringOut);

     fromPort = new VJBoundPort(this, inMethod1,
stringIn);
     toPort = new VJBoundPort(this, inMethod2,
stringIn);
     ccPort = new VJBoundPort(this, inMethod3,
stringIn);
     bccPort = new VJBoundPort(this, inMethod4,
stringIn);
     subjectPort = new VJBoundPort(this, inMethod5,
stringIn);
     bodyPort = new VJBoundPort(this, inMethod6,
stringIn);
     sendPort = new VJBoundPort(this, inMethod7,
stringIn);

     VJPort[] connectorList = {(VJPort)messagePort,
(VJPort)fromPort, (VJPort) toPort, (VJPort)subjectPort,
(VJPort)ccPort, (VJPort)bccPort, (VJPort)bodyPort,
(VJPort)sendPort};
     super.VJComponentInit((Object)eb, connectorList);
     eb.addEmailListener(this);

   }catch(Exception e){System.out.println(e.getMessage());
e.printStackTrace();}
  }

  public void emailBeanMessage(EmailEvent e){
    try{
      messagePort.sendMessage(e.getEventMessage());
    }catch(Exception
e1){System.out.println(e1.getMessage());}
  }
}
```

The *VJSendEmail* component implements *EmailListener* and outputs messages to the output connector whenever *SendEmailBean* fires an event. From the code you can also figure out how the input connectors and output connectors are hooked to the *SendEmailBean* methods.

## Developing an Info Class for the Component

To give more meaning to the *VJSendEmail* component, we will write an *info* class as we did for the *VJBooleanButton* class in Chapter 5, sample 2.

Below is the listing for *VJSendEmail VJComponentInfo,* which provides component information for the *VJSendEmail* component. For more information you may want to refer to Chapter 5.

**Listing 15-2**
Code that provides more information about VJSendEmail

```
VJSendEmailVJComponentInfo.java

import com.sun.jpropub.vj.vjcomp.*;
import com.sun.jpropub.vj.vjcomp.util.*;
import java.lang.reflect.*;

public class VJSendEmailVJComponentInfo extends
SimpleVJComponentInfo{
  public VJComponentDescriptor getVJComponentDescriptor(){
    try{
      Class vjcompClass = Class.forName("VJSendEmail");
      Class enclClass = Class.forName("SendEmailBean");

      VJComponentDescriptor c = new
VJComponentDescriptor(vjcompClass, enclClass, null);

      c.setManufacturerName("Tester");
      c.setDisplayName("Send Email");
      c.setShortDescription("Emails text to intended
recipients");

      return c;
    }catch(Exception e){e.printStackTrace(); return
null;}
  }

  public VJPortDescriptor[] getVJPortDescriptors(){
```

```
try{
   Class vjcompClass = Class.forName("VJSendEmail");

   VJPortDescriptor o1Desc = new
VJPortDescriptor("Status", "Sends status or error
messages", VJPortDescriptor.OUT_ONLY,
VJPortDescriptor.EAST_CENTER, vjcompClass);

   VJPortDescriptor i1Desc = new
VJPortDescriptor("From", "From Address",
VJPortDescriptor.IN_ONLY, VJPortDescriptor.WEST_CENTER,
vjcompClass);
   VJPortDescriptor i2Desc = new
VJPortDescriptor("To", "To Address",
VJPortDescriptor.IN_ONLY, VJPortDescriptor.WEST_CENTER,
vjcompClass);
   VJPortDescriptor i3Desc = new
VJPortDescriptor("Subject", "Email Subject",
VJPortDescriptor.IN_ONLY, VJPortDescriptor.WEST_CENTER,
vjcompClass);
   VJPortDescriptor i4Desc = new
VJPortDescriptor("Cc", "Cc To",
VJPortDescriptor.IN_ONLY, VJPortDescriptor.WEST_CENTER,
vjcompClass);
   VJPortDescriptor i5Desc = new
VJPortDescriptor("BCc", "BCc To",
VJPortDescriptor.IN_ONLY, VJPortDescriptor.WEST_CENTER,
vjcompClass);
   VJPortDescriptor i6Desc = new
VJPortDescriptor("Email Body", "Body Text",
VJPortDescriptor.IN_ONLY, VJPortDescriptor.WEST_CENTER,
vjcompClass);
   VJPortDescriptor i7Desc = new
VJPortDescriptor("Send Email", "Sends email to intended
recipients", VJPortDescriptor.IN_ONLY,
VJPortDescriptor.WEST_CENTER, vjcompClass);

   VJPortDescriptor[] desc = {o1Desc, i1Desc, i2Desc,
i3Desc, i4Desc, i5Desc, i6Desc, i7Desc};

   return desc;
```

```
        }catch(Exception e1){e1.printStackTrace(); return
null;}
    }


}
```

The complete source code can be found under the *chap15/sample1* directory on the CD-ROM. You will need to compile all the java files and generate VJSendEmail.jar using the steps described in Chapter 5. Then you'll need to import this bean component into Java Studio's User folder. Then you'll be set to develop an email application that will email text information to the intended recipients.

## Developing Email Client to Send Text Messages

Email client will have textfield components for typing the recipient information, textarea components to type in the email body, and a button to send the email. We will also hook up a menu component that can be used, instead of the button, to send the email message.

Here are the steps to follow to create the Email application for sending email:

1. Start Java Studio if you don't have it running yet.
2. Select File->New to create a new project.
3. From the User folder, place the Send Email component in the design window.
4. Place a Menu component from the GUI folder in the GUI window.
5. Double-click the Menu component in the design window to open the customizer window for the Menu component.
6. Change Menu Name to File. We use File as the name as a Windows standard. We also need to add menu items to the main menu File. Add two Menu Items, called New Message and Send Message, by typing **New Message** in the Item field and clicking on Add. Follow similar steps to add Send Message. Then click on OK to close the customizer window. You have set up the menu, they are not functional as yet.
7. Place a textfield component in the GUI window and resize it as shown in Figure 15-1.

8. In the design window, select the textfield component and click the right mouse button. Then select Copy... from the floating menu. Then by right-clicking the mouse button again, Paste... four more components. We need to do this to ensure that the height and width of the components remain the same.

9. You can switch on the Layout->Show Grid and place the components. You may want to use Layout->Align to align the components neatly, as shown in Figure 15-1.

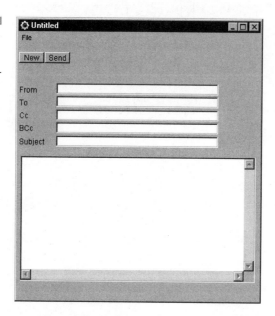

**Figure 15-1**
GUI for Send Email application

10. Name all the textfield components, as shown in Figure 15-2. All textfield components should have the Triggers that the component checkbox enabled. Except for the From address textfield, all the other textfield components should have the Clear textfield connector added. To do this, select the Connectors folder in the textfield Customizer window and check Clears text and Triggers the component as appropriate. Then click on OK.

11. Place a textarea component to type in the body of the message as shown in Figure 15-1. Open the customizer for this component and change the name to Body. Also, in the Connectors folder, check Clear text and Sends out text via output connector. Then click on OK.

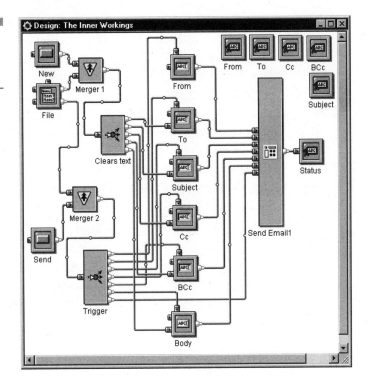

12. To display status, place a Label component at the bottom of the textarea. Name this label as Status. Delete the label text in the Label folder. Also, under the Connectors folder, check Sets the Label, then click on OK.

13. Add some more label components to name the textfields, as shown in Figure 15-1.

14. Place two buttons—one named New, and the other, Send. Place as shown in Figure 15-1. This is our Toolbar.

15. Hook up all the textfields and textarea to the respective connectors of the Email bean componen: for example, the output of the From textfield to the input connector of the Email bean that expects the From address.

16. Hook the menu item, New, we created earlier, and the button, New, to clear all the textfield and textarea. The New menu command and New button command are merged using a Merger component from the Data Flow window and given to a Distributor component, which will distribute the button or the menu command to all the textfields and textareas that have the Clear text connector at the input. Remember to customize the distributor to have the correct number of connectors as required.

17. Similarly, the Send button command and Send menu command need to be merged and distributed to trigger the components to the Send connector of the Email bean.

18. The output of the Email bean is connected to the Status label.

19. Set the SMTPHostName in your Email bean component Customizer window.

20. You are all set to test your Email application. In the GUI window type in the From address, To address, and Cc and Bcc addresses if needed. You can have multiple addresses for to, cc, and bcc; just separate them by a comma. Type in the subject and body. Click on Send.

21. You can save the application by choosing File->Save.

This email application is saved as "emailapp1.vj," which you'll find under the *chap15* subdirectory on the CD-ROM.

This is a very basic email application, and the basic concepts, whether building the application for basic or complex uses, remain the same. So, wasn't developing applications using Java Studio simple? The next time you want to use an email application to send a Hello to your friends, use the one developed by you.

In the next sections we will develop another application to view and print text-based emails.

# Developing an Email Client to Show Email Messages

In this section we will develop another email application that can view text-based email messages. To develop this application, use the *ShowMessageBean* we developed in Chapter 6. Since we'll be using Java Studio to wire the components to develop the application, we must first wrap ShowMessageBean into a Java Studio component class. Since we have done this exercise a couple of times, we won't go into the details of creating the Java Studio component again here.

## Converting ShowMessageBean to VJShowEmail

The *VJShowEmail* component will have the input connectors to accept the following information:

- Login Name
- Password
- Mailbox Name
- Connector that will get all message headers
- Connector that will get the body of the selected message

The *VJShowEmail* component will have the following output connectors:

- Connector that will output message header one at a time
- Connector that will output the body of the selected message

Listing 15-3 contains the code for VJShowEmail.java, which provides connectors and implements *ShowMessageBeanListener,* and VJShow-EmailVJComponent.java, which provides component information.

**Listing 15-3**
Code for
VJShowEmail and
VJShowEmailVJ-
ComponentInfo

**VJShowEmail.java**

```
import com.sun.jpropub.vj.vjcomp.*;
import com.sun.jpropub.vj.vjcomp.util.*;
import java.lang.reflect.*;

public class VJShowEmail extends VJComponent implements
ShowMessageBeanListener{
  VJBoundPort useridPort, passwordPort,
getAllHeaderPort, getMessageBodyPort, mailboxPort,
messageBodyPort, messageHeaderPort;

  public VJShowEmail(){
    super();
  }

  public void VJComponentInit(String nm){
    ShowMessageBean mb = new ShowMessageBean();
    StringToBasicOutputTransfer stringOut = new
StringToBasicOutputTransfer();
    BasicToStringInputTransfer stringIn = new
BasicToStringInputTransfer();
    ObjectInputTransfer objectIn = new
ObjectInputTransfer();

    Class emailClass = mb.getClass();
```

```
    Class myClass = this.getClass();

  try{
    Class outargs[] =
{Class.forName("ShowMessageBeanEvent")};
    Class inargs[] =
{Class.forName("java.lang.String")};

    Method outMethod1 =
myClass.getMethod("messageHeaderReceived", outargs);
    Method outMethod2 =
myClass.getMethod("messageBodyReceived", outargs);

    Method inMethod1 =
emailClass.getMethod("setUserName", inargs);
    Method inMethod2 =
emailClass.getMethod("setPassword", inargs);
    Method inMethod3 =
emailClass.getMethod("setMailBox", inargs);
    Method inMethod4 =
emailClass.getMethod("getAllMessageHeader", new
Class[0]);
    Method inMethod5 =
emailClass.getMethod("getMessageBody", inargs);

    messageHeaderPort = new VJBoundPort(this,
outMethod1, stringOut);
    messageBodyPort = new VJBoundPort(this,
outMethod2, stringOut);

    useridPort = new VJBoundPort(this, inMethod1,
stringIn);
    passwordPort = new VJBoundPort(this, inMethod2,
stringIn);
    mailboxPort = new VJBoundPort(this, inMethod3,
stringIn);
    getAllHeaderPort = new VJBoundPort(this,
inMethod4, objectIn);
    getMessageBodyPort = new VJBoundPort(this,
inMethod5, stringIn);

    VJPort[] connectorList =
```

```
{(VJPort)messageHeaderPort, (VJPort)messageBodyPort,
(VJPort)useridPort, (VJPort)passwordPort,
(VJPort)mailboxPort, (VJPort)getAllHeaderPort,
(VJPort)getMessageBodyPort};
    super.VJComponentInit((Object)mb, connectorList);
    mb.addShowMessageBeanListener(this);

  }catch(Exception e){e.printStackTrace();}
}

public void messageHeaderReceived(ShowMessageBeanEvent
e){
  try{
    messageHeaderPort.sendMessage(e.getMessage());
  }catch(Exception
e1){System.out.println(e1.getMessage());}
}

public void messageBodyReceived(ShowMessageBeanEvent
e){
  try{
    messageBodyPort.sendMessage(e.getMessage());
  }catch(Exception
e2){System.out.println(e2.getMessage());}
}
}
```

**VJShowEmailVJComponentInfo.java**

```
import com.sun.jpropub.vj.vjcomp.*;
import com.sun.jpropub.vj.vjcomp.util.*;
import java.lang.reflect.*;

public class VJShowEmailVJComponentInfo extends
SimpleVJComponentInfo{
  public VJComponentDescriptor
getVJComponentDescriptor(){
    try{
      Class vjcompClass = Class.forName("VJShowEmail");
      Class enclClass = Class.forName("ShowMessageBean");
```

```
        VJComponentDescriptor c = new
VJComponentDescriptor(vjcompClass, enclClass, null);

        c.setManufacturerName("Tester");
        c.setDisplayName("Receives Email");
        c.setShortDescription("Reads text based emails");

        return c;
    }catch(Exception e){e.printStackTrace(); return
null;}
    }

  public VJPortDescriptor[] getVJPortDescriptors(){
    try{
        Class vjcompClass = Class.forName("VJShowEmail");

        VJPortDescriptor o1Desc = new
VJPortDescriptor("Message Header", "Outputs message
header", VJPortDescriptor.OUT_ONLY,
VJPortDescriptor.EAST_CENTER, vjcompClass);
        VJPortDescriptor o2Desc = new
VJPortDescriptor("Message Body", "Outputs message body",
VJPortDescriptor.OUT_ONLY, VJPortDescriptor.EAST_CENTER,
vjcompClass);

        VJPortDescriptor i1Desc = new
VJPortDescriptor("Username", "Login id for the mailbox",
VJPortDescriptor.IN_ONLY, VJPortDescriptor.WEST_CENTER,
vjcompClass);
        VJPortDescriptor i2Desc = new
VJPortDescriptor("Password", "Password for the mailbox",
VJPortDescriptor.IN_ONLY, VJPortDescriptor.WEST_CENTER,
vjcompClass);
        VJPortDescriptor i3Desc = new
VJPortDescriptor("Mailbox", "Mailbox name. It is case
sensitive", VJPortDescriptor.IN_ONLY,
VJPortDescriptor.WEST_CENTER, vjcompClass);
        VJPortDescriptor i4Desc = new
VJPortDescriptor("Get Message Header", "Lists all
message headers from the specified mailbox",
VJPortDescriptor.IN_ONLY, VJPortDescriptor.WEST_CENTER,
vjcompClass);
```

```
        VJPortDescriptor i5Desc = new
VJPortDescriptor("Get Message body", "Gets message body
of the selected message", VJPortDescriptor.IN_ONLY,
VJPortDescriptor.WEST_CENTER, vjcompClass);

        VJPortDescriptor[] desc = {o1Desc, o2Desc, i1Desc,
i2Desc, i3Desc, i4Desc, i5Desc};

        return desc;
    }catch(Exception e1){e1.printStackTrace(); return
null;}
  }
}
```

You can find the complete source code for the bean and the component wrapper under the *chap15\sample2* subdirectory on the CD-ROM. Compile all the code and create the VJShowEmail.jar by following the steps in Chapter 5. Import the VJShowEmail component into the User folder in your Java Studio.

# Developing an Email Client to Receive Text Messages

An email client for receiving text-based email messages will have textfields where the user would enter a login ID, password, and the name of the mailbox from which he or she wants to view the messages. A button or menu event will ask the bean to list all the messages in that mailbox folder. The messages, in the form of headers, will be listed in a listbox. When one of the messages is selected from the list, its content will be displayed if the selected message is a textual message. There will also be provisions for printing the message.

Here are the steps to follow:

1. Start Java Studio if you don't have it running yet.
2. Select File->New to create a new project.
3. From the User folder, place the Receives EMail component in the design window.
4. Place a Menu component from the GUI folder in the GUI window.

5. Double-click the Menu component in the design window to open the customizer window for the Menu component.

6. Change Menu Name to File. Add two Menu Items, called Get Message and Print, by typing **Get Message** in the Item field and clicking on Add. Follow similar steps to add Print. Click on OK to close the customizer window.

7. Place a textfield component from the GUI window and resize it as shown in Figure 15-3.

**Figure 15-3**

GUI for receiving email

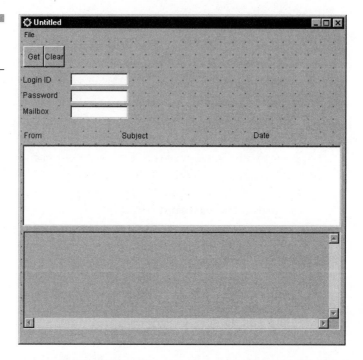

8. In the design window, select the textfield component and click the right mouse button. Then select Copy... from the floating menu. Then, by right-clicking the mouse button again, Paste... two more components. We need to do this to ensure that the height and width of the components remain the same.

9. You can switch on the Layout->Show Grid and place the components. You may want to use Layout->Align to align the components neatly, as shown in Figure 15-3.

10. Name all the textfield components as shown in Figure 15-3. All textfield components should have the Triggers the component checkbox enabled. To do this, select the Connectors folder in the textfield Customizer window and check Triggers the component, then click on OK.

11. Place a List component to display the message headers, as shown in Figure 15-3. Select the Connectors folder in the List Customizer and check "Clears the list." Click on OK.

12. Place a Textarea component below the List component and name it, as shown in Figure 15-3. Open the Textarea Customizer. Under the Textarea folder, uncheck "Make the component editable," and under the Connectors folder, check "Replaces existing text" and "Clears Text." Click on OK.

13. Add some label components to name the textfields, as shown in Figure 15-3.

14. Place a button named Get. Place it as shown in Figure 15-3. This is our Toolbar.

15. Hook up all the textfields to the respective connectors of the Receives Email bean component, as shown in Figure 15-4. For example, connect the Login ID textfield to the Username connector, the Password textfield to the Password connector, and so on.

16. The Output connector Message Header of the Receives Email Bean is connected to the Add input connector of the list component, which will display all the message headers.

17. The output of the List component is connected to the Get Message Body input connector of the Receives Email Bean.

18. The output connector Message Body of the Receives Email Bean is connected to the Set Text of the Textarea component.

19. The Menu Get Message and Get button of the toolbar are merged using a Merger component. This event is distributed using a Distributor and hooked to the triggers of the textfields and to the Get Message Header connector of the Receives Email bean.

20. You can save the application by choosing File->Save. This Email application is saved as "emailapp2.vj," which you'll find under the *chap15* subdirectory on the CD-ROM.

21. You are all set to test your application. In the customizer of the Receives Email bean, do not forget to enter the Host name and the Protocol.

22. Type in the username, password, and mailbox name. Click the Get button or the Get Message menu. Your listbox will be populated with the message headers. When you select one of the messages from the list, its body will be displayed in the listbox.

23. The only problem with the design of this application is that the list does not get cleared when you retrieve messages from other mailboxes, but gets appended to the already existing messages from the earlier mailbox. To work around this problem, we'll add another button and a menu item to clear the list, as well as the textarea. We need to clear the list manually before trying to fetch the messages from another mailbox. In the Menu component File, add another menu item called Clear. Similarly, add another toolbar button called Clear, as shown in Figure 15-3.

24. Via a Merger and Distributor component, hook up the Clear menu item and the Clear button to the Clear connector of List and the Textarea.

**Figure 15-4**

Wiring diagram for receiving email

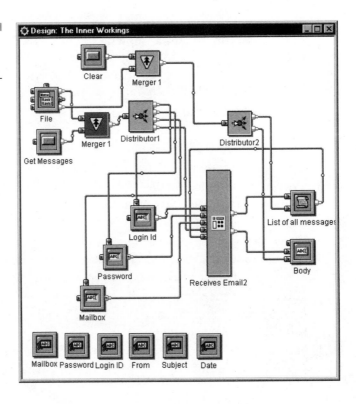

# Adding Print Capability to the Application

In this section we will learn how to use third party beans with Java Studio. Beans that can print text are available from other vendors. We will utilize one of the available printer beans to print our messages. TextPrinterBean from WildCrest is available for evaluation at *http://www.wildcrest.com*. Download the zip file and unzip it under some directory. You will find TextPrinter.jar in the directory where the contents were unzipped. The bean is also included on the CD-ROM.

Here are the steps to follow to import the components into Java Studio:

1. Open JavaStudio if it's not running already.
2. Click Import->JavaBeans...
3. In the popped-up wizard, click on Browse... to locate the TextPrinter.jar.
4. Click on Next.
5. Select Text Printer, click on Add>>, and click on Next.
6. Type **Prints Text** in the Description field, click Next.
7. Select print(String) from the list of methods, click on Add>>, and click on Next.
8. In the description field, type **Prints input String.** Click on Next.
9. Select mousePressed (mouseEvent) from the Mouse event list, click on Add>>, then click on Next.
10. Type **Prints input string when mouse pressed** in the description field, and click on Next.
11. Since the image is already chosen, click on Next.
12. Type in the filename you want to store the imported bean as or leave it as the default. Click on Next.
13. Click on Finish.
14. Select the user folder to make sure the Printer bean is there.

Now that we have created a printer bean, let's add the Printer capability to the email client we developed in the previous section.

Here are the steps to follow to add the printer capability to the email client:

1. Select File->Open, to open your emailapp2.vj project.
2. Place the printer bean in the GUI window as another toolbar button, as shown in Figure 15-5.

3. In the Customizer window of the Textarea component (which displays the body of the message), check Sends out text via output connector, and click on OK.

4. Merge the mouse-clicked event of the printer bean and the Print menu item to trigger the Textarea component.

5. The next time you click on Print menu item or the Print toolbar, the email message you are currently viewing will be printed.

Isn't that cool?

The complete GUI and the wiring for the print-enabled application is shown in Figures 15-5 and 15-6, respectively.

**Figure 15-5**
GUI diagram of receiving email application with print capabilities

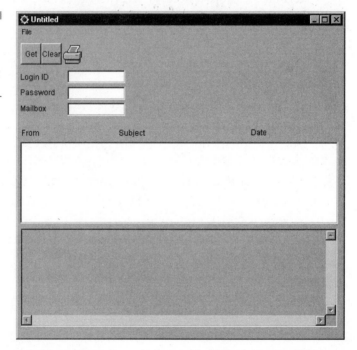

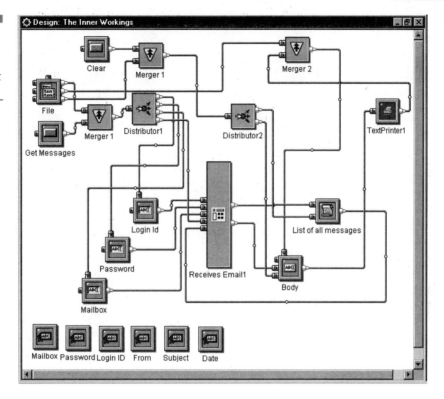

**Figure 15-6**
Wiring diagram of
receiving email
application with print
capabilities

# Summary

In this chapter we developed two simple email applications. This chapter elucidated the capabilities of Java Studio, and also showed how it can be used by non-Java Programmers to develop rapid applications with JavaBean components readily available from vendors. The power of component technology is to develop no-code applications, which is what we demonstrated in this chapter.

CHAPTER **16**

# Internet Chat
# Application

In this chapter we'll develop a simple chat application that can be used as an Internet/intranet discussion tool.

First we'll discuss certain design considerations for building this application. Then we'll see how to utilize the *HtmlGeneratorBean* we developed in Chapter 10 to present the chat dialogues to users.

# Design Considerations

These are the steps that the user will have to go through when using the client:

1. Use any browser as a client, such as Netscape Navigator or Internet Explorer.
2. A log-in page will be presented for the user.
3. If the login is successful, a discussion page will be presented.
4. The discussion page will have two frames: a top frame and a bottom frame.
5. The top frame will display the discussion dialogues and the bottom frame will have a form for typing in the dialogue.
6. Each dialogue typed will be submitted to a servlet.

These are the steps to follow to process the client response on the server:

1. The user is first presented with a log-in page where he can enter the user ID and password. Aservlet is used for validating the login. This is more of a dummy servlet. This servlet assumes that the login is successful.
2. Once the login is successful, a cookie is set to identify the user.
3. A chat page is presented to the client after log-in validation, and the cookie is set up.
4. Use the *HtmlGeneratorBean* for displaying the dialogues.
5. The servlet will generate an HTML file (output.html), placed in the *public_html* subdirectory under the server root. For example, it might look like: C:\JavaWebServer1.1\public_html\output.html.
6. The HTML file, output.html, will refresh automatically every 10 seconds (or as set by the developer). The refreshed page will show the latest dialogues. This is known as the *client pull* in technical terms. If we don't adopt this method, the servlet will have to maintain all the client information to notify the clients.

Now that you understand the design requirements, let's design the HTML files and servlet to build a chat application.

**NOTE**

Certain versions of the Java Web Server have a bug where *init()* and *destroy()* methods are called every time the servlet is accessed. Please refer to the TestServerBug.java sample for instructions on testing for the bug. You can find the complete source under *chap16\testbug* on the CD-ROM. In case our solution doesn't work for you, please check *http://archives.java.sun.com/archives/jserv-interest.html* for a number of solutions to resolve this bug.

# Logging In

Initially the login.html page will be loaded. This page will accept the user ID and password and pass it on to a servlet that is supposed to validate the login. The log-in page and servlet are discussed below. To see how our log-in page looks, check out Figure 16-1.

**Listing 16-1**
HTML code for
log-in screen

## login.html

```
<html>
<head>
<title>Login Page</title>
</head>
<body>
<center>
<h2>Login Screen</h2>
<strong>
Please enter Login and Password
</strong>
<pre>
<form action="/servlet/LoginServlet" method=POST>
<br>Login Name: <input type=text name="user">
<br>Password   : <input type=password name="pswd">
<br>
<br>        <input type=submit>
</form>
</pre>
</body>
```

**Figure 16-1**
Log-in screen

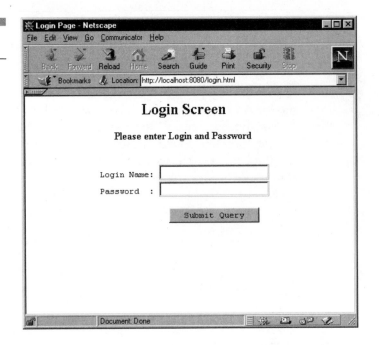

The log-in page is presented with two textfields for the user ID and password. These values are sent to the *LoginServlet* via an HTTP POST request. This servlet validates the user ID and password. Once this is done successfully, it will set the cookie on the client to retain the user's information. Our log-in servlet will not do any log-in validation, but will accept whatever information the user enters.

**Listing 16-2**
LoginServlet validates login and sets up a cookie

**LoginServlet.java**

```
import javax.servlet.*;
import javax.servlet.http.*;
import java.io.*;
public class LoginServlet extends HttpServlet{

  public void doPost(HttpServletRequest req,
HttpServletResponse res) {
    try{
      String userName =
req.getParameterValues("user")[0];
      String password =
req.getParameterValues("pswd")[0];
      Cookie userCookie = new Cookie("user", userName);
```

```
        res.addCookie(userCookie);

        res.setContentType("text/html");
        PrintWriter out = res.getWriter();
        out.println("<html><head><title>Servlet Chat</
title></head>");
        out.println("<frameset rows='70%,30%'>");
        out.println("<frame src='/output.html' noresize
border=0 name='result'>");
        out.println("<frame src='/input.html' noresize
border=0 name='input'>");
        out.println("</frameset></html>");
    }catch(IOException ioe){ioe.printStackTrace();}
  }
}
```

On the log-in page form, the username and password are obtained. The user textfield is named as "user" and the password textfield is named as "pswd".

The *LoginServlet* does not do any validation itself, but instead sets a cookie called "user."

```
Cookie userCookie = new Cookie("user", userName);
res.addCookie(userCookie);
```

After setting the cookie, we generate dynamic HTML to set up the chat page. Our client will have two frames, as shown in Figure 16-2.

```
res.setContentType("text/html");
PrintWriter out = res.getWriter();
out.println("<html><head><title>Servlet Chat</title></
head>");
out.println("<frameset rows='70%,30%'>");
out.println("<frame src='/output.html' noresize border=0
name='result'>");
out.println("<frame src='/input.html' noresize border=0
name='input'>");
out.println("</frameset></html>");
```

**Figure 16-2**

Chat screen

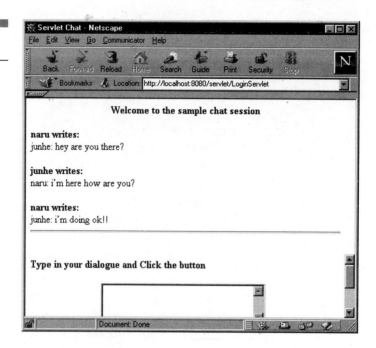

The frame at the bottom is for the user input and the frame at the top displays the chat dialogue.

The frame at the bottom is a form that accepts user input and submits the form data to the *ChatServlet*. Remember that the *ChatServlet* expects the data from a form element whose name is "*userInput*." The HTML is shown below:

**Listing 16-3**

HTML code for accepting user chat dialogues

**input.html**

```html
<html>
<body>
<strong>
Type in your dialogue and Click the button
<center>
<form action="/servlet/ChatServlet" target='result'>
<textarea rows=3 cols=30 name="text1"></textarea>
<br><input type=submit>
</form>
</body>


</html>
```

The HTML file submits the user input to the *ChatServlet* and redirects the output to the top frame, named *"result."* One of the output.html files may look like this:

**Listing 16-4**
Sample output file
that accumulates all
dialogues

**output.html**

```
<HTML>
<HEAD>
<META HTTP-EQUIV="Refresh" CONTENT="10" URL=http://
localhost:8080/output.html>
<META HTTP-EQUIV="Pragma" CONTENT=no-cache><TITLE>Chat
Servlet</TITLE>
</HEAD>
<BODY>
<CENTER><B>Welcome to the sample chat session</B></
CENTER>
<p><b>naru writes: </b><br>junhe: hey are you there?
<p><b>junhe writes: </b><br>naru: i'm here… how are you?
<p><b>naru writes: </b><br>junhe: i'm doing ok!!
<HR align=left width='100%'>
</BODY>


</HTML>
```

# ChatServlet

Now we will design the *ChatServlet* class that will initialize the bean, accept the user dialogue from the HTML form, and pass it on to the *HtmlGeneratorBean*. This bean will update the output.html file, which will be refreshed back to the client.

**Listing 16-5**
Complete code listing
for ChatServlet

**ChatServlet.java**

```
import javax.servlet.*;
import javax.servlet.http.*;
import java.beans.*;
import java.io.*;
import java.util.*;
import java.net.*;
```

```java
public class ChatServlet extends HttpServlet{
  HtmlGeneratorBean generateHtml;
  String fileName = "";

  public void init(ServletConfig conf){
    try{
      super.init(conf);
      generateHtml =
(HtmlGeneratorBean)Beans.instantiate(null,
"HtmlGeneratorBean");
    }catch(ClassNotFoundException
e){e.printStackTrace();}
    catch(IOException ioe){ioe.printStackTrace();}
    catch (ServletException se){se.printStackTrace();}

    if(generateHtml != null){
      fileName =
getServletContext().getRealPath("output.html");
      generateHtml.setFileName(fileName);
      generateHtml.setRefreshURL("output.html");
      generateHtml.setRefreshTime(10);
      generateHtml.setCache(false);
      generateHtml.writeHeaderFooter("ChatServlet",
"<b><center>Welcome to the sample chat session</
center></b>");
    }
  }

  public void doGet(HttpServletRequest req,
HttpServletResponse res) throws IOException{
    if(generateHtml != null){
      String userName = "";
      if(req.getCookies()[0].getName().equals("user")){
        userName = req.getCookies()[0].getValue();
      }
      generateHtml.writeBody("<b>" + userName + "
writes: </b><br>" +
req.getParameterValues("userInput")[0]);
      res.sendRedirect(getRedirectURL(req, res));
    }
  }
```

```
    private String getRedirectURL(HttpServletRequest req,
HttpServletResponse res){
      try{
        URL requestUrl = new
URL(HttpUtils.getRequestURL(req).toString());
        URL targetUrl = new URL(requestUrl, "/output.html");
        return(targetUrl.toExternalForm());
      }catch(MalformedURLException
m){m.printStackTrace();}
      catch(IOException ioe){ioe.printStackTrace();}
      return null;
    }
```

```
}
```

Now we'll take a look at some of the code snippets.
Method *init()* instantiates the *HtmlGeneratorBean:*

```
generateHtml = (HtmlGeneratorBean)Beans.instantiate(null,
"HtmlGeneratorBean");
```

We need a way to generate a physical path to write a file. Under Windows it may look like *C:\\Java WebServer1.1\\public_html\\output.html;* under Solaris it may look like */u/usr/Java WebServer1.1/public_html/output.html.*

```
fileName = getServletContext().getRealPath("output.html");
```

We use ServletContext's *getRealPath(),* which takes in the virtual path and translates into the real path. This is advantageous because we can use the code on any platform.

Method *doGet()* assumes that the HTML form on the client has a form element with the name "*userInput.*"

```
public void doGet(HttpServletRequest req,
HttpServletResponse res) throws IOException{
  if(generateHtml != null){
    String userName = "";
```

```
if(req.getCookies()[0].getName().equals("user")){
    userName = req.getCookies()[0].getValue();
}
generateHtml.writeBody("<b>" + userName + " writes:
</b><br>" + req.getParameterValues("userInput")[0]);
    res.sendRedirect(getRedirectURL(req, res));
}


}
```

Method *doGet()* extracts the HTML form data and passes it to the bean via *writeBody()*. Since *writeBody()* is already synchronized, we do not synchronize it here.

Instead of hard coding the URL that needs to be redirected back to the client from the servlet, we have written the following code snippet.

```
private String getRedirectURL(HttpServletRequest req,
HttpServletResponse res){
  try{
    URL requestUrl = new
URL(HttpUtils.getRequestURL(req).toString());
    URL targetUrl = new URL(requestUrl, "/output.html");
    return(targetUrl.toExternalForm());
  }catch(MalformedURLException m){m.printStackTrace();}
  catch(IOException ioe){ioe.printStackTrace();}
  return null;


}
```

# Running the Application

You can find the source for the chat application under the *chap16\app* subdirectory. Compile ChatServlet.java and LoginServlet.java and copy the corresponding class files into the *servlets* subdirectory under the web server root. Make sure to include HtmlGeneratorBean.jar in your CLASSPATH for compilation. You also need the JDK core classes and Servlet classes (jws.jar) for compilation, which needs to be included in CLASSPATH as well.

**NOTE**

Before compiling, make sure to change all the hostnames in the URL string to the hostnames that you are going to deploy the servlets on. Otherwise the examples may not work. All these examples have "localhost" as the hostname.

Copy HtmlGeneratorBean.jar developed in chapter 10 into the *lib* subdirectory under the server root directory. Restart the server if it is already running. Also copy login.html, output.html, and input.html and place them in the public_html directory.

If the server is running, you can type **http://host_name:8080/login.html**. The log-in page, as shown in Figure 16-1, will be displayed. Enter your user ID and password. You can enter any values since no serious validation is made of these on the server. Once you submit the form, the chat page is displayed. You are now set to chat with your other friends who have logged in.

**NOTE**

Make sure your browser supports cookies and that they are enabled. Otherwise this application may not work as expected because we use cookies.

# Summary

In this chapter we learned how to use existing beans to develop simple applications for enterprises. We have shown you a simple way of building an Internet chat application. You may want to use this as a base and add more features to it, such as validating the user, adding more graphics to the page, giving users display options like setting the refresh time, sending private messages, and so on. The possibilities are almost endless!

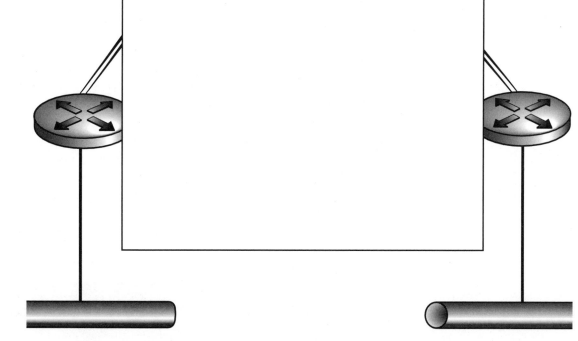

CHAPTER **17**

# E-Commerce
# Application

In this chapter we'll develop an e-commerce application that simulates a company selling computers. Customers will be able to use the application to select the computer configuration they want to order. Once they submit this configuration, the actual cost of a computer with the requested configuration is displayed. We won't be doing any credit card processing for the order.

We'll use the *CorbaBean* for developing this application, and we'll learn how to use the *HttpSession* class to maintain persistent information. Sessions will help us avoid accessing the database unnecessarily.

# Groundwork for the Application

Before running the application, we need to do some groundwork to set up the database. We need to create and populate tables so that the application can use them.

Here we assume that each computer component is represented in an individual table. Each table that represents a component will have two columns; the first column is a string that represents the component's size, and the second column is the price of the component for the specified size. We also assume that all the prices are represented as integers and that the component sizes do not have any embedded spaces in them (for example, if the memory's size is 128 MB, then it is represented as 128MB in the database). Since the available components can vary, another table called the Component will contain the names of all the components that are available. This table will just have one column, which will contain the component names. For this application it is sufficient to have three tables named Memory, Disk, and CPU. You can add more components, but remember to update the Component table also, which is the fourth table.

We'll run some of the programs developed in Chapter 7 to create tables and populate them. We'll demonstrate how to populate one table, and then you can use similar procedures to create and populate the other two tables.

Here are the steps you'll follow to populate the Component table. Make sure all your Oracle services are running before you execute the application. These steps assume that the Oracle database is installed on your local machine.

First, execute the example CreateTable, which is located under the *chap7\sample1* subdirectory on the CD-ROM. In the command line you'll be prompted for the following input:

- Enter database URL: **jdbc:oracle:thin:127.0.0.1:1521:ORCL** <Enter>
- Enter user ID: **admin** <Enter>
- Enter password: **admin** <Enter>
- Enter Table name: **Component** <Enter>
- Number of columns in table: **1** <Enter>
- Column Name 1: **COMPNAME** <Enter>
- Column Type 1: **Varchar(32)** <Enter>

If no exceptions are thrown, you have just created the table Component successfully. The next step is to populate the table. To do so, execute PopulateTable, which can be found under the *chap7\sample2* subdirectory on the CD-ROM. Here are the values you'll need to enter when prompted:

- Enter database URL: **jdbc:oracle:thin:127.0.0.1:1521:ORCL** <Enter>
- Enter user ID: **admin** <Enter>
- Enter password: **admin** <Enter>
- Enter Table name: **Component** <Enter>
- Number of columns in table: **1** <Enter>
- Number of entries you want to insert: **3** <Enter>
- Entry 1 Column Value 1: **Memory** <Enter>
- Entry 2 Column Value 1: **Disk** <Enter>
- Entry 3 Column Value 1: **CPU** <Enter>

The table Component is now populated and looks like the following example:

**Table 17-1**

Component table

| COMPNAME |
| --- |
| Memory |
| Disk |
| CPU |

Using similar methods, create three more tables and populate them as shown below:

**Table 17-2**

Memory table

| MEMORY SIZE | PRICE |
|---|---|
| 8MB | 15 |
| 16MB | 26 |
| 32MB | 45 |
| 64MB | 70 |
| 128MB | 100 |

**Table 17-3**

Disk table

| DISK CAPACITY | PRICE |
|---|---|
| 512MB | 75 |
| 1GB | 125 |
| 2GB | 200 |
| 5GB | 500 |

**Table 17-4**

CPU Table

| SPEED | PRICE |
|---|---|
| 100MHz | 75 |
| 133MHz | 125 |
| 166MHz | 150 |

In the next section we'll develop a servlet that uses the *CorbaBean* to access these tables. The table information is used to create the user interface, and that same stored information is used to calculate computer prices.

# Developing Servlets for the E-Commerce Application

Before seeing what the servlet does, let's take a look at the initial screen. The initial screen will look like Figure 17-1. It gives a brief introduction about the company. When the user hits the continue button, *CorbaServlet* is invoked with *Component* as the tablename parameter. Servlet than calls the CORBA service we developed in Chapter 12 and passes the *Component* table name to it. The table information is then used by the servlet to get information from all the other component tables. This information is used to generate dynamic HTML code. The table information obtained is also stored in an *HttpSession* instance for later use.

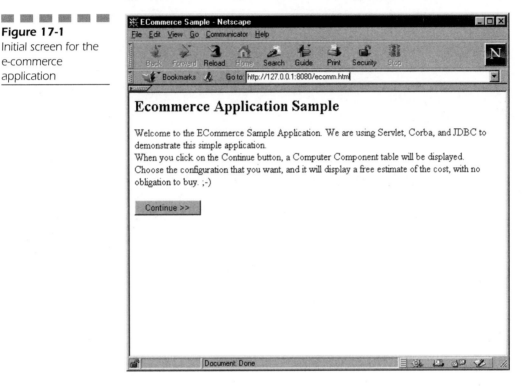

**Figure 17-1**
Initial screen for the e-commerce application

Here's the complete HTML code for the initial screen:

**Listing 17-1**
HTML code for the initial screen

**ecomm.html**

```
<html>
<head>
<title>
ECommerce Sample</title>
</head>
<body>
<h2>Ecommerce Application Sample</h2>
Welcome to the ECommerce Sample Application. We are
using Servlet, Corba, and JDBC to demonstrate this
simple application.
<br>
```

```
When you click on the Continue button, a Computer
Component table will be displayed. Choose the
configuration that you want, and it will display a free
estimate of the cost, with no obligation to buy. ;-)
<br>
<form action="/servlet/CorbaServlet">
<input type=hidden name=tablename value=Component>
<input type=submit value="Continue >>">
</form>
</body></html>
```

## Developing the CorbaServlet

In this section we will see how *CorbaServlet* uses the CORBA service we
developed in Chapter 12 to obtain the information from the database. Now
we will look at some of the code snippets of *CorbaServlet*.

All the initializations are done in the *init()* method.

```
public void init(ServletConfig conf)throws
UnavailableException{
  try
    super.init(conf);

    String[] arg = new String[2];
    arg[0] = "-ORBInitialPort";
    arg[1] = "1050";

    ORB orb = ORB.init(arg, null);
    org.omg.CORBA.Object obj =
orb.resolve_initial_references("NameService");
    NamingContext ncObj =
NamingContextHelper.narrow(obj);
    NameComponent nc = new NameComponent("PCConfig",
"");
    NameComponent path[] = {nc};
    config = ConfigHelper.narrow(ncObj.resolve(path));
    }catch(Exception e){e.printStackTrace(); throw new
UnavailableException(this, " CorbaServlet not
available");}
  }
```

Method *init()* searches for the CORBA service. This code is already explained in detail in Chapter 12.

Method *doGet()* first creates an *HttpSession* instance. Session tracking is a mechanism that can be used to maintain persistent data for individual users.

```
HttpSession session = req.getSession(true);
```

Servlets can create session objects for each user to maintain each user's state. These session objects are maintained by the Java Web Server. A new session object and an associated session ID are assigned for each user when he or she accesses the Web site for the first time. For subsequent requests the session ID matches with the session object.

```
String  tableNames =
config.getTableEntries(req.getParameterValues("tablename")[0]);
```

In the above code snippets, a call to the CORBA service is made. When the parameter passed is *Component,* all the table names that represent component tables are returned. In our case, the return would look like this:

```
<number of columns in table>, [<column name 1>, <column
name 2>...], [<column value 1>, <column value 2>], ...
```

Our CORBA service would return the following string when the service is requested upon the Component table:

```
1, COMPNAME, Memory, Disk, CPU
```

Here "1" represents the number of columns in the table, COMPNAME is the column name, and Memory, Disk, and CPU are the column values.

We have to parse the returned string to extract the value, which is what the following code does.

```
StringTokenizer st = new StringTokenizer(tableNames, "
,");
int i = 2;
for(; i != 0; i--){
```

```
    st.nextToken();
}
int numberOfTokens = st.countTokens();
Vector component = new Vector();
```

The first two tokens are skipped because they do not serve any purpose here. The vector component is created to store all the table names, as we'll see later.

Let's see how the required information is extracted:

```
for(i = 0; i < numberOfTokens; i++){
```

Here we loop to get all the table information. The length of the loop depends on the number of tables that are to be read as returned by the Component table.

After the unnecessary tokens are skipped, the pointer is set to the actual table names.

```
String tableName = st.nextToken();
component.addElement(tableName);
```

The table name is extracted by calling *st.nextToken()*, which is also added to the component vector for later use.

```
String tableContents = config.getTableEntries(tableName);
```

The same CORBA service is called again to obtain the other table information. When the loop is executed the first time, information about the Memory table is returned. The variable *tableContents* will hold the following string:

```
2, MEMORYSIZE, PRICE, 8MB, 15, 16MB, 26, 32MB, 45, 64MB,
70, 128MB, 100
StringTokenizer tempst = new
StringTokenizer(tableContents, " ,");
```

The resulting string, which is shown above, is tokenized again:

```
int j = 3;
for(; j != 0; j-){
  tempst.nextToken();
}
```

As shown in the previous code, we assume that the tables pointed to by the Component table have two columns, so we can safely skip the first three tokens.

We create two more vectors to save the size and price information for each of the Component's tables.

```
Vector size = new Vector();
Vector rate = new Vector();
```

We also assume that the first column of the table holds the size and the second column holds the price information.

We iterate through the tokens to separate the information and store it into different variables

```
while(tempst.hasMoreTokens()){
  size.addElement(tempst.nextToken());
  formBody += "<option value=" + j + ">" +
size.elementAt(j++) + "</option>";
  rate.addElement(tempst.nextToken());
}
```

The first token is added to the *size* instance and the second token is added to the *rate*. The iteration continues until all the elements are exhausted.

The rate and price information for each component is put into the *session* instance as shown below.

```
session.putValue(tableName + ".size", size);
session.putValue(tableName + ".rate", rate);
```

For the Memory table, the *session* instance holds the size vector under the name "*Memory.size*" and the rate vector under the name "*Memory.rate.*" The outermost *for* loop (see complete code below) is continued until all the tables are done.

```
session.putValue("component.names", component);
```

Once all the tables are complete, the information about the Component table is also put into the *session* instance under the name "*component.names.*" Simultaneously, all the necessary HTML is generated to populate the Web page.

At the end of *doGet()* method the *session* instance will contain the following:

- component.name, which holds the table of table names (i.e., Memory, Disk, and CPU)
- memory.size, which holds the MemorySize column info of the Memory table
- memory.rate, which holds the Price column info of the Memory table
- disk.size, which holds the DiskCapacity column info of the Disk table
- disk.rate, which holds the Price column info of the Disk table
- cpu.size, which holds the Speed column info of the CPU table
- cpu.rate, which holds the Price column info of the CPU table

Before *doGet()* exits, the HTML generated is sent back to the browser. Here's the complete code for CorbaServlet:

**Listing 17-2**
Complete listing for
CorbaServlet

**CorbaServlet.java**

```java
import javax.servlet.http.*;
import java.io.*;
import java.util.*;
import javax.servlet.*;
import PCSelect.*;
import org.omg.CosNaming.*;
import org.omg.CORBA.*;

public class CorbaServlet extends HttpServlet{
  protected Config config;

  public void init(ServletConfig conf)throws
UnavailableException{
    try{
      super.init(conf);

      String[] arg = new String[2];
```

```
        arg[0] = "-ORBInitialPort";
        arg[1] = "1050";

        ORB orb = ORB.init(arg, null);

        org.omg.CORBA.Object obj =
orb.resolve_initial_references("NameService");

        NamingContext ncObj =
NamingContextHelper.narrow(obj);

        NameComponent nc = new NameComponent("PCConfig",
"");

        NameComponent path[] = {nc};

        config = ConfigHelper.narrow(ncObj.resolve(path));
    }catch(Exception e){e.printStackTrace(); throw new
UnavailableException(this, "CorbaServlet not
available");}
   }

  public void doGet (HttpServletRequest req,
HttpServletResponse res) throws ServletException,
IOException{
     ServletOutputStream out;
     out = res.getOutputStream();
     res.setContentType("text/html");

     HttpSession session = req.getSession(true);

     String  tableNames =
config.getTableEntries(req.getParameterValues("tablename")[0]);

     StringTokenizer st = new StringTokenizer(tableNames,
" ,");

     int i = 2;

     for(; i != 0; i--){
       st.nextToken();
     }
```

```
    int numberOfTokens = st.countTokens();
    Vector component = new Vector();

    String formBody = "<pre><form action='/servlet/
ECommerceServlet'>";

    for(i = 0; i < numberOfTokens; i++){
      String tableName = st.nextToken();
      component.addElement(tableName);

      String tableContents =
config.getTableEntries(tableName);

      StringTokenizer tempst = new
StringTokenizer(tableContents, " ,");

      int j = 3;

      for(; j != 0; j—){
        tempst.nextToken();
      }

      Vector size = new Vector();
      Vector rate = new Vector();

      formBody += "<br><br><b>" + tableName + "</b><br>"
+ "<select name='" + tableName + "'>";

      j = 0;

      while(tempst.hasMoreTokens()){
        size.addElement(tempst.nextToken());
        formBody += "<option value=" + j + ">" +
size.elementAt(j++) + "</option>";
        rate.addElement(tempst.nextToken());
      }

      session.putValue(tableName + ".size", size);
      session.putValue(tableName + ".rate", rate);

      formBody += "</select>";
    }
```

```
        session.putValue("component.names", component);

        formBody += "<br><input type=submit></form></pre>";

        sendDataToClient(out, formBody);

        out.close();
    }

    private void sendDataToClient(ServletOutputStream
out, String dataToSend) throws IOException{
        out.println("<html><head><title>");
        out.println("Electronic Commerce</title></head>");
        out.println("<body><center><h1>Welcome to ECommerce
Sample</h1></center>");
        out.println("Please specify the configuration you
want. Once you submit your configuration we will give
you a free estimate. <p>");
        out.println(dataToSend);
        out.println("</body></html>");
    }
}
```

Here's the complete code of the HTML file that is generated by
*CorbaServlet:*

**Listing 17-3**
Sample listing of
dynamic HTML
generated by
CorbaServlet

```
<html><head><title>
Electronic Commerce</title></head>
<body><center><h1>Welcome to ECommerce Sample</h1></
center>
Please specify the configuration you want. Once you
submit your configuration we will give you a free
estimate. <p>
<pre><form action='/servlet/ECommerceServlet'><br><br>
<b>Memory</b><br><select name='Memory'>
<option value=0>8MB</option>
<option value=1>16MB</option>
<option value=2>32MB</option>
<option value=3>64MB</option>
<option value=4>128MB</option></select><br><br>
<b>Disk</b><br><select name='Disk'>
<option value=0>512MB</option>
```

```
<option value=1>1GB</option>
<option value=2>2GB</option>
<option value=3>5GB</option></select><br><br>
<b>CPU</b><br><select name='CPU'>
<option value=0>100MHz</option>
<option value=1>133MHz</option>
<option value=2>166MHz</option></select><br>
<input type=submit></form></pre>
</body></html>
```

In the previous HTML code generated by the *CorbaServlet*, each table in the database is represented as a choice list, with the table's first column (representing the size of the component) displayed as the items in the list. These list items have the values 0, 1, 2, and so on. We used integer values to make it easy to reference the respective vector element to calculate the rate. We'll see how this works in the next section.

To compile CorbaServlet.java code, be sure to point to rt.jar, which is packaged with JDK 1.2. Also, you must point to jws.jar, which is packaged with your Java Web Server. You must also copy the PCSelect directory, which can be found under the *chap7\sample2* directory on the CD-ROM.

In the next section we'll develop an e-commerce servlet that is responsible for calculating the price for the configuration chosen by the user.

## Developing the E-Commerce Servlet

In the last section we obtained database information from a CORBA service. This information was used to generate the HTML file that the user can use to select a PC configuration. In addition, all the database information was stored in the session object for calculating the total cost. We store persistent information in the session object to eliminate another database access.

In this section we'll see how to calculate the total cost of the PC for the user's specified configuration.

Once the user chooses the configuration that he or she wants, he or she submits the form. All the form data is submitted to the EcommerceServlet, which is responsible for calculating the total cost. We will see how the EcommerceServlet uses the session object to calculate the total cost.

In the *doGet()* method we obtain the session object.

```
HttpSession session = req.getSession(false);
```

Once the *session* instance is obtained we can extract the stored information, which is shown below.

```
Vector componentNames =
(Vector)session.getValue("component.names");
```

We get "*component.names*" from the session to obtain all the existing component tables. This code snippet, which is the heart of this servlet, may look complicated, but it is very simple. All it does is obtain the selection from the choice list we created earlier.

```
for(i = 0; i < componentNames.size(); i++){
  String comp = (String)componentNames.elementAt(i);
  htmlString += "<br><b>" + comp + ": ";
  String selectedSize = req.getParameterValues(comp)[0];
  htmlString += ((Vector)session.getValue(comp +
".size")).elementAt(Integer.parseInt(selectedSize)) +
"</b>";
  price +=
Integer.parseInt((String)((Vector)session.getValue(comp
+ ".rate")).elementAt(Integer.parseInt(selectedSize)));
}
```

Every choice list represents a component table, which is also the table name, and the values in the choice list represent the component size, which is the first column of the table. The components in the choice list were named 0, 1, 2, and so on, so it is easier for us to know which element was selected. Then we can extract the corresponding element from the vector that holds the price information for the same component. This is what we did in the snippet shown above. The prices for each component are added together and the total is displayed.

Here's the complete code for the *ECommerceServlet*:

**Listing 17-4**
Complete listing for
EcommerceServlet

**ECommerceServlet.java**

```
import javax.servlet.http.*;
import java.io.*;
import java.util.*;
import javax.servlet.*;
```

```
public class ECommerceServlet extends HttpServlet{


    public void doGet (HttpServletRequest req,
HttpServletResponse res) throws ServletException,
IOException{
        HttpSession session = req.getSession(false);

        if(session == null){
            System.out.println("Cannot find session,
exiting...");
            return;
        }

        int i = 0;
        int price = 0;
        String htmlString = "<html><head><title>Estimate</
title></head>";
        htmlString += "<body><h2><center>Price Estimate</
center></h2>";
        htmlString += "Thank you for showing interest in our
product.";
        htmlString += "You selected the following
configuration for your computer:<br> ";

        ServletOutputStream out;
        out = res.getOutputStream();
        res.setContentType("text/html");

        Vector componentNames =
(Vector)session.getValue("component.names");

        for(i = 0; i < componentNames.size(); i++){
            String comp = (String)componentNames.elementAt(i);
            htmlString += "<br><b>" + comp + ": ";
            String selectedSize =
req.getParameterValues(comp)[0];
            htmlString += ((Vector)session.getValue(comp +
".size")).elementAt(Integer.parseInt(selectedSize)) +
"</b>";
            price +=
Integer.parseInt((String)((Vector)session.getValue(comp
```

```
+ ".rate")).elementAt(Integer.parseInt(selectedSize)));
    }

    htmlString += "<p>The total estimate for this
configuration is roughly $" +
        + price + " (USD). Shipping and handling charges
are extra.</body></html>";
    out.println(htmlString);
    out.close();
  }
}
```

When you compile this code, make sure your CLASSPATH also points to jws.jar and to the JDK core classes.

# Running the Application

Before you run the application, copy *CorbaServlet* and *ECommerceServlet* to the *servlets* subdirectory under the Java Web server root. Also, copy ecomm.html to the *public_html* subdirectory, which is present under the Java Web server root.

Here are the steps you follow to run the application:

1. On the command line, type **tnameserv -ORBInitialPort 1050** (tnameserv is found under the JDK 1.2 bin directory).

2. Make sure CLASSPATH is pointing to rt.jar and to the JDBC drivers for Oracle.

3. Make sure all your Oracle services, OracleServiceORCL, OracleStartORCL, and OracleTNSListener80, are running.

4. From the command line, start the Corba service developed in Chapter 12. You'll find ConfigServer.class under the *chap12\sample2* on the CD-ROM. Copy JDBCBean.jar, which is present in the *chap7\sample5* subdirectory, to the *chap12\sample2* subdirectory. Type **java -CLASSPATH %CLASSPATH%;.\JDBCBean.jar ConfigServer -ORBInitialPort 1050**. You should see "Server Object registered" printed in the command line.

5. Make sure your Java Web Server is also running. If it's not, run the httpd.exe that is present under the bin directory of the server root.

6. From the Web browser access *http://<hostname>:8080/ecomm.html*.

7. You'll see the initial screen (shown previously in Figure 17-1).

8. Press the Continue button.

9. You'll see another screen (shown in Figure 17-2). Select the configuration you would like and submit. For demonstration purposes, we'll choose the default values displayed.

10. Another screen (shown in Figure 17-3) is displayed, which gives the price information.

**NOTE**

In case JavaWebServer throws an exception, you may want to change your CLASSPATH so that *JDK 1.2 core* classes (rt.jar) are after the *Java Web Server* classes (jws.jar), and test the application again after restarting the Web server.

**Figure 17-2**

Screen displaying all the components

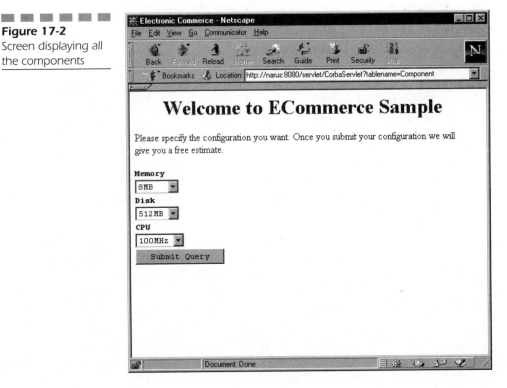

The HTML file generated by the *ECommerceServlet* for the selected configuration is shown here:

**Listing 17-5**
Sample listing of dynamic HTML generated by ECommerceServlet

```
<html>
<head><title>Estimate</title>
</head>
<body><h2><center>Price Estimate</center></h2>
Thank you for showing interest in our product.You
selected the following configuration for your
computer:<br> <br>
<b>Memory: 8MB</b><br>
<b>Disk: 512MB</b><br>
<b>CPU: 100MHz</b>
<p> The total estimate for this configuration is roughly
$165 (USD). Shipping and handling charges are extra.
</body></html>
```

**Figure 17-3**
Screen displaying the estimated price for the specified configuration

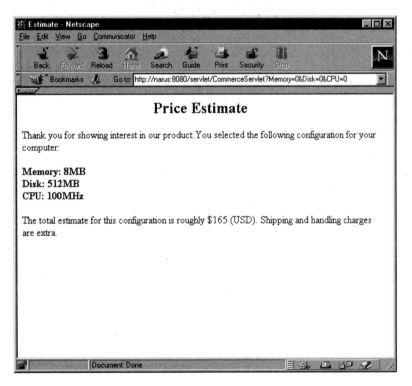

You can modify the database so it represents your business and try using this application yourself. You can also write code for credit card processing to make this example more complete. A brief discussion on credit card processing is presented in Chapter 14.

# Summary

In this chapter we learned how to use a Servlet to access the CORBA service. We also learned how to use *session* objects to maintain persistent information for a particular user. Unlike the previous chapter, the generated HTML data is directly written to the client. You can also use the *HtmlGeneratorBean* developed in Chapter 10 for writing the HTML data to the client.

CHAPTER **18**

# Project
# Tracking System

In this chapter we will see how to develop a simple project tracking system. We assume that the database has all the project information updated in a timely manner by the Project Managers. Clients within and outside the company may want to see the project status periodically. Depending on the type of person viewing the site, they will be able to see a given part of the project status, based on their privilege level. This same idea can also be extended to product tracking in a company, for external customers using an extranet. The idea is still the same although we call it project tracking.

In this sample, we will use two tables. One table, named Privilege, will contain usernames and associated privilege levels. The other table, ProjectTracker, will contain project information for every privilege level.

The sample we'll develop will make use of the Enterprise JavaBeans we developed in Chapter 13. For authorization, we'll use the Security Bean developed in Chapter 11. If you use the new HomeBase server, remember to refer to Appendix D for code changes and deployment instructions.

# Creating Users in a Database

Our example assumes that under a real situation in an enterprise, an administrator will create entries in a database and associate each user with a privilege level. For demonstration purposes, we will assume that you are the administrator and allow you to create entries in the database.

We'll assume that users can have a privilege level of 0, 1, or 2, with 0 being the highest privilege level. In other words, users with a privilege level of 0 can see the project information of all users, while users with a privilege level of 1 can only see the project information of users with privilege levels 1 and 2, and users with a privilege level of 2 can only see the project information of users with a privilege level of 2.

In Chapter 13 we learned how to create users in a database using EJB. We wrote a dedicated client program that did this. Here we will port that client program to a servlet so that the database can be populated using a Web interface. Our sample will have the Web interface shown in Figure 18-1.

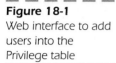

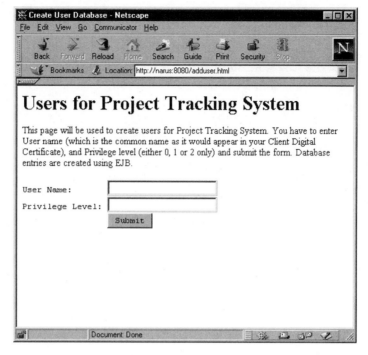

We perform all the validation of the fields on the client itself using Javascript, so that the server can use the fields directly.

```
function validate(){
  if(document.form1.username.value == ""){
    alert("Enter User name");
    return false;
  }

  var x = parseInt(document.form1.level.value);
  if(x > 2 || isNaN(x)){
    alert("Enter Privilege level between 0 and 2");
    return false;
  }
  document.form1.submit();
  return true;
}
```

The Javascript function *validate()* does all the client validation. It makes sure that the entry in the first field, which holds the username, is not empty, and that the second field is a whole number between 0 and 2. Once the fields are validated, the form is submitted. The complete HTML file for the GUI is shown in Listing 18-1.

**Listing 18-1**

*HTML interface for adding users into database*

```
adduser.html
<html>
<head>
<title>
Create User Database
</title>
<script>
function validate(){
  if(document.form1.username.value == ""){
    alert("Enter User name");
    return false;
  }

  var x = parseInt(document.form1.level.value);
  if(x > 2 || isNaN(x)){
    alert("Enter Privilege level between 0 and 2");
    return false;
  }
  document.form1.submit();
  return true;
}
</script>
</head>
<body>
<h1>Users for Project Tracking System</h1>
This page will be used to create users for Project
Tracking System.
You have to enter User name (which is the common name as
it would appear in your Client Digital Certificate),
and Privilege level (either 0, 1 or 2 only)
and submit the form. Database entries are created using
EJB.
<form action=" /servlet/AddUserServlet" Method=Post
name="form1">
<pre>
```

```
User Name:          <input type=text name="username">
Privilege Level: <input type=text name="level">
                    <input type=button value="Submit"
onClick="validate()">
</pre>
</form>
</body>
</html>
```

When the form is submitted, *AddUserServelet* is invoked and the form data is submitted to it.

## Creating Entries Using EJB via Servlets

Once the form data are posted to the servlet, the servlet will extract the data and call EJB's *create()* method to create an entry in the database. The code in method *init()* in the servlet should be familiar to you, because it is the same as the client program that we wrote for sample 1 in Chapter 13. So, if you need to refresh your memory, please refer to that section of the book. Listing 18-2 contains the source code for the servlet.

**Listing 18-2**
Servlet that creates
user using EJB

**AddUserServlet.java**

```java
import javax.servlet.*;
import javax.servlet.http.*;
import javax.naming.*;
import java.util.*;
import sample1.*;
import java.io.*;
import java.rmi.*;
import javax.ejb.*;

public class AddUserServlet extends HttpServlet{
  protected Properties env;
  protected Context ctx;
  protected PrivilegeHome home;

  public void init(ServletConfig conf)throws
ServletException{
    try{
```

```
        super.init(conf);

        env = new Properties();
        env.put("java.naming.factory.initial",
"com.ejbhome.naming.spi.rmi.RMIInitCtxFactory");
        ctx = new InitialContext(env);
        home = (PrivilegeHome)ctx.lookup("Privilege");
      }catch(NamingException e){e.printStackTrace();}
  }

  public void doPost(HttpServletRequest req,
HttpServletResponse res){
    try{
      String userName;
      int level;
      PrintWriter out;

      res.setContentType("text/plain");
      out = res.getWriter();

      userName = req.getParameterValues("username")[0];
      level =
Integer.parseInt(req.getParameterValues("level")[0]);

      if(home != null){
        home.create(userName, level);
        out.println("User " + userName + " with
privilege level " + level + " created successfully.");
      }
      else{
        out.println("Can't find Privilege EJB. Make sure
the server is running and EJB is loaded." +
          " Otherwise, please start the EJB server so
that the EJB is loaded and restart Java WebServer");
      }

      out.close();
    }catch(RemoteException e){e.printStackTrace();}
    catch(IOException ioe){ioe.printStackTrace();}
    catch(CreateException ce){ce.printStackTrace();}
  }
}
```

You can find the complete code for Listing 18-2 under the *chap18\app1* subdirectory on the CD-ROM. To compile the code, make sure your CLASSPATH is also pointing to *C:\chap13*, which is where we assume you have stored the code for the Privilege EJB. Your CLASSPATH should also point to jws.jar, rt.jar, and ejbhome.jar, which are the archive files packaged with Java Web Server, JDK 1.2, and EJBHome respectively.

Once you successfully compile the code, you are all set to add some entries into the database.

## Running the Sample to Create Users

To run the sample that we developed, you need to copy adduser.html into the *public_html* subdirectory and AddUserServlet.class into the *servlets* subdirectory, which are both under the server root directory. Before running the sample, make sure Privilege EJB is loaded and running. All your Oracle services should be running too. For more details on how to run the EJB, refer to Chapter 13, "Testing the Privilege EJB." In addition, make sure your CLASSPATH is also pointing to *C:\chap13* and *C:\chap13\sample1*, because we assume that the EJB container classes for Privilege EJB, which were developed in Chapter 13, are stored in these subdirectories. Once this groundwork is complete, you must start your Java Web Server if it is not already running. Assuming that the Java Web Server is running in localhost, type **http://localhost:8080/adduser.html**. The GUI shown in Figure 18-1 will be displayed.

Enter your username and privilege level. Make sure the username that you enter is same as the Common Name that your certificate displays. This requirement is important because later in this chapter, we will get your privilege level from the database after verifying your certificate. Once your certificate is verified, we'll extract the Common Name from the certificate and use this Common Name to extract your privilege level from the database. Once the entry is successfully created, you will see the following output in your browser (shown in Figure 18-2).

**Figure 18-2**
Servlet output when entry is successfully created in privilege table

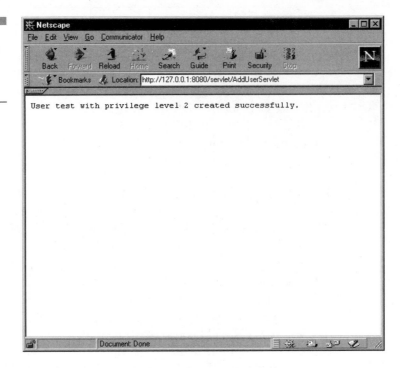

By clicking the Back button of the browser you can create as many entries as you wish. Make sure that you do not repeat usernames, because we identified name as the primary key while creating the database in Chapter 13. If your EJB is not running, or if the CLASSPATH is not set properly for servlets to find the EJB, then servlet outputs this message:

```
Can't find Privilege EJB. Make sure the server is
running and EJB is loaded. Otherwise, please start the
EJB server so that the EJB is loaded and restart Java
Web Server.
```

In such a situation, correct the CLASSPATH and restart Java Web Server or make sure EJB is running.

# Viewing the Project Information

Assuming that all of the project information is preloaded into the ProjectTracker table, in this section we'll demonstrate how to view this information using servlet.

This application will run on a secured server. Here's what the whole application is going to do. Once you view the indicated URL, you'll be asked to submit your client certificate. The server validates the certificate obtained and returns the Common Name of the certificate owner. Privilege EJB will use this Common Name information and return the privilege that is stored for this user. In our case, the privilege level has been entered by you in the previous section. ProjectTracker EJB will use this privilege level to obtain the string that is stored for that particular privilege level.

Since this application is very simple, we'll just look into the relevant snippets of code. The first screen will look like Figure 18-3.

**Figure 18-3**

First screen view of the project information

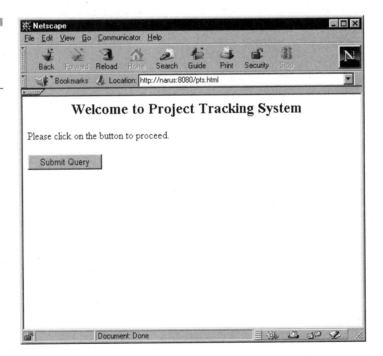

Once you click on the button, a servlet is invoked. In the next section, we will look at what the servlet does for us. The complete listing of the HTML file for the initial screen is shown in Listing 18-3.

**pts.html**

```html
<html>
<body>
<h2><center>Welcome to Project Tracking System</
center></h2>
<p>Please click on the button to proceed.
<form action="/servlet/ProjectInfoServlet" method=post>
<input type=submit>
</form>
</body>
</html>
```

The complete source code for pts.html can be found under the *chap18\app2* subdirctory on the CD-ROM.

## Servlet for Viewing Project Information

This servlet is responsible for a series of activities, including obtaining the client certificate, validating the client certificate, and invoking EJB for displaying the project information.

We have declared some final strings to avoid repeating code, as shown below:

```java
protected final String FORMTAG = "<p><pre><form
action='/servlet/ProjectInfoServlet'>";
protected final String SELECTTAG = "<select
name='privilege'>";
protected final String OPTION0 = "<option value='0'>File
0</option>";
protected final String OPTION1 = "<option value='1'>File
1</option>";
protected final String OPTION2 = "<option value='2'>File
2</option></select>";
protected final String SUBMIT = "<p><input
type=submit></form></pre>";
```

When the servlet is loaded, its *init()* method is called and some initialization is performed, as shown below:

```
env = new Properties();
env.put("java.naming.factory.initial",
"com.ejbhome.naming.spi.rmi.RMIInitCtxFactory");
ctx = new InitialContext(env);
home = (PrivilegeHome)ctx.lookup("Privilege");
ptHome =
(ProjectTrackerHome)ctx.lookup("ProjectTracker");
```

The code shown above searches for privilege and project tracker EJB and instantiates the security bean.

Once the button in Figure 18-3 is clicked, the *doPost()* method of servlet is called. The servlet first obtains the *SSLSession,* as shown here:

```
sslSession =
(SSLSession)req.getAttribute("javax.net.ssl.session");
```

To make sure that the application is running on a secured Web server, checks are made:

```
if(sslSession == null){
   htmlString += "Not an SSL session, cannot continue</
html></boby>";
   out.println(htmlString);
   out.close();
   return;
}
```

If the *sslSession* is *null,* then it means the application is not running on a secured server and we print the error string and return. If the *sslSession* is not *null,* then we initialize the Security bean:

```
securityBean.setSSLSession(sslSession);
```

We set the *SSLSession* object for the Security bean.
We have to obtain the client certificate in order to proceed:

```
userName = securityBean.getCertCN();
```

We call the Security bean's *getCertCN()* method. This method will return the Common Name (CN) of the certificate owner, which will be stored in the variable *userName*.

Next we have to invoke the Privilege bean to obtain the privilege level the value stored in *userName*.

If the servlet finds the Privilege EJB in its *init()* method, then we proceed. We call the *getPrivilegeLevel()* business method of the privilege bean, as shown:

```
Privilege p = home.findByPrimaryKey(new
PrivilegePKey(userName));
int level = p.getPrivilegeLevel();
```

Method *getPrivilegeLevel()* will return the privilege level associated with the name from the Privilege table.

We generate a dynamic HTML that depends on the privilege level:

```
if(level == 0){
  htmlString += "<p>You have privilege level 0" +
    ". You can access files that belong to user with " +
    "privilege level 0, 1 and 2. Select the file you
want " +
    "to view and click on the button.";

  htmlString += FORMTAG;
  htmlString +=  SELECTTAG +
    OPTION0 +
    OPTION1 +
    OPTION2 +
    SUBMIT;
}
```

If the privilege level is 0, then that user can view files belonging to all the users. In this case, we create a drop-down list of three choices, so the user can decide which files they would like to see.

Similarly, if the privilege level is 1 or 2, we will display those choices as appropriate. The code snippets for privilege level 1 and 2 are shown below:

```
else if(level == 1){
  htmlString += "<p>You have privilege level 1" +
    ". You can access files that belong to user with " +
    "privilege level 1 and 2. Select the file you want "
+
    "to view and click on the button.";

  htmlString += FORMTAG;
  htmlString += SELECTTAG +
    OPTION1 +
    OPTION2 +
    SUBMIT;
}
```

If the level is 1, then the drop-down list contains two choices as shown above.

```
else if(level == 2){
  htmlString += "<p>You have privilege level 2" +
    ". You can access files that belong to user with " +
    "privilege level 2. Click on the button to view the
file.";

  htmlString += FORMTAG;
  htmlString += SELECTTAG +
    OPTION2 +
    SUBMIT;
}
```

If the privilege level is 2, then the drop-down list has a single choice as shown above.

If the level holds any other value, the servlet does not support it, and the following message is printed:

```
htmlString += "Privilige level " + level + " not
supported.";
```

The HTML page that is generated by the servlet for a user with privilege level 2 is shown in Listing 18-4:

```
<html>
<head>
<title><Project information></title>
</head>
<body>
<h1><center>Project Tracking System</h1></center><p>
You have privilege level 2. You can access files that
belong to user with privilege level 2. Click on the
button to view the file.
<p><pre>
<form action='/servlet/ProjectInfoServlet'>
<select name='privilege'>
<option value='2'>File 2</option></select>
<p><input type=submit>
</form>
</pre>
</body>
</html>
```

Once the user selects their choice and submits the code, the same servlet is called again. But this time *doGet()* is called.

Method *doGet()* retrieves the string from the ProjectTracker database and displays it to the client as shown below:

```
ProjectTracker p = ptHome.findByPrimaryKey(new
ProjectTrackerPKey(level));
out.println(p.getProjectInfo());
```

Listing 18-5 contains the complete code for the servlet.

**ProjectInfoServlet.java**

```
import javax.servlet.*;
import javax.servlet.http.*;
import javax.naming.*;
import java.util.*;
import sample1.*;
import sample2.*;
import java.io.*;
import java.rmi.*;
```

```
import javax.ejb.*;
import javax.net.ssl.*;
import java.beans.*;

public class ProjectInfoServlet extends HttpServlet{
  protected Properties env;
  protected Context ctx;
  protected PrivilegeHome home;
  protected ProjectTrackerHome ptHome;

  protected final String FORMTAG = "<p><pre><form
action='/servlet/ProjectInfoServlet'>";
  protected final String SELECTTAG = "<select
name='privilege'>";
  protected final String OPTION0 = "<option
value='0'>File 0</option>";
  protected final String OPTION1 = "<option
value='1'>File 1</option>";
  protected final String OPTION2 = "<option
value='2'>File 2</option></select>";
  protected final String SUBMIT = "<p><input
type=submit></form></pre>";

  public void init(ServletConfig conf)throws
ServletException{
    try{
      super.init(conf);

      env = new Properties();
      env.put("java.naming.factory.initial",
"com.ejbhome.naming.spi.rmi.RMIInitCtxFactory");
      ctx = new InitialContext(env);
      home = (PrivilegeHome)ctx.lookup("Privilege");
      ptHome =
(ProjectTrackerHome)ctx.lookup("ProjectTracker");
      }catch(NamingException e){e.printStackTrace();}
  }

  public void doPost(HttpServletRequest req,
HttpServletResponse res){
    String userName;
    SSLSession sslSession;
    PrintWriter out;
```

```
        SecurityBean securityBean;

        try{
          res.setContentType("text/html");
          out = res.getWriter();

          securityBean =
(SecurityBean)Beans.instantiate(null, "SecurityBean");

          String htmlString = "<html><head><title><Project
information></title></head>";
          htmlString += "<body><h1><center>Project Tracking
System</h1></center>";

          sslSession =
(SSLSession)req.getAttribute("javax.net.ssl.session");

          if(sslSession == null){
            htmlString += "Not an SSL session, cannot
continue</html></boby>";
            out.println(htmlString);
            out.close();
            return;
          "
          securityBean.setSSLSession(sslSession);

          userName = securityBean.getCertCN();

          if(home != null){
            Privilege p = home.findByPrimaryKey(new
PrivilegePKey(userName));
            int level = p.getPrivilegeLevel();

            if(level == 0){
              htmlString += "<p>You have privilege level 0"
+". You can access files that belong to user with "
+"privilege level 0, 1 and 2. Select the file you want "
+"to view and click on the button.";

              htmlString += FORMTAG;
              htmlString +=  SELECTTAG +
                OPTION0 +
```

```
                    OPTION1 +
                    OPTION2 +
                    SUBMIT;


        }
      else if(level == 1){
         htmlString += "<p>You have privilege level 1"
+". You can access files that belong to user with "
+"privilege level 1 and 2. Select the file you want "
+"to view and click on the button.";

         htmlString += FORMTAG;
         htmlString += SELECTTAG +
             OPTION1 +
             OPTION2 +
             SUBMIT;
      }
      else if(level == 2){
         htmlString += "<p>You have privilege level 2"
+". You can access files that belong to user with "
+"privilege level 2. Click on the button to view the
file.";

         htmlString += FORMTAG;
         htmlString += SELECTTAG +
             OPTION2 +
             SUBMIT;
      }
      else{
         htmlString += "Privilige level " + level + "
not supported.";
        }
      htmlString += "</body></html>";
      out.println(htmlString);
    }
   else{
      out.println("Can't find Privilege EJB. Make sure
the server is running and EJB is loaded." +
          " Otherwise, please start the EJB server so
that the EJB is loaded and restart Java WebServer");
      }
```

```
      out.close();
    }catch(RemoteException e){e.printStackTrace();}
    catch(IOException ioe){ioe.printStackTrace();}
    catch(FinderException fe){fe.printStackTrace();}
    catch(ClassNotFoundException cnf){cnf.printStackTrace();}
  }

  public void doGet(HttpServletRequest req,
HttpServletResponse res){
    try{
      PrintWriter out;
      res.setContentType("text/html");
      out = res.getWriter();

      int level =
Integer.parseInt(req.getParameterValues("privilege")[0]);

      if(ptHome != null){
        ProjectTracker p = ptHome.findByPrimaryKey(new
ProjectTrackerPKey(level));
        out.println(p.getProjectInfo());
      }
      else{
        out.println("Can't find Project Tracker EJB.
Make sure the server is running and EJB is loaded." +
          " Otherwise, please start the EJB server so
that the EJB is loaded and restart Java WebServer");
      }
      out.close();
    }catch(RemoteException e){e.printStackTrace();}
    catch(IOException ioe){ioe.printStackTrace();}
    catch(FinderException fe){fe.printStackTrace();}
  }
}
```

You can find the complete source code for Listing 18-5 under the *chap18\app2* subdirectory on the CD-ROM. To compile the sample you'll need the SecurityBean that we developed in Chapter 11. Make sure that your CLASSPATH also points to SecurityBean.jar. CLASSPATH should also point to jws.jar, rt.jar, and ejbhome.jar, which are packaged with Java Web Server, JDK1.2, and EJBHome server respectively. To import the sample1 and sample2 packages created in Chapter 13, you'll also need to be sure that your CLASSPATH points to C:\chap13, or to the subdirectory that is one level below the subdirectory in which your EJB Bean classes are stored.

# Running the Project Tracking System Application

To run the project tracking system application, first copy pts.html to the *public_html* subdirectory and copy the ProjectInfoServlet.class to the *servlets* subdirectory. Both of these subdirectories are under the Java Web Server root directory. You will have to make sure that the EJB server (see Chapter 13 for more details) and all your Oracle services (see Chapter 7 for more details) are running. Also make sure that your CLASSPATH is also pointing to *C:\chap13, C:\chap13\sample1,* and *C:\chap13\sample2,* or to the subdirectories where the EJB container classes that were developed in Chapter 13 are located. Populate the ProjectTracker table to load your project information there. In this case, we'll assume that you'll use the default values that we used in Chapter 13. Here are the steps required to run the application:

1. First make sure you enable the server to ask for client certificate. For more information, refer to the section "Obtaining the Client Certificate from a Servlet" in Chapter 11. After enabling the *endpoint.main.ssl.need-clnt-auth* to *true,* restart Java Web Server if already running. Access *https://host_name:7070/pts.html* from your browser. You'll be asked if you want to accept the Server Certificate. Go through all the steps, if any, as indicated by your browser.

2. You'll see a screen like the one shown in Figure 18-3. Click on the button.

3. The server will also ask you to submit your Client Certificate. The browser will pop up a dialog as shown in Figure 18-4 asking you to select your certificate and submit it. Select a certificate from the list and submit it. You'll also have to type in the password to submit your certificate.

**Figure 18-4**
Certification selection
screen

4. Once everything is validated, and if you have an entry in the Privilege table (that matches your Common Name as stored in the Certificate), then you will see an output like the one shown in Figure 18-5. Make your selection from the drop-down list and submit.

**Figure 18-5**
Output from
certificate submission

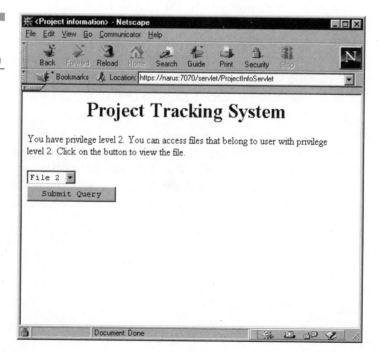

5. If the selection is File 2, then you'll see *This is level 2 String* printed in your browser by the servlet.

**NOTE**

In case you are unable to access *https://host_name:7070/pts.html,* make sure secure Web server is running. To do this, access *http://host_name:8080* and click on "Administer the Web Server" link. Login with 'admin' as user ID and password and start the Secure Web server.

## Summary

In this chapter we learned how easy it is to use EJB to develop a fairly complex application. Our examples made it clear that the development time is less than the traditional way of programming servlets for database access, and development is easy too. We also learned how to run applications on a secure Web server.

# CHAPTER 19

# Employee Tracking System

If you are employed in a large company with thousands of employees, it is often difficult to make contact with employees who don't work in your immediate area. While it is difficult to know all the employees in a single building, it is impossible to know everyone in facilities that may be spread around the globe. Suppose you know the name, but not the email address, of an employee to whom you want to send an email message. If you're lucky, your company will have designed a Web-based employee tracking system for you to use to find the employee's email address.

In this chapter we'll develop a Web-based employee tracking system that allows you to enter an employee's name or email ID and receive detailed information about the employee. We will also develop an application that will allow the administrator to modify employee details, such as the phone number, office location, and so on.

# Developing a Servlet for Tracking Employee Information

In this section we'll design a Web-based employee tracking system that can be used on an office intranet. We'll design two versions of the tracking system; in the first version we'll use the LDAP Bean we developed in Chapter 8, and in the second version we'll use the JNDI Bean we developed in Chapter 9.

## Developing a Servlet Using LDAPBean

In this section, we'll design a servlet that uses the *LDAPBean* to search and display the results. In this case, we'll assume that all the required employee information is present on the LDAP server.

Before we examine how the servlet works, let's look at the initial screen. A frame-based HTML page is displayed first when the user accesses the Employee Tracking System, as shown in Figure 19-1.

The complete code for the HTML is shown below.

```
ets.html
<html>
<head>
<title>Employee Tracking System</title>
</head>
<frameset rows="40%,60%">
<frame src=search.html noresize name='search' border=0>
<frame src=result.html noresize name='result' border=0>
</frameset>
</html>
```

You must enter the search criteria in the top frame. You can enter either the email ID or the name of the person for whom you are searching.
(Either the complete name or email ID or a partial name will do.) For
example, if you want to search for the name "Torrey Clow," you could
enter "T", "Tor", "tor", or "Torrey." You will also have to select the proper
option from the "Search By" list. In this example, you'd select "Name." The

same rules apply to the email ID search. When you have finished entering the data, click on the submit button. This action will pass the values to the *ETSServlet* we'll develop later.

Below is the complete code for the top frame.

**search.html**
```
<html>
<body>
<center>
<h2>Welcome to Employee Tracking System</h2>
</center>
<strong>
Please enter a Search String and click on Submit.
</strong>
<pre>
<form action="/servlet/ETSServlet" TARGET='result'>
Search for: <input type=text name="text1">
Search by: <SELECT NAME="type">
<OPTION VALUE="name">Name</OPTION>
<OPTION VALUE="email">Email</OPTION></select>
<input type=submit>
</form>
</pre>
</body>
</html>
```

When the *ETSServlet* is finished with the search, the result, whether or not it is successful, is displayed in the bottom frame. Initially, a dummy message is displayed in the bottom frame, as shown in Figure 19-1. The complete HTML that displays the dummy message in the bottom frame is shown below.

**result.html**
```
<html>
<body>
<center>
<b>
Search result will be displayed here.
</b>
</center>
```

```
</body>
</html>
```

Now we'll develop the *ETSServlet,* which will take care of searching the LDAP server and displaying the results. Once the form data is submitted for the search, the data and result processing is taken care of by this servlet. Let's look at some of the code snippets that put this servlet into action:

In *doGet()* we initialize the LDAPBean. If the bean is successfully instantiated then we set the properties for the bean as shown.

```
try {
   ldapBean = (LDAPBean)Beans.instantiate(null,
"LDAPBean");
} catch(ClassNotFoundException e) { e.printStackTrace();
}
catch(IOException ioe) { ioe.printStackTrace(); }

if(ldapBean != null) {
   htmlString += "<html><head><title>Employee Tracking
System</title></head>"
+ "<body><center><h1>Search results.</h1>Powered by
Netscape LDAP Server 3.1</center>";
   ldapBean.setOrganization("Airius.com");
   ldapBean.addLDAPListener(ldapListener);
```

We initialize the *LDAPBean* by adding a listener whose implementation class is shown later in this section and setting the database to Airius.com. Here we are assuming that all the searches are done on Airius.com.

Next, a search is done in the LDAP server, for the user input. Before searching, we must set the search criteria too, using the user input.

```
if((req.getParameterValues("type")[0]).equals("name")) {
   ldapBean.setSearchCriteria("cn=" +
req.getParameterValues("text1")[0] + "*");
} else {
   ldapBean.setSearchCriteria("uid=" +
req.getParameterValues("text1")[0] + "*");
}
```

Here we check the search criteria to determine whether the search should be based on the name or the email ID. If the search is by name, then we set the search criteria to "cn," otherwise it is set to "uid" as shown above.

We then call the *searchLdapServer()* of the *LDAPBean,* which will search the LDAP server.

```
ldapBean.searchLdapServer();
```

Here we assume that the LDAP server is installed locally at the default port of 389. Otherwise you have to set the appropriate properties to set the hostname and the port. See Chapter 8 for more details.

Next, we wait for the LDAP event to occur for the result:

```
while(!(resultAvailable =
ldapListener.resultAvailable()) && i < 10){
  try{
    Thread.sleep(1000);
    i++;
  } catch(InterruptedException ie){ie.printStackTrace(); }
```

Our servlet will wait for about ten seconds for the event to occur. Once the event occurs, the loop exits.

If the event does not occur within ten seconds, we assume that the LDAP server is not running.

```
if(!resultAvailable){
  htmlString += "<b>No result from LDAP. Make sure the
server is running</b>";
}
```

Sometimes the event may occur with no result.

```
else if(resultAvailable &&
(ldapListener.getData().size() == 0)){
  htmlString += "<b>Please try a different search</b>";
}
```

We get a null result when the user's entry is not found in Airius.com. If the event occurs with a non-null result, we must process some data.

```
else{
  htmlString += lutil.extractData(ldapListener.getData());
}
```

Method *extractData()* of *LDAPUtil,* which is listed in Listing 19-5, will help in extracting the data. If there are multiple results, we separate entries by their distinguished names (DN).

We then write the HTML string servlet created back to the client.

Here's the class that implements *LDAPListener,* which our servlet uses to read the data available from LDAP server. For more information on LDAP events fired by the *LDAPBean,* please refer Chapter 9.

**Listing 19-4**
LDAP listener
implementation class

**LDAPListenerImpl.java**

```
import java.util.*;

public class LDAPListenerImpl implements LDAPListener {
  private boolean result;
  private Vector data = null;

  public LDAPListenerImpl(){
    result = false;
  }

  public void result(LDAPEvent e){
    data = e.getResult();
    result = true;
  }

  public Vector getData(){
    return data;
  }

  public boolean resultAvailable(){
    return result;
  }
}
```

Here's the *LDAPUtil* class, which our servlet uses to extract the data from the vector returned by the *LDAPBean* to generate formatted output. This class separates entries by their distinguished names (DN), which is what the *for* loop in *extractData()* does. After being separated, each entry is formatted and put in a table by *generateTable()*. Since this class does simple string manipulation, we will not go into greater detail here.

**Listing 19-5**

Class responsible for formatting vector data into a table format

**LDAPUtil.java**

```java
import java.util.*;

public class LDAPUtil{

    public String extractData(Vector data){
        String htmlString = "";
        Vector temp = new Vector();

        for(int i = 0; i < data.size(); i++){
            String dataElement = (String)data.elementAt(i);
            if((dataElement.substring(0, 2)).equals("DN") &&
(temp.size() > 0)){
                htmlString += generateTable(temp);
                htmlString += "<p><hr><p>";
                temp.removeAllElements();
            }
            temp.addElement(dataElement);
        }
        return (htmlString += generateTable(temp));
    }

    private String generateTable(Vector data){
        String htmlString = "<table border cols=2
width='100%'>";

        for(Enumeration e = ((Vector)data).elements();
e.hasMoreElements();){
            String s = (String) e.nextElement();
            htmlString += "<tr><td>" + s.substring(0,
s.indexOf('=')) + "</td><td>" +
s.substring(s.indexOf('=') + 1) + "</td></tr>";
        }
```

```
            return (htmlString += "</table>");


    }
}
```

Complete code for ETSServlet.java is shown below.

■■ ■■ ■■ ■■ ■■ ■■

**Listing 19-6**

Servlet responsible for
executing the
Employee Tracking
System using
LDAPBean

**ETSServlet.java**

```java
import javax.servlet.*;
import javax.servlet.http.*;
import java.beans.*;
import java.io.*;
import java.util.*;
import java.net.*;

public class ETSServlet extends HttpServlet{

  public void doGet(HttpServletRequest req,
HttpServletResponse res) throws IOException{
    LDAPUtil lutil = new LDAPUtil();
    String htmlString = "";
    LDAPBean ldapBean = null;
    LDAPListenerImpl ldapListener = new
LDAPListenerImpl();
    boolean resultAvailable = false;

    try{
      ldapBean = (LDAPBean)Beans.instantiate(null,
"LDAPBean");
    }catch(ClassNotFoundException
e){e.printStackTrace();}
    catch(IOException ioe){ioe.printStackTrace();}

    if(ldapBean != null){
      htmlString += "<html><head><title>Employee
Tracking System</title></head>" +
        "<body><center><h1>Search results.</h1>Powered
by Netscape LDAP Server 3.1</center>";
```

```
ldapBean.setOrganization("Airius.com");
ldapBean.addLDAPListener(ldapListener);


if((req.getParameterValues("type")[0]).equals("name")){
      ldapBean.setSearchCriteria("cn=" +
req.getParameterValues("text1")[0] + "*");
      }
      else{
      ldapBean.setSearchCriteria("uid=" +
req.getParameterValues("text1")[0] + "*");
      }

      ldapBean.searchLdapServer();

      int i = 0;

      while(!(resultAvailable =
ldapListener.resultAvailable()) && i < 10){
      try{
        Thread.sleep(1000);
        i++;
      }catch(InterruptedException
ie){ie.printStackTrace();}
      }

      if(!resultAvailable){
      htmlString += "<b>No result from LDAP. Make sure
the server is running</b>";
      }
      else if(resultAvailable &&
(ldapListener.getData().size() == 0)){
      htmlString += "<b>Please try a different
search</b>";
      }
      else{
      htmlString +=
lutil.extractData(ldapListener.getData());
      }
      htmlString += "<hr align=left width='100%'></
body></html>";
```

```
            res.setContentType("text/html");
            PrintWriter out = res.getWriter();
            out.println(htmlString);
            out.close();
        }
    }
}
```

The source code for listings 19-4 through 19-6 can be found under the *chap19\app1* subdirectory on the CD-ROM. When you compile the source, make sure that LDAPBean.jar, jws.jar, and the JDK core classes are present in your CLASSPATH. Once you compile the source successfully, copy ETSServlet.class, LDAPUtil.class, and LDAPListenerImpl.class into the *servlets* subdirectory under your server root directory. You should also copy LDAPBean.jar under the *lib* subdirectory of the server root if it's not already there, and restart the server if it's already running.

**NOTE**

In our example we have hard-coded the hostname as *http://localhost:8080.* You may have to change the source to fit your settings.

Also, this servlet re-opens the LDAP connection each time. You could optimize this by changing the LDAPBean to re-use ldap connection between requests.

## Running the Employee Tracking System Application

Copy ets.html, result.html, and search.html, which are present under the *chap19\app1* subdirectory on the CD-ROM into the *public_html* subdirectory under the server root directory. Here are the steps you should follow to run the Employee Tracking System.

1. Open the browser window and enter **http://hostname:8080/ets.html.** The screen shown in Figure 19-1 will be displayed.
2. Type **tclow** in the Search for field.
3. Select Email from the Search by list.
4. Click on the Submit Query button.
5. You'll see the display (shown in Figure 19-2).

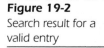

**Figure 19-2**

Search result for a
valid entry

6. Type **Torrey Clow** instead of **tclow**, select Name from the list, and click the Submit Query button.

7. You'll see the same result as in Figure 19-2.

8. Now type **tclow** in the Search for field, select Name from the list, and click the Submit Query button.

9. Since there is no such entry, your result screen will look like Figure 19-3.

10. You can also try typing just a **T** in the Search for field. If you select name, then all the names starting with "T "will be displayed. If you had selected Email, then all the entries whose email ID starts with "T" are displayed.

**Figure 19-3**
Search result for an
invalid entry

## Developing a Servlet Using JNDIBean

A servlet that uses *JNDIBean* will work the same as a servlet that uses the LDAPBean. Since most of the code remains the same we will not elaborate on the details here.

Complete source code for this application is available under the *chap19\app2* subdirectory on the CD-ROM. To compile the code, make sure the CLASSPATH is also pointing to ldap.jar, jndi.jar, and providerutil.jar. You acquired these files when you installed the JNDI development kit in Chapter 9. Also, point the CLASSPATH to JNDIBean.jar, and jsdk.jar. After you compile ETSJNDIServlet.java and JNDIListenerImpl.java, copy ETSJNDIServlet.class and JNDIListenerImpl.class to the *servlets* directory under the Java Web Server root directory. You can also copy ldap.jar, jndi.jar, and providerutil.jar into the *lib* subdirectory under the Java Web Server root directory. Remember this example also uses LDAPUtil.class for formatting the data. In case you have not executed the previous example, you'll have to copy LDAPUtil.class into the *servlets* subdirectory under server root.

## Running the Application

Copy all the HTML files, for example, jndiets.html, jndiresult.html and jndisearch.html, under the *chap19/app2* subdirectory into the *public_html* subdirectory under the server root. Make sure all the files indicated in the previous section are present under the *servlets* and *lib* subdirectories under the Java Web Server root. To test the Servlet, open jndiets.html by typing **http://hostname:8080/jndiets.html** in your browser. The steps to run the application are the same as in the previous example.

# Developing a Servlet for Modifying Employee Information

What if the information about a person in the LDAP database needs to be modified? If, for example, a person's location or phone number changes, then the LDAP database should reflect the new information. Otherwise, when somebody uses the tracking system, false information will be presented. In this section we will develop an application that allows the administrator of the LDAP database to modify the user information.

We will assume that the administrator has access to the information about the person whose entries need to be modified. This application will use a single servlet to process two HTML files, the log-in screen and the update information screen. This servlet will use the *LDAPBean* for modifying information.

## Logging In

The first thing that the administrator should do is to log-in. If the login is correct, a form will be displayed to enter the values that need to be modified. Otherwise, the administrator will have to log-in again.

The log-in screen will look like Figure 19-4.

**Figure 19-4**
Log-in screen

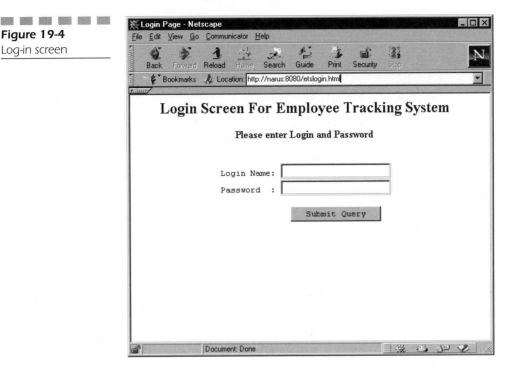

The code for the log-in screen is shown below.

**Listing 19-7**
HTML page for log-in
screen

**etslogin.html**

```
<html>
<head>
<title>Login Page</title>
</head>
<body>
<center>
<h2>Login Screen For Employee Tracking System</h2>
<strong>
Please enter Login and Password
</strong>
<pre>
<form action="/servlet/LoginUpdateServletForETS"
method=POST>
<br>Login Name: <input type=text name="user">
<br>Password  : <input type=password name="password">
<br>
<br>        <input type=submit>
```

```
</form>
</pre>
</body>
```

Once the log-in name and password are entered and submitted, the *LoginUpdateServletForETS* servlet validates the login using the *LDAPBean*.

*LoginUpdateServletForETS* is a single servlet that processes two different HTML data files. One of the HTML files sends the data using the POST method and the other sends the data using the GET method. When the log-in screen data is submitted, the *LoginUpdateServletForETS* servlet's *doPost()* is called. Let's see what this method does.

```
userid = req.getParameterValues("user")[0];
password = req.getParameterValues("password")[0];
```

First it obtains the user ID and password and assigns them to the two variables shown above. Then the values are validated by calling the LdapBean's *login()* method.

```
if(ldapBean.login("cn=" + userid, password))
```

The method returns true if the login is valid, otherwise it returns false. If the login is valid, we first store the user ID and password in a session object. For more on sessions, refer to Chapter 17.

```
HttpSession session = req.getSession(true);
session.putValue("userid", userid);
session.putValue("password", password);
```

After valid login, administrator is presented with an HTML page that allows him or her to modify the information. For this we dynamically generate two frames.

```
out.println("<html><head><title>Modify LDAP Entries</
title></head>");
out.println("<frameset rows='50%,50%'>");
out.println("<frame src='/etsldapmodify.html'
name='modify'>");
```

```
out.println("<frame src='/etsldapmodifyresult.html'
name='result'>");
out.println("</frameset></html>");
```

The top frame displays a form that can be used to update the entries and the bottom frame initially displays a dummy message. Later it will be used to display the updated result. The valid log-in screen is shown in Figure 19-5.

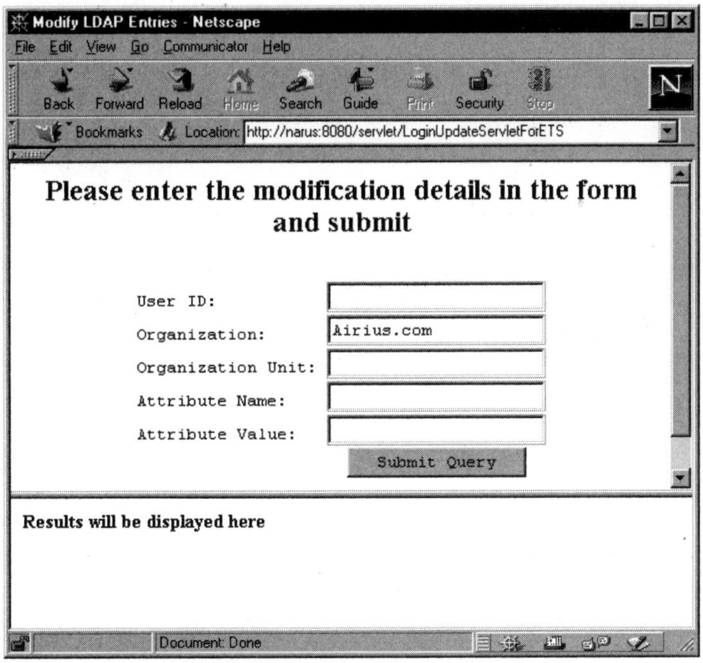

**Figure 19-5**
User interface for modifying LDAP entries

If the login is invalid, the invalid log-in screen is displayed, as shown in Figure 19-6. The code responsible for displaying this page is shown below.

```
res.setContentType("text/html");
out.println("<html><head><title>Invalid Login</title></
head>");
out.println("<body><b>Invalid login id or
password....<p>Please try again</b></body></html>");
```

**Figure 19-6**
Result of invalid login

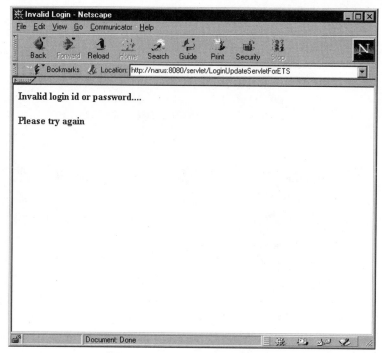

The top frame displays etsldapmodify.html, whose code is shown below:

**Listing 19-8**
HTML page where
the administrator will
enter the fields for
modification

**etsldapmodify.html**

```
<html>
<head>
<title>
Modify Employee Information
</title>
</head>
<body>
<center>
<h2>Please enter the modification details
in the form and submit</h2>
<pre>
<form action="/servlet/LoginUpdateServletForETS"
target='result'>
User ID:            <input type=text name='user'>
Organization:
<input type=text name='organization' value='Airius.com'>
```

```
Organization Unit:
<input type=text name= 'organizationunit'>
Attribute Name:   <input type=text name='attributename'>
Attribute Value: <input type=text name='attributevalue'>
                        <input type=submit>
</form>
</pre>
</body>
</html>
```

The bottom frame displays a dummy message initially, as shown in Figure 19-5. The HTML code displayed in the bottom frame is shown below:

**Listing 19-9**
HTML page that displays dummy result initially

**etsldapmodifyresult.html**

```
<html>
<body>
<b>
Results will be displayed here
</body>
</html>
```

You should fill out the form details to update an LDAP entry. When the form is filled and submitted, the same *LoginUpdateServletForETS* servlet is invoked, but this time the *doGet()* method is called because the form uses the GET method to send the data. We'll look at some of the code snippets of the *doGet()* method.

*LDAPBean* is initialized to the values as entered in the form.

```
ldapBean.setOrganization(req.getParameterValues("organization")[0]);
ldapBean.setAttributeName(req.getParameterValues("attributename")[0]);
ldapBean.setAttributeValue(req.getParameterValues("attributevalue")[0]);
```

Since a search has to be performed to view the modified result, we also set some criteria as shown below.

```
ldapBean.setSearchCriteria("uid=" +
req.getParameterValues("user")[0]);
```

```
ldapBean.setDN("uid=" +
req.getParameterValues("user")[0] + ", " +
"ou" + "=" +
req.getParameterValues("organizationunit")[0] + ", " +
"o=" + req.getParameterValues("organization")[0]);
```

The Search criteria and the DN of the *LDAPBean* are again set using the form data that was entered by the user.

First, LDAP server is updated with the new values, and then a search is performed.

```
ldapBean.updateLdapServer();
ldapBean.searchLdapServer();
```

After the update, a search is made on the same user, so that the modified data can be displayed. The rest of the code is similar to the examples in the previous sections. Here's the complete listing for Login-UpdateServletForETS.java.

**Listing 19-10**

Servlet responsible for validating the login and updating the LDAP database

**LoginUpdateServletForETS.java**

```
import javax.servlet.*;
import javax.servlet.http.*;
import java.io.*;
import java.beans.*;
import java.util.*;
import java.net.*;

public class LoginUpdateServletForETS extends
HttpServlet{

  public void doPost(HttpServletRequest req,
HttpServletResponse res){
    PrintWriter out = null;
    LDAPBean ldapBean = null;
    String userid = "", password = "";

    res.setContentType("text/html");

    try{
```

```
        ldapBean = (LDAPBean)Beans.instantiate(null,
"LDAPBean");
        userid = req.getParameterValues("user")[0];
        password = req.getParameterValues("password")[0];
        out = res.getWriter();

        if(ldapBean.login("cn=" + userid, password)){
          HttpSession session = req.getSession(true);
          session.putValue("userid", userid);
          session.putValue("password", password);

          out.println("<html><head><title>Modify LDAP
Entries</title></head>");
          out.println("<frameset rows='50%,50%'>");
          out.println("<frame src='/etsldapmodify.html'
name='modify'>");
          out.println("<frame src='/
etsldapmodifyresult.html' name='result'>");
          out.println("</frameset></html>");
        }
        else{
          out.println("<html><head><title>Invalid Login</
title></head>");
          out.println("<body><b>Invalid login id or
password....<p>Please try again</b></body></html>");
        }

      out.close();
    }catch(IOException ioe){ioe.printStackTrace();}
    catch(ClassNotFoundException
e){e.printStackTrace();}
  }

  public void doGet(HttpServletRequest req,
HttpServletResponse res){
    LDAPUtil lutil = new LDAPUtil();
    String htmlString = "";
    LDAPBean ldapBean = null;
    LDAPListenerImpl ldapListener = new LDAPListenerImpl();
    boolean resultAvailable = false;
```

```
    try{
      ldapBean = (LDAPBean)Beans.instantiate(null,
"LDAPBean");

      if(ldapBean != null){
        htmlString += "<html><head><title>Employee
Tracking System</title></head>" +
          "<body><center><h1>Search results.</h1>Powered
by Netscape LDAP Server 3.1</center>";

        ldapBean.addLDAPListener(ldapListener);
ldapBean.setOrganization(req.getParameterValues("organization")[0]);

ldapBean.setAttributeName(req.getParameterValues("attributename")[0]);

ldapBean.setAttributeValue(req.getParameterValues("attributevalue")[0]);

        ldapBean.setSearchCriteria("uid=" +
req.getParameterValues("user")[0]);

        ldapBean.setDN("uid=" +
req.getParameterValues("user")[0] + ", " +
        "ou" + "=" +
req.getParameterValues("organizationunit")[0] + ", " +
        "o=" +
req.getParameterValues("organization")[0]);

        HttpSession session = req.getSession(false);

        ldapBean.login("cn=" +
((String)session.getValue("userid")),
(String)session.getValue("password"));
        ldapBean.updateLdapServer();
        ldapBean.searchLdapServer();

        int i = 0;

        while(!(resultAvailable =
ldapListener.resultAvailable()) && i < 10){
          try{
            Thread.sleep(1000);
            i++;
```

```
            }catch(InterruptedException
ie){ie.printStackTrace();}
        }

        if(!resultAvailable){
            htmlString += "<b>No result from LDAP. Make
sure the server is running</b>";
        }
        else if(resultAvailable &&
(ldapListener.getData().size() == 0)){
            htmlString += "<b>Error!! Please make sure all
the information provided are correct</b>";
        }
        else{
            htmlString +=
lutil.extractData(ldapListener.getData());
        }

        htmlString += "<hr align=left width='100%'></
body></html>";

        res.setContentType("text/html");
        PrintWriter out = res.getWriter();
        out.println(htmlString);
        out.close();
    }
    }catch(ClassNotFoundException
e){e.printStackTrace();}
    catch(IOException ioe){ioe.printStackTrace();}
  }
}
```

The complete source code can also be found under the *chap19\app3* subdirectory on the CD-ROM. When you compile the source, make sure that LDAPBean.jar, jws.jar, and the JDK core classes are present in your CLASSPATH. Once you compile the source successfully, copy LoginUpdateServletForETS.class *servlets* subdirectory under your server root directory. Also, copy LDAPListenerImpl.class and LDAPUtil.class into the *servlets* subdirectory, if you haven't done this already. You should also have LDAPBean.jar in the *lib* subdirectory under server root. Now you are ready to modify the employee information.

# Running the Application

Copy etslogin.html, etsldapmodifyresult.html, and etsldapmodify.html (which can be found under the *chap19\app3* directory on the CD-ROM) into the *public_html* subdirectory under your server root directory. Make sure all the files indicated in the previous section are present under the *servlets* subdirectory under your Java Web server root. To test, open etslogin.html by typing **http://hostname:8080/etslogin.html** in your browser. Now we'll show you how to modify tclow's location from San Jose to San Francisco. Here are the steps you follow to modify the LDAP entry:

1. Type in **Directory Manager** and **admintest** as the Lo-gin name and Password.
2. After a successful login, you will see the screen shown in Figure 19-5.
3. Type **tclow** for the User ID, **Airius.com** for the Organization, **People** for the Organization Unit, **1** for the Attribute name, and **San Francisco** for the Attribute Value. Click on the Submit Query button.
4. The LDAP location field for tclow is modified and the latest updated result is displayed in the bottom frame (shown in Figure 19-7)

**Figure 19-7**

Result after the LDAP entry is modified

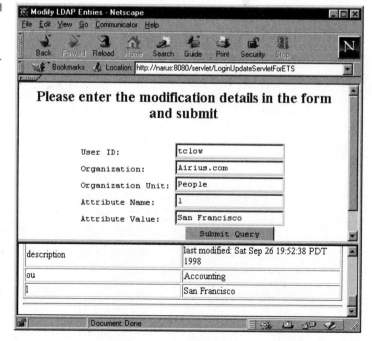

Along similar lines, you can design another Servlet that uses JNDIBean to update the LDAP entries..

# Summary

In this chapter we learned how to combine the *LDAPBean* and *JNDIBean*, which we discussed in Chapters 8 and 9, and to develop a typical intranet application that tracks employee information.

PART

4

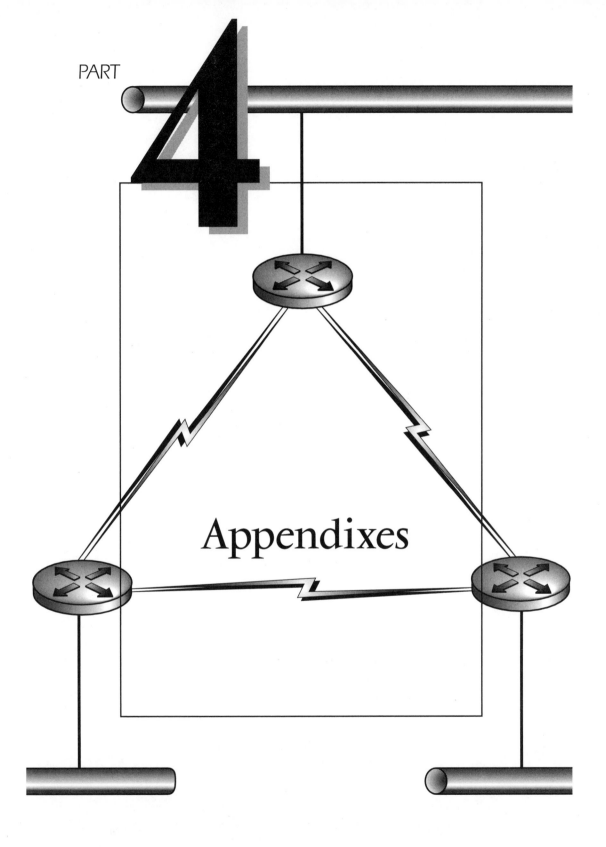

Appendixes

APPENDIX **A**

# A Sample on Infobus

# Introduction

In Chapter 3 we learned about a number of frameworks that JavaBeans can use. One such framework is InfoBus. In this Appendix we'll review a simple example that demonstrates two different Java classes communicating with each other and exchanging data. This demonstration uses Java classes. However, the same would work for JavaBeans too.

# Implementing InfoBus

For our example we need a data producer and a data consumer. The data producer will send a "Hello" string, and the consumer will print the data received by the producer. Let us briefly review the Producer and Consumer.

## Data Producer

Any class that wants to listen on InfoBus should implement *InfoBusMember*.

```
public class ProducerBean implements InfoBusMember,
InfoBusDataProducer{
```

*ProducerBean* implements *InfoBusMember*, which means it can join the InfoBus. It also implements *InfoBusDataProducer*, which means it will announce the availability of data on the bus.

There is an *InfoBusMemberSupport* class that implements InfoBusMember. We'll use this class to ease our implementation.

```
public ProducerBean(){
   infoBusHolder = new InfoBusMemberSupport(this);
}
```

In the constructor, we create an instance of *InfoBusMemberSupport*. *InfoBusMemberSupport* provides high level methods that can be called to join or leave the InfoBus.

```
infoBusHolder.joinInfoBus(infoBusName);
```

We call the *joinInfoBus()* method to join a named InfoBus, as in *infoBusName*.

Data producers will have to register themselves on the InfoBus so that they can listen to the data request notification from the consumers.

```
InfoBus infoBus = getInfoBus();

if(infoBus != null){
  infoBus.addDataProducer(this);
}
```

*ProducerBean* registers itself as a data producer, as shown above.

Whenever the data is available the producer will announce it on the InfoBus, as shown below:

```
infoBus.fireItemAvailable("HelloString", null, this);
```

The producer announces that a data item by name "HelloString" is available on the bus. When a consumer requests the data, then the data item is set, as shown below:

```
e.setDataItem(dataItem);
```

When the InfoBus producer leaves, it has to do some cleanup activity, as shown below:

```
InfoBus infoBus = getInfoBus();
if(infoBus != null){
  infoBus.removeDataProducer(this);
}
infoBusHolder.leaveInfoBus();
```

The producer un-registers itself as a producer, which means it is no longer a data producer. If a class does not want to stay on the bus, then it calls *leaveInfoBus()*.

Here's the complete code listing for the *ProducerBean*:

**ProducerBean.java**

```java
import java.beans.*;
import javax.infobus.*;

public class ProducerBean implements InfoBusMember,
InfoBusDataProducer{
  protected String dataItem = "Hello";
  protected InfoBusMemberSupport infoBusHolder;

  public ProducerBean(){
    infoBusHolder = new InfoBusMemberSupport(this);
  }

  public void start(String infoBusName){
    try{
      infoBusHolder.joinInfoBus(infoBusName);
      InfoBus infoBus = getInfoBus();
      if(infoBus != null){
        infoBus.addDataProducer(this);
      }
    }catch(Exception e){e.printStackTrace();}
  }

  public void destroy(){
    try{
      InfoBus infoBus = getInfoBus();
      if(infoBus != null){
        infoBus.removeDataProducer(this);
      }

      infoBusHolder.leaveInfoBus();
    }catch(Exception e){e.printStackTrace();}
  }

  public void send(){
    InfoBus infoBus = infoBusHolder.getInfoBus();
    if(infoBus != null){
      infoBus.fireItemAvailable("HelloString", null,
this);
    }
  }
```

```
   public void
dataItemRequested(InfoBusItemRequestedEvent e){
     e.setDataItem(dataItem);
   }

   public void propertyChange(PropertyChangeEvent e){
   }

   public InfoBus getInfoBus(){
     return infoBusHolder.getInfoBus();
   }

   public void setInfoBus(InfoBus newInfoBus){
     try{
       infoBusHolder.setInfoBus(newInfoBus);
     }catch(Exception e){e.printStackTrace();}
   }

   public void
addInfoBusVetoableListener(VetoableChangeListener vcl){
   }

   public void
removeInfoBusVetoableListener(VetoableChangeListener
vcl){
   }

   public void
addInfoBusPropertyListener(PropertyChangeListener pcl){
   }

   public void
removeInfoBusPropertyListener(PropertyChangeListener
pcl){
   }

}
```

# Data Consumer

Consumers implement *InfoBusDataConsumer* in addition to implementing *InfoBusMember*.

```
public class ConsumerBean implements InfoBusMember,
InfoBusDataConsumer{
```

*ConsumerBean* implements *InfoBusMember* to listen on the bus and also implements *InfoBusDataConsumer,* which means it will consume the data if it is interested in it.

Consumers always check for the data when the producer announces it. If the data interests them, then they consume it, otherwise the announcement is ignored.

```
public void dataItemAvailable(InfoBusItemAvailableEvent
e){
   if(e.getDataItemName().equals("HelloString")){
     System.out.println(e.requestDataItem(this, null));
   }
}
```

*ConsumerBean* checks for the data name. If the data is "HelloString" data, then it asks for more information and prints it to the Standard output.

The rest of the code remains almost same as the *ProducerBean.* Here's the complete code listing for *ConsumerBean.*

**Listing A-2**
Complete listing for
data consumer

**ConsumerBean.java**

```
import java.awt.*;
import java.beans.*;
import javax.infobus.*;

public class ConsumerBean implements InfoBusMember,
InfoBusDataConsumer{
   protected InfoBusMemberSupport infoBusHolder;

   public ConsumerBean(){
     infoBusHolder = new InfoBusMemberSupport(this);
   }
```

```java
public void start(String infoBusName){
  try{
    infoBusHolder.joinInfoBus(infoBusName);
    InfoBus infoBus = getInfoBus();
    if(infoBus != null){
      infoBus.addDataConsumer(this);
    }
  }catch(Exception e){e.printStackTrace();}
}

public void destroy(){
  try{
    InfoBus infoBus = getInfoBus();
    if(infoBus != null){
      infoBus.removeDataConsumer(this);
    }
    infoBusHolder.leaveInfoBus();
  }catch(Exception e){e.printStackTrace();}
}

public void
dataItemAvailable(InfoBusItemAvailableEvent e){
  if(e.getDataItemName().equals("HelloString")){
    System.out.println(e.requestDataItem(this, null));
  }
}

public void dataItemRevoked(InfoBusItemRevokedEvent
e){
}

public void propertyChange(PropertyChangeEvent e){
}

public InfoBus getInfoBus(){
  return infoBusHolder.getInfoBus();
}

public void setInfoBus(InfoBus newInfoBus){
  try{
    infoBusHolder.setInfoBus(newInfoBus);
```

```
        }catch(Exception e){e.printStackTrace();}
    }

    public void
addInfoBusVetoableListener(VetoableChangeListener vcl){
    }

    public void
removeInfoBusVetoableListener(VetoableChangeListener
vcl){
    }

    public void
addInfoBusPropertyListener(PropertyChangeListener pcl){
    }

    public void
removeInfoBusPropertyListener(PropertyChangeListener
pcl){
    }
}
```

## Testing the Bus

Below is the listing of a program that tests the communication between the ProducerBean and the ConsumerBean:

**Listing A-3**
Complete listing for testing InfoBus

**TestInfoBus.java**

```
import javax.infobus.*;

public class TestInfoBus{
    public static void main(String[] args){
    try{
        ProducerBean p = new ProducerBean();
        ConsumerBean c = new ConsumerBean();
        p.start("Test");
        c.start("Test");
        p.send();
```

```
        p.destroy();
        c.destroy();

    }catch(Exception e){e.printStackTrace();}
    }
}
```

The complete source code for all the java files in this appendix can be found under the *appendixa\infobus* subdirectory on the CD-ROM. To compile the source code you'll need infobus.jar. You have to download InfoBus from *http://java.sun.com/beans/infobus/index.html*. When you unzip the contents, you will see infobus.jar under the unzipped directory. Make sure your CLASSPATH points to Java core classes (either classes.zip or rt.jar, depending on the JDK version) and to infobus.jar. Once the source compiles successfully, you can run the test by running TestInfoBus from the command line.

You'll see **Hello** printed on the console.

## Summary

InfoBus is just one of the frameworks used to extend the component technology. It is the best means for components to communicate with each other, and exchange data too. Additionally, the latest BeanBox provides support for InfoBus-aware JavaBean components.

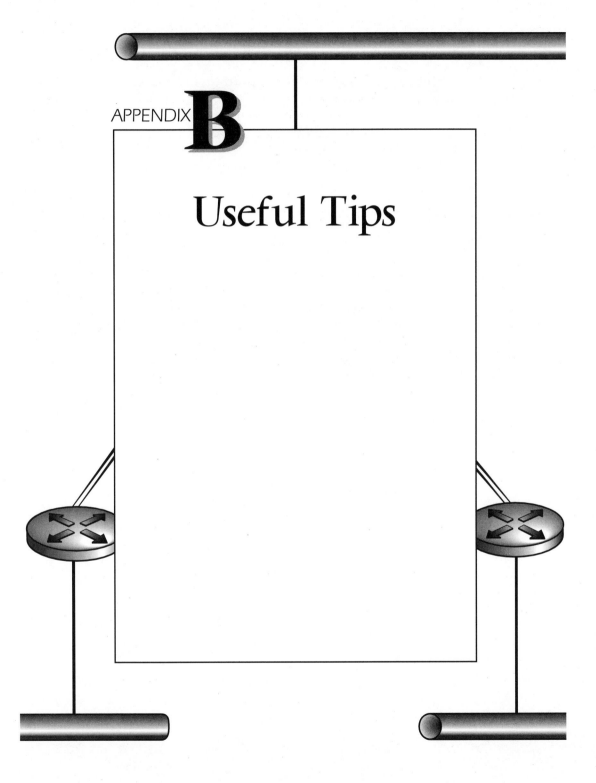

APPENDIX **B**

# Useful Tips

# Introduction

This appendix suggests some tips that will be useful if you need to enhance the performance or the look of your code or component. These tips are not necessarily to be used with our examples, although they can be used any time in your work. Since these are just tips, you can also get away without following them at all.

# String Buffer

Generally we manipulate strings using the *String* class. We basically use the *String* class as a buffer to append strings by the use of the + operator. This is OK for demonstrations, but for more efficient code you may want to use *StringBuffer*. Since the *String* class is immutable, the Java compiler really creates a *StringBuffer* and a *String* object for every string manipulation. This is obviously not very efficient because of the number of objects being created and the garbage that accumulates. It would be better to create a *StringBuffer*, manipulate the string value, and at the end, convert the buffer to a *String* object. Here's a small code snippet that demonstrates how to do this:

```
String s = "Hello";
s += " World";
System.out.println(s);
```

Here's the equivalent of the above code using *StringBuffer*.

```
StringBuffer sb = new StringBuffer(50);
sb.append("Hello");
sb.append(" World");
System.out.println(sb.toString());
```

## Utility Class

If you have followed our examples carefully, you have noticed that we have repeated some of the code, like *sendDataToClient()*, *getRedirectURL()* and so on. It would be a good idea for you to create some type of utility class— maybe with static functions—so that these methods could be reused again and again, instead of relying on the traditional cut and paste strategy.

## Setting Icons for Java Studio Components

When we built Java Studio components in Parts 2 and 3 of this book, we did not add any icon representation for our components, so they used the default representations. It is a good idea to have a visual representation of the components by loading an image that represents your bean. When providing design time information for your component, it is a good idea to override *getSmallImage()*, *getMediumImage()*, or *getLargeImage()*, as shown below:

```
public class VJSendEmailVJComponentInfo extends
SimpleVJComponentInfo{
   ...
   ...
   ...

   public Image getSmallImage(){
     return loadImage(resourceName);
   }
}
```

Method *loadImage()* is a utility method in the *SimpleVJComponentInfo* class for loading images.

# Separate Business Logic and Presentation Logic in Servlets

In our samples we have demonstrated using servlets for processing business logic and presentation logic. This is acceptable because our applications are small. For large enterprise applications it will be better to use servlets for processing business logic only and use Java Server Pages (JSP) for presentation logic. This will provide a clean separation between business logic and presentation logic. This will also help you to manage the presentation using HTML editors and have business logic in the form of a reusable component.

# Putting all JAR Files Together

Since Java is growing, you are sure to acquire a number of classes as you download more and more frameworks and tools. If you keep setting the CLASSPATH variable for every class, zip, or jar file, the CLASSPATH would grow very large. Some operating systems will not permit you to have huge environment variables. It is a good idea to put all your Java-dependent files into a common directory and make CLASSPATH smaller in size, to reduce the compilation time.

APPENDIX **C**

# Tools Usage

# Introduction

In this appendix we'll review how to use some of the tools discussed in this book. While writing this book, we assumed that readers are Java programmers, so the usage of common tools, such as *javac*, are not discussed. Appendix C just covers the *jar* and *serialver* utility.

# JAR Utility

Most of the JAR archives that we created do not indicate the bean class among the set of the classes in the archive. We did not do this because it wasn't necessary. But if you are using the beans that we have provided with any builder tool, this distinction—of explicitly indicating the JavaBean class—is a must, unless, of course, all the classes in the JAR are beans. Here are some commands that you will execute to create a JAR, manipulate the Manifest file, and repackage the same.

To create the JAR archive you have to execute the command below:

```
Jar cvf <jarname.jar> *.class
```

The command to unpack the jar to extract the Manifest.mf is shown below:

```
Jar xvf <jarname.jar> META-INF
```

Edit the Manifest.mf file present under *META-INF/Manifest.mf*. Make sure every JavaBean class carries Java-Bean:True, and every VJComponent class carries VJComponent:True (specific to Java Studio components).

Delete the old jar file, <jarname.jar>. Re-create the JAR file with the latest Manifest information with the command shown below:

```
Jar cvfm <jarname.jar> META-INF/Manifest.mf *.class
```

# Using Serialver for Bean Versioning

In Chapter 2 we learned how to maintain the compatibility between different versions of the JavaBean component. We also talked about using the *serialver* utility packaged with the JDK for obtaining SerialVersionUID. Here's how to run the tool from the command line:

```
serialver SimpleServlet
```

If SimpleServlet is in CLASSPATH, the output may appear as shown below:

```
SimpleServlet: static final long serialVersionUID = -
966405302967357572L;
```

Just cut and paste the version number in your Bean class.

You can also use the GUI version of serialver by using the parameter *-show*. You have to type the following on the command line for the GUI version:

```
serialver -show
```

This will pop up a GUI, which is simple to use.

APPENDIX **D**

# Using
# EJBSamples
# with HomeBase
# Server

# Introduction

As is often the case with computer books, after writing the book software used in the book is revised. In our case it was done prior to publication, so we have the opportunity to include this appendix about HomeBase—the new version of EJBHome server. Since there are few changes between version .4 (discussed in Chapter 13) and the version .5 (which was still in beta when this book went to press), we have dedicated this appendix to showing you how to deploy the Chapter 13 samples with the new HomeBase server.

# Installing and setting up HomeBase

Download the HomeBase server from *http://www.ejbhome.com/download*. Unzip the contents into *C:\ejbhome0.5*, so that ejbhome.jar is under the *C:\ejbhome0.5* subdirectory. Note that to deploy the beans, in addition to Java, HomeBase needs JFC. In case you do not have JFC already installed, download JFC 1.1.x from *http://java.sun.com/products/jfc/* (or install the version available on the accompanying CD-ROM). We used JFC 1.1.1 beta for the purpose of testing. Once you install JFC under *C:\swing*, you'll find *swingall.jar* installed along with the other libraries. Add *ejbhome.jar* and *swing.jar* to your CLASSPATH.

Under *C:\ejbhome0.5* create two subdirectories—conf and logs. Copy the contents from *chap13\conf* and logs (found on the accompanying CD-ROM) to *C:\ejbhome0.5\conf* and *C:\ejbhome0.5\logs*, respectively. Your sever setup is now complete.

# Using our samples with HomeBase

In this section we'll both discuss the changes that need to be made to the two samples developed in Chapter 13 and how to test them with HomeBase.

# Generating Container classes for the Privilege EJB

Here are the steps you'll follow

1. Under *C:\ejbhome0.5* directory create a subdirectory called sample1.
2. From *chap13\sample1* on the CD-ROM copy all the files to *C:\ejbhome0.5\sample1*.
3. Now change your working directory to *C:\ ejbhome0.5\sample1*.
4. Delete all the files that start with EJB
5. Except *PrivilegeTest.class*, delete all the .class files.
6. Open *PrivilegeBean.java* , add this dummy method in the class public void ejbPostCreate(String name, int privilegeLevel){}. This is needed because EJB 1.0 specification specifies it.
7. Save and exit *PrivilegeBean.java*.
8. Add *C:\ejbhome0.5* to the CLASSPATH. Also make sure to use JDK 1.1.x to compile *PrivilegeBean.java* and *PrivilegeHome.java*.
9. To generate container classes, create a file called *privilege.ejbml* under *C:\ejbhome0.5\sample1*. Copy the contents in Listing D-1 and save the file.

**Listing D-1**
Complete listing for privilege.ejbml

```
<ejbml>
<entity-bean name="Privilege"
home="sample1.PrivilegeHome" remote="sample1.Privilege"
bean="sample1.PrivilegeBean" package="sample1" primary-
key="sample1.PrivilegePKey">
<container-managed storage-
helper="com.ejbhome.generator.helpers.RelationalPersistenceCodeHelper"
table="privilege" data-source="jdbc/PrivilegeDB"
username="admin" password="admin">
<field name="privilegeLevel"/>
<field name="name"/>
</container-managed>
</entity-bean>
</ejbml>
```

Type in the following command from C:\ejbhome0.5 to generate the container classes.

```
java com.ejbhome.Deployer sample1\privilege.ejbml
```

If everything is fine, the generated container classes should compile.

## Testing the Privilege EJB

We already developed a client in Chapter 13 to test Privilege EJB. HomeBase server needs ejbml files to load the beans. From *C:\ejbhome0.5\sample1* copy privilege.ejbml to the *C:\ejbhome0.5\conf* subdirectory. Make sure to specify the JDBC drivers in the CLASSPATH. Start the HomeBase server by typing the following command from *C:\ejbhome0.5*

```
start java com.ejbhome.Server
```

The server should be able to load the Privilege EJB.

To test the client, type the following on the command line from *C:\ejbhome0.5\sample1*

```
java PrivilegeTest user 1
```

You'll see the following output on the console

```
Privilege level for user1 : 0
```

## Generating Container classes for the ProjectTracker EJB

Here are the steps you'll follow

1. Under the *C:\ejbhome0.5* directory create a subdirectory called sample2.
2. From *chap13\sample2* on the CD-ROM copy all the files to *C:\ejbhome0.5\sample2*

3. Now change your working directory to *C:\ ejbhome0.5 \sample2*
4. Delete all the files that start with EJB
5. Except ProjectTrackerTest.class, delete all the .class files.
6. *\ejbhome0.5* directory should be specified in the CLASSPATH. Also make sure to use JDK 1.1.x to compile *ProjectTrackerBean.java* and *ProjectTrackerHome.java*.
7. To generate container classes create a file called *projectTracker.ejbml* under *C:\ejbhome0.5\sample1*. Copy the contents in Listing D-2 and save the file.

■ ■ ■ ■ ■ ■ ■
**Listing D-2**
Complete listing for projectTracker.ejbml

```
<ejbml>
<entity-bean name="ProjectTracker"
home="sample2.ProjectTrackerHome"
remote="sample2.ProjectTracker"
bean="sample2.ProjectTrackerBean" package="sample2"
primary-key="sample2.ProjectTrackerPKey">
<container-managed storage-
helper="com.ejbhome.generator.helpers.RelationalPersistenceCodeHelper"
table="projecttracker" data-source="jdbc/ProjectDB"
username="admin" password="admin">
<field name="projectInfo"/>
<field name="privilegeLevel"/>
</container-managed>
</entity-bean>
</ejbml>
```

Type in the following command from *C:\ejbhome0.5* to generate the container classes.

```
java com.ejbhome.Deployer sample2\projectTracker.ejbml
```

If everything is fine, the generated container classes should compile.

# Testing the ProjectTracker EJB

We already developed a client in Chapter 13 to test ProjectTracker EJB. From *C:\ejbhome0.5\sample2* copy *projectTracker.ejbml* to the *C:\ejbhome0.5\conf* subdirectory. Make sure to specify the JDBC drivers in CLASSPATH. Start the HomeBase server by typing the following command from *C:\ejbhome0.5*

```
start java com.ejbhome.Server
```

This time the server should be able to load the Privilege EJB and ProjectTracker EJB.

To test the client, type the following on the command line from *C:\ejbhome0.5\sample2*

```
java ProjectTrackerTest
```

You'll see the following output on the console

```
Zero level string
```

# INDEX

# Oracle No-Charge 30 day Trial License

Oracle offers the following trial products for a 30-day evaluation period under the terms of the No Charge 30 Day Trial License. You may purchase these and other products at any time from the Oracle Store. Please visit Free Software for downloadable products free of charge, including Oracle ODBC Drivers.

USE OF SOFTWARE: Any use of software and accompanying documentation from this CD is subject to the terms of a software license agreement between you and Oracle. You must read the license agreement below and indicate your agreement to its terms prior to installing or using the software and by registering using either Oracle's online registration at *http://www.oracle.com/products/trial/html/trial.html* (select product and then fill in registration information) or by mailing your name, address, and phone number to Alex C. Ho, 500 Oracle Parkway, Redwood Shores, CA 94065.

CAUTION: Loading this software onto a computer indicates your acceptance of the following terms. Please read them carefully.

TRIAL LICENSE: Oracle Corporation ("Oracle") grants you a no-charge trial license to use the software selected ("Software") solely for evaluation purposes for a period of 30 days. You may not use the Software for any development, commercial, or production purpose. You may not run any benchmark tests with the program. You may give trial copies of the Software to others to permit them to use the Software under the same restrictions as are in this License, provided that you do not charge a fee for doing so. At the termination of this sublicense, you agree to discontinue use and destroy all copies of the Programs and Documentation, or you must purchase a full-use license if you wish to do any of the following: (a) use the Software after the end of the 30-day trial period, or (b) use the Software for any development, commercial, or production purpose, or (c) distribute the Software for any such use.

COPYRIGHT: The Software is the proprietary product of Oracle and is protected by copyright law. You acquire only the right to use the Software and do not acquire any rights of ownership. You agree not to remove any product identification, copyright notices, or other notices or proprietary restrictions from the Software. You agree not to cause or permit the reverse engineering, disassembly, or decompilation of the Software. You shall not disclose the results of any benchmark tests of the Software to any third party without Oracle's prior written approval.

WARRANTY DISCLAIMER: Oracle is providing this license on an "as is" basis without warranty of any kind; Oracle disclaims all express and implied warranties, including the implied warranties of merchantability or fitness for a particular purpose.

LIMITATION OF LIABILITY: LIMITATION OF LIABILITY: ORACLE SHALL NOT BE LIABLE FOR ANY DAMAGES, INCLUDING DIRECT, INDIRECT, INCIDENTAL, SPECIAL OR CONSEQUENTIAL DAMAGES, OR DAMAGES FOR LOSS OF PROFITS, REVENUE, DATA OR DATA USE, INCURRED BY YOU OR ANY THIRD PARTY, WHETHER IN AN ACTION IN CONTRACT OR TORT, EVEN IF YOU OR ANY OTHER PERSON HAS BEEN ADVISED OF THE POSSIBILITY OF SUCH DAMAGES.

EXPORT: Customer shall comply fully with all laws and regulations of the United States and other countries ("Export Laws") to assure that neither the Software, nor any direct products thereof are (1) unexported, directly or indirectly, in violation of Export Laws, or (2) are used for any purpose prohibited by Export Laws, including, without limitation, nuclear, chemical, or biological weapons proliferation.

RESTRICTED RIGHTS: Software delivered subject to the DOD FAR Supplement is "commercial computer software" and use, duplication and disclosure of the Software shall be subject to the licensing restrictions set forth in the applicable license agreement. Otherwise, Software delivered subject to the Federal Acquisition Regulations are "restricted computer software" and use, duplication and disclosure of the Software shall be subject to the restrictions in FAR 52.227-14, Rights in Data — General, including Alternate III (June 1987).

Personal Oracle 8i " 1997, 1999 Oracle Corporation. All rights, title and interest not expressly granted are reserved.

Oracle Corporation World Headquarters, 500 Oracle Parkway, Redwood Shores, CA 94065 USA

Worldwide Inquiries: 650.506.7000, Fax: 650.506.7200

## Software and Information License

The software and information on this diskette (collectively referred to as the "Product") are the property of The McGraw-Hill Companies, Inc. ("McGraw-Hill") and are protected by both United States copyright law and international copyright treaty provision. You must treat this Product just like a book, expect that you may copy it into a computer to be used and you may make archival copies of the Products for the sole purpose of backing up your software and protecting your investment from loss.

By saying "just like a book," McGraw-Hill means, for example, that the Product may be used by any number of people and may be freely moved from one computer location to another, so long as there is no possibility of the Product (or any part of the Product) being used at one location or on one computer while it is being used at another. Just as a book cannot be read by two different people in two different places at the same time, neither can the Product be used in two different places at the same time (unless, of course, McGraw-Hill's rights are being violated).

McGraw-Hill reserves the right to alter or modify the contents of the Product at any time.

This agreement is effective until terminated. The Agreement will terminate automatically without notice if you fail to comply with any provisions of this Agreement. In the event of termination by reason of your breach, you will destroy or erase all copies of the Product installed on any computer system or made for backup purposes and shall expunge the Product from your data storage facilities.

## Limited Warranty

McGraw-Hill warrants the physical diskette(s) enclosed herein to be free of defects in materials and workmanship for a period of sixty days from the purchase date. If McGraw-Hill receives written notification within the warranty period of defects in materials or workmanship, and such notification is determined by McGraw-Hill to be correct, McGraw-Hill will replace the defective diskette(s). Send request to:

Customer Service
McGraw-Hill
Gahanna Industrial Park
860 Taylor Station Road
Blacklick, Ohio 43004-9615

The entire and exclusive liability and remedy for breach of this Limited Warranty shall be limited to replacement of defective diskette(s) and shall not include or extend any claim for or right to cover any other damages, including but not limited to loss of profit, data, or use of the software, or special, incidental, or consequential damages or other similar claims, even if McGraw-Hill has been specifically advised as to the possibility of such damages. In no event will McGraw-Hill's liability for any damages to you or any other person ever exceed the lower of suggested list price or actual price paid for the license to use the Product, regardless of any form of the claim.

The McGraw-Hill Companies, Inc. specifically disclaims all other warranties, express or implied, including but not limited to, any implied warranty of merchantability or fitness for a particular purpose. Specifically, McGraw-Hill makes no representation or warranty that the Product is fit for any particular purpose and any implied warranty of merchantability is limited to the sixty day duration of the Limited Warranty covering the physical diskette(s) only (and not the software or information) and is otherwise expressly and specifically disclaimed.

This Limited Warranty gives you specific legal rights; you may have others which may vary from state to state. Some states do not allow the exclusion of incidental or consequential damages, or the limitation on how long an implied warranty lasts, so some of the above may not apply to you.

This agreement constitutes the entire agreement between the parties relating to use of the Product. The terms of any purchase order shall have no effect on the terms of this Agreement. Failure of McGraw-Hill to insist at any time on strict compliance with this Agreement shall not constitute a waiver of any rights under this Agreement. This Agreement shall be construed and governed in accordance with the laws of New York. If any provision of this Agreement is held to be contrary to law, that provision will be enforced to the maximum extent permissible and the remaining provisions will remain in force and effect.